D0262173

Current
Widowhood

Understanding Families

Series Editors: *Bert M. Adams, University of Wisconsin*
                      David M. Klein, University of Notre Dame

This book series examines a wide range of subjects relevant to studying families. Topics include parenthood, mate selection, marriage, divorce and remarriage, custody issues, culturally and ethnically based family norms, theory and conceptual design, family power dynamics, families and the law, research methods on the family, and family violence.

The series is aimed primarily at scholars working in family studies, sociology, psychology, social work, ethnic studies, gender studies, cultural studies, and related fields as they focus on the family. Volumes will also be useful for graduate and undergraduate courses in sociology of the family, family relations, family and consumer sciences, social work and the family, family psychology, family history, cultural perspectives on the family, and others.

Books appearing in **Understanding Families** are either single- or multiple-authored volumes or concisely edited books of original chapters on focused topics within the broad interdisciplinary field of marriage and family.

The books are reports of significant research, innovations in methodology, treatises on family theory, syntheses of current knowledge in a family subfield, or advanced textbooks. Each volume meets the highest academic standards and makes a substantial contribution to our understanding of marriages and families.

The National Council on Family Relations cosponsors with Sage a book award for students and new professionals. Award-winning manuscripts are published as part of the **Understanding Families** series.

Multiracial Couples
Paul C. Rosenblatt, Terri A. Karis, and Richard D. Powell

Understanding Latino Families
Edited by Ruth E. Zambrana

Current Widowhood
Helena Znaniecka Lopata

Helena Znaniecka Lopata

Current
Widowhood

Myths & Realities

UNDERSTANDING
FAMILIES

SAGE Publications
International Educational and Professional Publisher
Thousand Oaks London New Delhi

Copyright © 1996 by Sage Publications, Inc.

All rights reserved. No part of this book may be reproduced or utilized in any form or by any means, electronic or mechanical, including photocopying, recording, or by any information storage and retrieval system, without permission in writing from the publisher.

For information address:

SAGE Publications, Inc.
2455 Teller Road
Thousand Oaks, California 91320
E-mail: order@sagepub.com

SAGE Publications Ltd.
6 Bonhill Street
London EC2A 4PU
United Kingdom

SAGE Publications India Pvt. Ltd.
M-32 Market
Greater Kailash I
New Delhi 110048 India

Printed in the United States of America

Library of Congress Cataloging-in-Publication Data

Lopata, Helena Znaniecka, 1925-
        Current widowhood: Myths and realities/Helena Znaniecka Lopata.
          p. cm. — (Understanding families).
        Includes bibliographical references and index.
        ISBN 0-8039-7395-0 (cloth: alk. paper). — ISBN 0-8039-7396-9
    (pbk.: alk. paper)
          1. Widows—United States—Psychology. 2. Widows—United States—
    Social conditions. 3. Widows—Services for—United States.
        I. Title. II. Series.
        HQ1058.L64   1996
        305.48′9654—dc20   95-35750

This book is printed on acid-free paper.

96 97 98 99 10 9 8 7 6 5 4 3 2 1

Sage Production Editor: Gillian Dickens
Sage Typesetter: Janelle LeMaster

Contents

Preface

Some time ago, the distinguished dyad of editors for this series on the family, Bert Adams and David Klein, invited me to talk with them at the meetings of the National Council on Family Relations. They then convinced me to pull together into one volume much that I know about widowhood from both my own research and that of other scholars, students, widowed women, and people working with and providing resources to widowed women. It really did not take much convincing, for such a project would culminate my years of interest in this very important subject studied through a variety of sociological concepts and perspectives.

My research on role modifications, support systems, and the situation of widows in America, as well as in other places in the world, began in a rather serendipitous way. I had come to the United States during World War II, completed my PhD at the University of Chicago a number of years later, and then could not find an academic position in the Chicago area, where my husband was determined to remain. We moved with two small children to a suburb, and there I became fascinated by the gap between the apologetic way women in the community talked about themselves and the creativity and competence with which they actually carried out their roles and developed a completely new lifestyle (a lifestyle that male sociologists deprecated in a number of 1950s books). This interest led me into a study of suburban and urban homemakers, and the Midwest Council for Social Research on Aging (MCSRA) granted me several fellowships to analyze the interviews, sociograms, and other data that I had been collecting. The result was published as *Occupation: Housewife* in 1971 (Lopata, 1971b). While I was finishing that project, Warren Peterson and Al Westin, MCSRA honchos, kiddingly asked me what I was going to do on aging to pay back the psychological and financial support I had received from their organization. I immediately responded that I would study widowhood. Actually, this response was not as ridiculous as its spontaneity might suggest. Homemakers do age, and I was curious as to what happened to their roles when their children left home and their husbands died. When I was developing a proposal and starting the research, I knew of only two studies that focused on widows: Peter Marris's research in London and Felix Berardo's study of both widows and widowers in Washington State. The field was ready for greater exploration with a variety of theoretical tools.

I was funded in the late 1960s by the Administration on Aging. (Considering how long, on and off, I have been doing such studies, I should know something about the subject!) That research on role modifications in widowhood, which was published as *Widowhood in an American City* (Lopata, 1973d), was followed by an even more ambitious cross-cultural project supported by the Social Security Administration (SSA). Doctor Henry Brehm, then Director of Research Grants and Contracts at the SSA and an expert in quantitative research methodology, became the project officer. The SSA had permission to use the U.S. counterpart funds (Pub. L. No. 480) for this project in Egypt, Poland, and Yugoslavia. These funds accumulated in countries where the United States sold grain but whose money our government did not wish to receive. Instead, the moneys were diverted for embassies, research, and humanitarian uses. My team at the Center for the Comparative Study of Social Roles at Loyola University of Chicago and Hank Brehm of the SSA were joined by Dr. Nada Smolic Krkovic and her research team at the Institute of Social Work in Zagreb, Yugoslavia; Dr. Adam Kurzynowski of the Szkola Glowna Planowa nia i Statystyki of Warsaw, Poland; and Dr. Nawal Nadim of the American University in Cairo, Egypt. Dr. Jacqueline Touba of the University of Teheran, Iran, obtained funds from her own government, and we all started the long process of working up an interview that could be applicable cross-culturally. That was not as easy a task as it may sound. In fact, the original theoretical framework for the research, based on a symbolic interactionist perspective of social roles, proved too complex at this level of comparison. We finally hit on the concept of support systems by breaking down into segments of rights and duties the relations between the central social person and the social circle in each role. Defining a support as any object or action that the receiver or giver regarded as contributory to a lifestyle, we developed four systems of supports: economic, service, social, and emotional. The reader will learn more of these in this volume.

Political reality interfered with the project when the Yugoslav version of the interview was sent (for reasons we were unable to discover) to the Department of War—and it wanted no such project. The Polish government also nixed the project in the last minute. Dr. Nadim left the results of their interviews behind when she left the American University due to internal conflicts, and those data were never analyzed. Luckily, Dr. Touba got out of Iran with her data. The theoretical framework and the interview, or parts of it, have been used in research on widowhood in Korea, India, China, the Philippines, Australia, Turkey, Israel, Canada, and several locations in America (Lopata, 1987d, 1987e).

In the meantime, Hank and I pulled together material on the economic situation of widows with special emphasis on the history and consequences of the policies of the United States toward women and children (Lopata & Brehm, 1986). My part of the cross-cultural study was published in *Women as Widows: Support Systems* (Lopata, 1979).

I have been lucky to have been invited to many conferences dealing with aging or the roles of women, where I met scholars interested in the same subjects and exchanged ideas and sources—a vital link to the world outside of one's space. I have written many chapters, articles, and papers for scientific meetings resulting from these stimulating interchanges.

It is really impossible for me to thank each and every person who has helped me during these 26 years of work on widowhood. This includes both the many widowed women who have contributed their life experiences to our knowledge and the scholars in America and the world over who have used various ideas and methodologies in their own work on widowhood. Many thanks go to all those sociologists and others involved in the Center for the Comparative Study of Social Roles at Loyola University of Chicago. As always, my colleagues in the sociology and anthropology department at Loyola have lent support, both social and emotional. In addition, they helped me to deal with all the technological changes that have made knowledge retrieval and writing so much easier now than when I first started this work. Of additional help have been all the friends and colleagues involved in my other projects. (As a symbolic interactionist, I look at the world construction of a variety of people, using a variety of concepts.)

It is hard for me to thank my family at this time. My husband, Richard Lopata, to whom a number of my books have been dedicated and to whom I have expressed gratitude in many prefaces, died on July 13, 1994. We found out that he had inoperable cancer and insulin-dependent diabetes 18 months before that. I had started working on this book before we knew he was ill. I continued developing the ideas and pulling together the material throughout that time, except for a 5-month period surrounding his death when I could not even look at the then almost-completed manuscript. There is much truth to the statement that there is a vast difference between understanding and feeling empathy for the emotions and sentiments of others and understanding and feeling such emotions oneself. Living through the devastating illness and death of someone with whom one has shared everything for 49 years and all the aftereffects of these events is a different kind of pain from any that I had ever experienced before. On the other hand, knowing what others have gone through and the many different, ambivalent, and intensive ways they have felt has helped me personally. Also, having to put all this on paper has, I believe, eased the grieving. I only wish that Dick were alive to share the results.

My daughter Teddy and my son Stefan have been marvelous throughout all this, as always. Their contributions followed the gender-specific lines expected from my research, and I am glad that they complemented each other so well in providing me with different supports. They and their families have always added to the pleasures of my life.

And so, what is this book all about? Since the 1960s, the amount of knowledge about widowhood has exploded due to the contributions of both widowed women and many scholars studying the role changes, support systems, problems, and results of widowhood. In this work, I have organized this vast database around two major themes. The first theme focuses on the uneven and often convoluted influence of changes in societies, communities, and personal resources resulting from modernization or social development. The second theme focuses on the presence of numerous myths, stereotypes, and assumptions that surround widowhood and all the circumstances of becoming and being a widow. Even I found myself influenced by these at the start of the research. Many of these myths present a dismal and limiting picture of women, which has grown out of a variety of traditional and even modern cultures and subcultures. I discuss these throughout the book, pointing, when possible, to research showing the realities of actual life. I also indicate areas in which we need more research to test the assumptions behind the myths.

Current Widowhood: Myths & Realities is organized with an initial comparative and historical perspective on the situation of widows in other parts of the world and in special communities in America. In Chapter 4, I proceed to show the effects on a woman of the role of wife and the circumstances by which a woman experiences the illness and death of her husband. These circumstances move her first into the temporary role of widow and then into a pervasive identity of widowed woman. This pervasive identity enters her various social roles more or less significantly. Following this discussion are analyses of the effects of widowhood on the roles of mother, kin member, friend, and participant in the larger community.

This book ends with an overall picture of the major themes of the effects of social development and of the myths surrounding widowhood. These themes had led me from the beginning, along with the help of Herbert Blumer's (1969) "sensitizing concepts." Most of my analysis evolved gradually as I tried to systematize the vast body of knowledge in the grounded-theory method now so common in sociology. I am a symbolic interactionist, concerned with the construction of reality, or the meanings of life, for people who are going through an experience. I hope that this perspective is evident throughout.

The methods used to pull all this together are quite varied. They include interviews, questionnaires, participant observations, personal experiences, census and other statistical resources, and the unexpected findings through which all of us carry forth our studies. Above all, they include the guiding concepts through which organizational structure emerges. The reader must remember that many scholars contributed to this volume through their works, which I have used selectively. I have obviously benefited from my own research. The analytical concepts and perspectives used in the various projects range from the broad macrolevel of societal change to the intermediary stress on social role, role modification, and support systems, to the microlevel of personal experiences, such as loneliness and grief. Always present for sociologists are the questions of the representativeness and validity of the data.

I consider one of the major contributions of this book to be the set of conceptual themes through which I have been able to analyze, organize, and present an extensive body of scholarly knowledge. Another major contribution is making available to many readers this world of knowledge from so many different studies, which were conducted by means of a great variety of methodologies. I have an advantage over other scholars working with the general subject of widowhood and its various topic areas in that I was present at the beginning and helped to influence the development of this broad area. My theoretical perspective has supplied some of the concepts and areas of focus that have defined this research. Luckily, other social scientists have approached widowhood with other conceptual and technical methodologies. We have all added cumulatively to knowledge and to the concepts used in other areas of investigation.

In the meantime, I have learned much from all the work of others and from the maturation of my own ideas. The recent work to which I refer in Chapter 9 has helped pull away the dismal image (with which even I first approached this subject) of the ever-limited, ever-suffering, ever-dependent widow. The picture of widowhood that now emerges is much more complicated and varied than I had been able to grasp in my first study in the late 1960s.

In addition, of course, ideological and sociocultural changes in American society, as well as changes in the social life spaces and self-concepts of women, have resulted in new cohorts of widowed women and of women who will at some point in their lives become widowed. These changes will help dissolve any remaining old myths. The feminist movement has been a major change agent influencing directly both American women and many of us scholars. As a result, while providing opportunities for women to express themselves, we have been reexamining the images of women in general, of different "types" of women, of women in many different situations, and of individual women. This reconstruction of womanhood extends, of course, to widowed women. We are learning much in recent years, and I hope that this book will help others in their learning processes.

Fortunately, this particular book has had help from new sources. Annette Prosterman came on this scene during the past 2 years as my research assistant. She became so interested in this volume (especially in the community and societal responses to widowhood) and was of such assistance with its preparation that I asked her to contribute a chapter on this topic. She has worked with me on the references (always a painful job) and is an excellent editor who forced me to think out many questions. David Klein and Bert Adams have also asked the penetrating questions and pushed me to greater clarity and consistency. Kirsten Gronbjerg and Judith Wittner also guided me in these directions.

To all of them, I owe a great debt.

1

Studying Widowhood

S tudying widowhood is not easy. People become widowed in several ways, and there are numerous influences on the consequences of this process. For these reasons, I have selected widowhood as it affects women only and will focus on American women, with some comparative and historical foundations. We can agree that a widowed woman is a woman who had been married and whose husband has died. We do not need to eliminate women who were not living with their husbands, who were perhaps even divorced from their husbands, when these men died. Their living and marital arrangements form part of the influences on widowhood. Women who were widowed but who have remarried will also be included, because remarriage is one of the ways widowhood is changed.

The bare situational essentials defining widowhood camouflage great variations the world over by many societal, community, and personal factors. Societies differ considerably in their social structure and culture. In addition, societies are not stable, changing rapidly in recent times.[1] The more complex the structure, the greater the resources for social integration at all stages of life. At the same time, complex societies require considerable knowledge and individuated, voluntaristic, social integration. The more heterogeneous the culture, the greater the variety of ways people are integrated through a variety of social roles. One of the problems for members of changing societies is that social change removes traditional forms of social integration without adequately replacing them before the people are socialized into new methods of social engagement.

A person is also affected by the community in which she or he is located, in terms of its size and availability of resources for all members, as well as for different kinds of members, to develop lifestyles. Social class, minority, and gender identification influence choices and restrictions.

Finally, a person's characteristics determine if she or he is able to take advantage of opportunities or is limited to a narrow set of social roles—that is, life space—within the society and community. To understand this statement, we must reach an agreement as to the definition of concepts, including social development, social role, social life space, the role of wife, the role of widow, widowhood as a pervasive identity, and myths and reality.

Basic Concepts

SOCIAL DEVELOPMENT

Several concepts summarize the direction of change in societies of the past century or so, including social development, modernization, and complexity of scale. Although there is quite a bit of debate as to which of these concepts best represents both the changes and the differences between societies, depending on the extent and kind of change, I prefer to use the concept of social development.

Generally speaking, societies have been moving in the past couple of centuries, at varying rates in different areas, toward increasing complexity of social structure and social units with the help of the industrial, technological, and knowledge revolutions; mass education; urbanization; and mobility of population. At an ideal-typical level, societal members expand their social life space (see discussion later), construction of reality, and social roles as they broaden awareness and identification. With this expansion comes increasing rationality in problem solving, individualization, and choice. In addition, these changes are influencing more and more of the population, providing people with personal resources to choose from extensive societal resources. These people can build flexible social life spaces in cooperation with equally self-developed others.

An additional complicated factor in our understanding of widowhood is the unevenness in the development of various aspects of societal life and community and personal resources even in the 1990s. Many older Americans, let alone members of other societies, were socialized in traditional settings, with ascribed—that is, assigned—social roles. Those socialized in transitional times suffered much strain from the anomalies of contradictory norms and relations. People needed to develop their own solutions to problems throughout the life course, or they might have had the help of a limited number of role associates. Modern times still contain many contradictions and vestiges of the past social class, racial, ethnic, rural-urban, gender, and other constraints. Relatively few people have really been socialized to take advantage of existing resources or create their own resources to build complex, flexible, and satisfying life courses. This is particularly true of older American women, many, if not most, of whom have been systematically disadvantaged in their ability to reach even existing resources. This is reflected in their role as wife and in widowhood.

SOCIAL ROLE

A social role is a set of patterned, interdependent relations between a social person and a social circle encompassing rights and privileges, duties, and obligations on all sides. The social person is the title bearer: mother, father, student, professor, and so forth. Each role is organized around a purpose. A total individual is not involved in each social role. Rather, only certain characteristics, physical, sociopsychological, and behavioral, are required for each role because of the nature of the duties and rights. The person must somehow prove to the social circle, through various testing methods, that she or he has the characteristics assumed to be necessary to perform the negotiated duties and receive the negotiated rights. The circle consists of everyone with whom the social person relates in the role, those who provide the cooperative rights and privileges and who are recipients of the person's duties and obligations.

In general, most social circles contain beneficiaries of the role, assistants who help meet obligations to the beneficiaries, suppliers of necessary objects and services, colleagues or others with whom the person works, and administrators, in the case of an organized group. Sometimes the person pulls together her or his own circle, but frequently the circle precedes the person, seeking, testing, and then accepting and cooperating with the appointee. The person needs to win acceptance of each segment of the circle. The duties are directed not only to the beneficiaries but also to all members of the circle, if only in recognition of their presence and their contributions. Thus, the duties and obligations of a wife are deeply influenced by not only her husband but also by other members of her social circle as a wife. She has duties not only to her husband but also to all the people in the social circle who make it possible for her to be the kind of wife that all of them, including her, have negotiated to accept. The social circle members, in turn, have obligations to her and must give her the rights and resources she needs to be that kind of wife.

Although each role is unique in that the relations are negotiated between a social person and a specific circle of people, the culture within which they interact contains the model for the role, and other persons and circles are usually involved in that kind of role at the same time.

With social development, social roles have become increasingly open to selection, much more negotiable, less institutionalized, and able to flow with the needs of the social person and circle members (Turner, 1962, 1970). We shall see this throughout the book.

SOCIAL LIFE SPACE

At any one time and throughout the life course, each individual is involved in a variety of roles. Some of these roles are more similar than other roles, sharing a somewhat common institutional base. For example, the roles of daughter, sister, wife, mother, and kin member in general all fall into the family institution, defined as a set of established procedures organizing a major area of life. Social life space refers to the figurative portrayal of the complexity of the role cluster of any member of society. Some people have a relatively flat social life space, being involved in social roles that fall into one institution. The richness of their involvement in that dimension can vary by the number of roles in which they are active. Other people have a multidimensional social life space, being involved in social roles in several institutions.

MYTHS

The concept of myth also has multiple meanings, being used very differently by philosophers, psychiatrists, anthropologists, and sociologists. I use the concept here narrowly, not as a whole story, often with supernatural themes or historical foundations, passed on from generation to generation, and shared by a social group. That is more an anthropological than a sociological usage. Here, *myth* is used to signify a belief, assumption, or stereotype that influences behavior of persons toward each other. As part of a socially constructed reality, a myth can even consist of beliefs about the self, but it is usually a set of expectations about others, influencing everyday interaction between categories of people who do not know each other very well.

Myths can present a neutral, negative, or positive picture of the subject, but the problem with them is their stereotypical nature. That is, they classify people into categories on the basis of only one or, at most, a limited number of characteristics. Any statement that begins with "adolescents are . . ." or "older people prefer . . ." is likely to be a myth unless it is founded on scientific evidence or is so generalized as to be meaningless (e.g., "Older people prefer to eat rather than starve").

Referring to Shaic and Willis (1986), Hunter and Sundel (1989) state in *Midlife Myths* that "myths are dangerous when they result in oversimplified stereotypes that influence personal perceptions, social interaction, and social policy. . . . Myths can be refuted or qualified with contradictory evidence based on objective sources or scientific methods" (p. 21). Ethel Shanas (1979), in her Robert W. Kleemeier Award Lecture, "Social Myth as Hypothesis: The Case of the Family Relations of Old People," stated the following:

> Every society has its own social myths. Such myths are those collective beliefs which everyone within a given society knows to be "right," and which everyone accepts as "true." . . . Social myths act as a cohesive force within a society. However, such myths or beliefs may also serve to obstruct both thought and action by encouraging people to accept as fact that which may really be a fiction. (p. 3)

Shanas then analyzes the realities concerning the generally accepted myth of the alienation of old people "from their families, particularly from their children."

Myths cover categories of objects of various generalizability. Thus, my own research and that of other social scientists, even the work of poets and other literary artists and scholars find several levels of myths stereotyping widows: those applicable to members of different kinds of societies, to women, to old people, to old women, directly to widows, and to widows of varied characteristics, such as race or class. It is sometimes difficult to separate the base for any of the assumptions or myths about such people from other bases, and it is nearly impossible to trace these to their origins. In fact, one of the characteristics of myths is their acceptance without historical or current evidence. They are just believed, by many people, by those surrounding that category of people, and sometimes even by the self. A great deal of scientific analysis is devoted to tracing the origins and dissemination of myths about different racial groupings.

The interesting aspect of myths about widows and widowhood in such a society as the American one is their varied and heterogeneous nature. They can originate from peasant cultures of immigrants, or they can arise from often faulty generalizations drawn from current lives. They are often contradictory, as are many other folk beliefs and commonsense notions. Annette Prosterman (see Chapter 8) and I have used many of these to accentuate the gap between beliefs and realities, contrasting them to the findings of social scientific research or to each other to show their contradictory nature.

The psychologist Mort Lieberman (1994) states that "widows are probably one of the most misunderstood groups in America today. . . . As pernicious as they are pervasive, the myths about widowhood are far more harmful than its realities." Lieberman adds another source of the myths about widowhood, in addition to the commonsense ones I found in my studies, and that is psychiatry, its practitioners viewing "widowhood as a disease requiring therapy and even tranquilizers before recovery is possible." Of course, not all myths are negative, but like all typifications, they simplify and stereotype complex phenomena, which usually has limiting consequences on the situation. Another characteristic of myths about widows, as with many myths, is that they often negate each other. For example, widows are seen by some people as asexual and by others as sexually starved and seeking gratification from any available man. We will find these characteristics as we go through the experiences of widowhood.

Changes in Marriage
and Widowhood With
Social Development

For the sake of simplicity in my analysis of widowhood, I have organized the social development changes in the lives of women in families into three overall periods: traditional (the frequently used concept), transitional, and modern. The traditional has been in most places patriarchal in authority and patrilineal in descent and inheritance, the strongest form accompanied by patrilocal residence. This most frequent family system gave considerable control to the patriarchal unit over all family subinstitutions: mate selection, marital roles, and relations within the nuclear and with the extended family. The control extended over socialization of the young and the life of the widowed. Its sources and forms were contained in the culture, supported by religion, and reinforced by other social units.

The transitional era, accompanying rapid urbanization, industrialization, and all the related changes, resulted in the weakening of past support networks and systems with the decrease of control by the patriarchal family and the small community. This has been accompanied by only limited attempts from the expanding-in-complexity society to help members and families deal with the changes. The most modern or developed era, which most societies and most members in even allegedly modern societies have not reached, provides a multiplicity of resources to members but requires that they engage in these voluntaristically, developing their own support networks, social roles, and interdependencies.

The changes from the traditional to the transitional family systems decreased the power of the patriarchal lineage but made the wife and children personal dependents on the husband and father (Eichler, 1973). His power over his family of procreation increased as his lineage power decreased and with the dependence of the wife and children on his income with the substitution of a money economy for the previous subsistence economy. Modern marriages, where so developed, negotiate egalitarian relations within roles that maintain cooperatively reached purposes.

MATE SELECTION

There have been many methods of mate selection in human history and in different places in the world, basically dependent on the way the marital unit fits into a broader social unit. Frequently, the method has been family selection through which the parents and other relatives of a potential groom and bride, with the possible help of official matchmakers, select and negotiate the relationship. In those cases, the significant characteristics of the potential bride include (a) family position relative to the groom's, (b) what the woman can bring to the man's family or what the man's family must offer for the marriage to take place, and (c) the personal resources of both bride and groom.

Transitional families still involve the parental generation in mate selection to the extent of the granting of permission and arrangements of marriage ceremonial.

In more modern, urbanized, and industrialized societies with complex social structures, mate selection is by choice of the future spouses. Varying and changing rituals have evolved by which women and men decide not only whom to marry but also the forms of interaction preceding and during the actual ceremony. All societies insist that there be some form of legal recognition of the marriage. This form of mate selection places a heavy burden on marital roles, because "love" and happiness are supposed to follow into death. Divorce is possible for those who see that their expectations are not being met or who change over the course of the marriage.

THE ROLE OF WIFE

Although there are many ways in which social roles are carried forth, there are similarities within a specific society and its subunits. In the case of the role of wife, a required characteristic is that she be a woman and go through a marriage ceremony, almost invariably to a man who then becomes a husband.[2] Other criteria are introduced by the husband and anyone else who has the power to select or reject a candidate. The anthropologist Paul Bohannan (1963) concluded from a study of many societies that men traditionally acquired certain rights to women after marriage. One was the right to share a "domicile" in which the couple lived, forming and maintaining it. The second right was that of sexual access, and the third of filiation of the resultant children with the patrilineal line. Finally, a husband had economic rights to the wife: to the goods she brought with her, to those they created together, and to those she created independently. The stronger the patriarchy, the stronger these rights. Of course, the flip side was that the wife also acquired rights to sharing a domicile, to sexual intercourse (even if only for procreation in societies in which her pleasure was not the purpose), to the filiation of the children to the male line that was therefore responsible for their welfare and inheritance, and to her own support. The whole picture emphasizes the importance of the already formulated social circle into which the wife entered at marriage. In traditional societies, the husband's family of orientation (into which he was born), especially his mother, and his male relatives had a great deal of control over his wife's life.

Women vary considerably in what being married means and in their relationship with their husbands and how it is embedded in other relationships. Polygamous marriages, in which one man has more than one wife, or polyandrous marriages (rare), in which one wife has several husbands, are certainly different from each other and from monogamous ones. Even within the same society, marriages vary by social class or caste, race, religion, ethnicity, rural-urban location, and the other roles of both husband and wife. The age difference between the husband and wife has an important effect in that older men generally have more power in the relationship than do younger men.[3] Groups other than the kinship group that can have influence, even considerable control, over the marriage, are the community, the employer, or the state. Finally, the interpersonal dynamics within a marriage differ considerably, depending on mate selection, the cultural expectations of egalitarianism or patriarchy, stage in the life course, prior relations with other men and women, role clusters, commitments, and emotions and sentiments.

The influence of the patriarchal family on the son and on his family of procreation decreased during the transitional era. The son could obtain the knowledge he needed for participation in the broader society from schools and his own means of economic support from a job. He was free to jointly select a wife, move away from his family, and establish his own household. The wife was also freed from the control of her in-laws. Much of the patriarchal nature of the social structure, however, still restricted her sphere of operation. Starting about the 18th century, increasing societal complexity pulled much of life away from the household and its territory into the public sphere

(Lopata, 1993a, 1994b). Much of traditional work, as well as of the numerous new forms of work, became organized into jobs in employing structures. Political life formed around the ever-growing state. A very influential ideology of "separate spheres" emerged in societies such as America that defined the public sphere as the province of men and as of greater importance than the private sphere that was assigned to women. The main purpose of the private sphere was to provide support to the breadwinner and new, properly socialized members to the society in appropriate gender roles (Bernard, 1983). Wifehood and motherhood acquired primary importance as "natural" social roles for women, discouraging women with these roles from active participation in the public sphere. This made them and their children, as well as others who were unable to work for money, into personal dependents of the man (Eichler, 1973).

The freedom gained by the nuclear unit from the patriarchal line brought with it certain disadvantages, in that it simultaneously weakened the prior support systems from the extended family. The male kinship network could be ignored. So could the woman's own family of orientation, although it tended to increase in importance as the husband's family began to lose its traditional rights. The social circle of the role of wife became increasingly one of choice on the part of the couple. The emphasis on voluntary marriage increased the importance of the marital unit, expected now to provide all the main supports, economic, service, social, and emotional. This was a heavy burden during these transitional times, with decrystallizing gender roles and increasing consciousness of women.

The middle-class wife of the transitional era may have been deeply involved in what is called a two-person single career (Papanek, 1973, 1979). Her role may have included obligations to the husband's employer and work associates, especially if he was in a salaried position with organizational responsibility. In addition to providing emotional and service supports expected from the primary sphere, she may have had to contribute social support in the form of entertainment or attendance at meetings and instrumental work assisting his career. These supports included protection of the husband from problems arising at home (such as those confronting the children, for whom she had almost exclusive responsibility), care of his personal needs (such as laundry and meals), emotional "stroking," and maintenance of the home. Societies such as the American one were built on what Coser

(1974) called "greedy institutions," especially in the economic and political arenas, that assumed total commitment and loyalty to the employer or organization. The worker was the man; the support person, the wife, devoted full-time to her private-sphere responsibilities, except when she was directly involved in helping her husband with his job. The family was her "greedy institution" (Coser & Coser, 1974), demanding total loyalty and noninterference from external social roles and commitments.

Bohannan's (1963) conclusions as to the rights men acquire in marriage may have been universal in the past, but they have certainly changed in recent years. Even the right to sexual access is being questioned in American courts. The marital unit can live anywhere it wishes, and wives can even have an independent domicile. How economic goods are handled is another of the negotiated aspects of modern marriage.

Modern marriages tend to assume ideologically greater equality between husband and wife, because each spouse is involved in both public and private lives. Whether in response to the consciousness raised by the feminist movement, opening opportunities, or economic necessity, most women are now active in the labor force and in other public arenas. They tend to remain in these after marriage and even after the birth of children. Servants and extended family members are mainly gone from the modern household, and each couple has to solve its own support problems.

Despite the ideological trend toward egalitarian marriage, reality finds that vestiges of patriarchy still abound, as evidenced in studies such as Hochschild's (1989) *The Second Shift*. This sociologist found that even in two-career, or at least two-earner, marriages, the woman contributes much more time and energy and carries much more responsibility to household management and to the role of parent than does the man. In fact, in most cases, the man whose wife has a full-time job behaves not very differently from the husband of a full-time homemaker. The problems contained in the role of wife in modern times have turned many a woman away from such involvement or delayed her entering it. Bernard (1973) concluded that there are actually two marriages, his and hers, and that hers has fewer advantages and creates more emotional and physical problems than does his marriage. Although we can write off such situations by defining them as true of only transitional marriages, they are very prevalent even in the 1990s. Maybe we need to include a second stage of transitional marriages, when the wife is already spending considerable ability, time, and energy in contributing to the "good provider" function (Bernard, 1983) that had formed part of the husband's role, without much cooperation from others, husband, family, or community. The myth of the economically dependent homemaking wife ignored the fact that the husband was also dependent on all her unpaid labor and support. The myth continues in the image of the wife who is sharing the provider function with no backup person of her own—if she does not earn as much as he earns. We can but speculate on the changes that need to be made in the society, community, and family for a truly egalitarian marriage to proliferate. In the meantime, the solutions to role conflict problems are still worked out on an individual level, the burden usually carried by the wife, with much strain and broken marriages.

DEATH

Death of a group member is disturbing to survivors. Each society that we know of has developed complex rituals to establish and acknowledge this event, dispose of the body, and reintegrate itself (Rosenblatt, Walsh, & Jackson, 1976). The mourning rituals vary by complexity but generally surround the declaration of the actual death by someone who has the authority to make that decision and provide some explanation of its causes, which is especially important in deaths of leaders and deaths involving inheritance. Specified people have the societally defined obligation to care for the body; arrange for funeral or memorial services, if these are to take place; and dispose of the body. Religious beliefs and ceremonies are usually involved or even dominant in all the rituals and have important historical functions in documenting a death, enabling not only continued social life but also disposal or dispersal of the property of the deceased.

In prior centuries, and in places where belief in the afterlife was strong, many items of property, including wives and concubines, went into the grave or crypt with the deceased to help him (sometimes her) on the journey to the spiritual resting place and life within it. Numerous Egyptian tombs provide perfect examples of such practices, the use of the goods and people illustrated by biographical pictographs on the walls.

An example of the complexity of funeral and mourning rituals is found in the orthodox Jewish religion. The care of the body is very important; autopsies and embalming are discouraged, even forbidden, because they are seen as a desecration of the body. Permission for the former must be given by a "competent rabbinic authority" and only under specified conditions (see Lamm, 1969, pp. 9-15). There are exact ways that the body must be prepared for burial, and it should never be left alone until that time.

Orthodox Jews also define who has the right to be an *onen,* that is, the close relative who is *obliged* to mourn, distinguishing that person from others who are not allowed to be an *onen.* Those obliged to mourn must follow a complex set of rules concerning eating, drinking, self-adornment, business, study of the Torah, and participating in pleasurable activities. The rights of an *onen* include release from certain other duties.

The right to mourn and take part in the funeral, as well as the norms of appropriate behavior by each person are strong in every society. As Rosenblatt et al. (1976, p. 16) found, however, appropriate behavior is quite varied. In Bali, for example, instead of the expressions of grief and anger so typical of the Western world, there is laughter and smiling. Anthropologists sometimes assume that all survivors of the death of a significant other must feel anger and aggression, and when they do not find ritualistic expressions of such emotions, they explain their absence as purposeful concealment or suppression (see also Stroebe & Stroebe, 1987, for such explanations). We will deal here only with the cross-cultural analysis of behavior deemed appropriate in different places, leaving the discussion of the sentiments and emotions of grief to Chapter 4.

Common to funeral and mourning behavior in most cultures are all forms of crying, ranging from quiet release of tears to wailing. Self-mutilation and mutilation of clothing are practiced in several societies. Ritual expressions or suppressions of anger are usually highly controlled so as not to create serious disruption of the group. Many of the rituals keep the close survivors either isolated in numbness or too busy to consider all the consequences of death. The funeral itself performs many functions of group solidarity identified by Durkheim (1915/1946) and described in my earlier work:

> One of the functions of the funeral is to insure that the body of the deceased is buried or handled in a sanitarily appropriate manner in spite

of the expected emotional instability of the immediate survivors. In addition, of course, the funeral accomplishes other functions: reminding the society of the deceased and building a collective representation . . . of him, especially in cases in which he can serve as a symbol of the group; uniting the survivors with new bonds in spite of the death; facilitating disengagement and temporary limbo location of those who are expected to have their lives disorganized by the event; and insuring the living that they too will be remembered. (Lopata, 1973d, p. 53)

One of the common fears of human beings is that they will soon be forgotten and life will go on as if they never lived and were important to others. The funeral, especially the eulogy, serves to frame the memory of the deceased in pleasant terms. The Jewish shiva organizes the memories of the life and the circumstances of death (see Lamm, 1969, pp. 86-146). The shiva starts right after the funeral, takes place in the home of the mourners and lasts 7 days. Strict norms as to the appearance of the house and participants are observed, and shiva visitors pay condolences and allow the main survivors to grieve openly, not bringing their own problems into the home. According to Gorer (1967), many of the rituals of mourning have become deinstitutionalized in the modern, Western world, to the detriment of people who must accomplish their grief work individually, without public guidelines (see Chapter 4).

The frequency of and age at death in any society are affected by natural events, such as floods or plagues, and societal events, such as wars. Longer life expectancy exists in societies with more scientific public health and medical care. Barring events such as wars that create young widows or death in childbirth that creates young widowers, widowhood tends to occur increasingly late in life. One of the characteristics of American society is that more marriages are dissolved through divorce than through widowhood.

THE ROLE OF WIDOW

Defining a social role as a set of relations between a social person and a social circle clarifies one of the confusions surrounding the study of widowhood. People often speak of the role of widow. The pervasive nature of widowhood as an experience of losing one's husband through death and of *widow* as one of the characteristic of a woman, varies considerably, as we shall see, by society. For the role of widow to exist, there would have to be some function or purpose that ties together the duties and rights between a widowed woman and some sort of circle. The purpose would be to separate a widowed woman from other women not only by the fact of widowhood but also through some sort of function that widowed women perform that nonwidowed women do not perform. It is possible to speak of a lifelong role of widow in traditional India, in which widowed women were assigned a completely different set of duties and rights from other women. The movie *Zorba the Greek* portrayed women in black clothing, forming part of each other's circle as widows, relating to other people as widows, able and needing to perform certain functions in the community, such as assisting at funerals.

American society lacks such a distinct role that lasts beyond the funeral and the earliest stages of widowhood. One can logically say, however, that there is a transitory role of widow in America, with a definite circle and with duties and rights surrounding the funeral. That role is central in a woman's role cluster for the duration of the mourning period. It is then dropped at some indefinite and varied time, becoming a characteristic of the woman that enters more or less significantly into her social roles, such as friend, mother, or neighbor. The fact that a woman is widowed may affect her friendships or her role as mother, but there is no translation of the role of wife into a role of widow. As with the role of student, accountant, or nun, exit from the role of wife carries certain remaining obligations, such as keeping the husband's social self alive through memory and through reminders of him to others. According to my definition of social role, there is no role of "ex-wife."[4]

Widowhood as a Pervasive Identity

What happens to the wife when her husband dies depends on the degree of her dependence on being married and being married to that particular husband, the degree of disorganization in her various roles and support systems, and her status as a widow. Her life need not be heavily disorganized in traditional marital systems if she simply continues residence and participation in the family work and social group, especially if she can remarry within it or have a *levir* provided from the husband's male relatives.[5] According to Bohannan (1963, p. 120), a levir carries forth the obligation of the late husband to impregnate the widow but is not considered the father of the children she bears, the late husband remaining the father. Also, the levir does not carry forth other duties of the role of husband and does not receive all the rights. Other scholars disagree with this view, considering the levirate system similar to widow remarriage within the husband's family. Widow remarriage to a brother or other male agnate (close relative) of the deceased occurs when he gains the same rights as any husband. Highly patriarchal families almost invariably do not want the widow to marry outside of the family if she already has children because the descent line is thus confused. In fact, one of the indexes of modernization is the removal of norms controlling the remarriage of a widow. In some societies, such as Hindu India, even the religion forbids a widow's entrance into another marriage, because the first one is for eternity.

Generally speaking, widowed women in traditional societies often face a strong drop in status and limited life choices. In some communities in which a woman cannot support herself independently, a widow can leave the husband's family and return to her family of origin, as long as the couple did not have children and she is not pregnant. Of course, such a move depends also on whether her family of orientation is willing to receive her back, which it might not be if it has to return a bride-price to the late husband's family. It is more likely to accept her if her return brings back the dowry that she carried with her on marriage, but that is not likely to happen.

In transitional societies, a woman's life could be highly disrupted if she does not have economic means of support, because she is not likely to have skills with which to obtain a well-paying job after full-time homemaking. Social security has introduced some decrease of poverty and worry, but in America it does not cover the "gray" years after the children are grown and before the widow reaches beneficiary age. Family support is usually possible only if she moves in with her married children and contributes to the care of their home and offspring.

In modern societies, remarriage is less and less possible the older the widow. When it does occur, it must be entered through a renewal of mate selection rituals. In societies such as the American one, there are no formal norms about remarriage, although objections can be raised by children afraid of losing their inheritance in community property states. A widow who has been active in social roles in circles in which the husband was not fully involved may continue these with little disruption.

What a widow can do with the rest of her life depends also on the societally developed resources, such as inheritance laws defining and protecting her property, paid labor force participation, geographical mobility, organizational affiliation, and the roles available to her at her particular stage of life. She herself must enter new roles if social barriers do not prevent her from doing so. This means she must have the necessary knowledge to prepare for and enter these roles.

In fact, one of the variations in widowhood is the amount of control other people may have over the woman after the death of her husband. As we shall see, in traditional India, this control can be all-encompassing and her whole life can depend on her in-laws (Patil, 1990). On the other hand, most Chicago-area widowed women whom I studied hardly ever saw their former in-laws unless there were important reasons for continuing contact, such as inheritance of position or goods by the children (Lopata, 1979). Even less frequent was interaction with the late husbands' work associates, who appeared to drop the women once the connecting link died, often causing the women feelings of abandonment and anger.

The decrease of control by other people can lead to isolation or freedom of life choices on the part of the widow. In general, widowed women in modern societies do not face loss of status or in relations with others of the type experienced in other places. The main situation in which they do feel like a "second-class citizen" or "a fifth wheel" is in the company of couples, especially married friends, as we shall see in Chapter 6. The most frequently expressed feeling is personal loneliness. Widows are unlikely to be living with relatives, even married children, preferring and being able to live independently.

Summary

This introductory chapter provides the definition of some basic concepts to be used throughout this book as well as a framework for organizing the social changes affecting widowhood in general. Defining a social role as a set of functionally interdependent, negotiated relations between a social person and a social circle involving duties and obligations, rights and privileges, we concluded that there is no role of widow in modern American society. Many other societies isolate widows from other women, providing them functions and a social circle or allowing them to pull together such a circle. In America and in many other Western societies, that role is a transitory one, surrounding the funeral and of an indefinite ending. Widowhood then becomes a pervasive identity or characteristic of a woman, entering her social roles to varying degrees. In many social roles this identity may not even be known, although it may be an important component of her relations with friends and family. The wider and more complex a woman's social life space, the less likely is her identity as a widow to enter the social relationships of each role.

Social development or modernization has introduced tremendous changes in the lives of societal members, but even in societies defined as most developed, there is great variation in how it has influenced any particular individual. Traditional family systems dominated lives of members, with patriarchal, patrilineal, and patrilocal ones controlling the wives brought into the unit and the widows remaining in it. A drop in status was common in the absence of the men from whom it was vicariously obtained—fathers, husbands, and sons. Remarriage or the levirate custom decreased the amount of disorganization faced by the widow.

The transitional era of social development, full of vestiges of the traditional mixed in with modernizing life circumstances, makes the role of wife and the situation of widows full of role conflict and strain. The decrease of the power of the extended, patriarchal family has turned the wife and children into personal dependents on the husband and father and restricted the woman mainly to the private sphere, the husband providing one of the few links to the outside world. Widowhood has brought dependence on the children, usually the daughter, unless the woman has a multidimensional life space, which few have had.

The so-called modern family system, reached unevenly and least often among older, less educated women, attempts to develop egalitarian, role-negotiated relationships between men and women who are involved in both the private and public worlds, pulling them together and blurring the boundaries. There are many vestiges of patriarchy in that few wives and husbands really share responsibility and work in their lives. Communities have not as yet returned to feelings of concern and responsibility for "other people's children"; each family unit must solve its role conflicts and strains independently, with few resources provided by the society (Grubb & Lazerson, 1983). The amount of disorganization brought about by widowhood in modern America depends to a great extent on the degree to which a wife was dependent on being married and dependent on that husband in all her roles and life space.

The organization of *Current Widowhood: Myths & Realities* is as follows: Chapter 2 introduces some of the differences in widowhood experiences in several rather varied countries, leading then into Chapter 3, which examines the variations within American society alone. The places that I have selected to examine the ways in which widowhood can affect women are ones for which I have the greatest amount of information and that provide the strongest contrasts. Chapters 4 and 5 are devoted to the processes by which wives become widows and the various problems surrounding this major life transition. Changes in kin roles, especially that of mother, produced by these processes are covered in Chapter 6. Chapter 7 analyzes the effect of being a widowed woman on friendships, old and new, same gender and cross-gender, concluding with remarriage. The involvement of widowed women in the community and the resources provided by the American society to widows, older women, and the elderly in general are discussed in Chapter 8. The final chapter brings together the theoretical and empirical ideas from the book as a whole, stressing the importance of social development and of the myths about widowhood.

The reader must remember that these descriptions do not apply to each woman but simply generalize patterns learned from many different women. Throughout, we will be guided not only by social development theory but also by the social role framework, a paradigm or prism organizing the wealth of characteristics surrounding the subject of widowhood.

Throughout the discussion, we will examine some of the myths concerning the characteristics and lives of widows as these myths apply to societies, women within them, old women, widows, and certain categories of widows.

Notes

1. Social scientists and historians have made many attempts to analyze the social changes through which societies have been going in the past two centuries or so. There is a great deal of debate concerning the concepts that best summarize these changes, because they often appear patronizing to some people and their polarization (as in traditional-modern) camouflages the complexities. As Gusfield (1967) pointed out, there are many myths about the mutual exclusiveness of traditional and modern social systems.

The concept of social development presents more of an image of continuity of change, and the concept of scale of social complexity provides the direction of change.

2. There are now a few lesbian marriages, but not enough is known about them to allow separate analysis.

3. As late as 1980, some of the "less developed" (by the United Nations definition) countries recorded an average age difference between men and women at marriage—as high as 8 years in Afghanistan and Bangladesh (see Koo, 1982, p. 15).

4. In this, I do not agree with Ebaugh (1988) that being an "ex" is a role lasting forever, but it can be a transitional one during the process of role exit. It becomes a vestige of the role and a characteristic affecting other roles. To call a woman a widow or divorcée or a man an ex-priest does not identify a role unless there is a social circle within which there are duties and rights because of the ex status. Most of Ebaugh's examples are of temporary stages of role exit or even of temporary roles within something like a halfway house, although a few appear to be long lasting.

5. The concepts "levir" and "agnate" are specific anthropological concepts that apply to such relationships in many societies. The Oxford Universal Dictionary (1955) defines an agnate as "a descendant by male links from the same common male ancestor" (p. 36). A levir is less clearly specified as a brother-in-law acting under the custom of a levirate. Levirate is defined as "a custom among Jews and some other nations, by which the brother or next of kin to the deceased man was bound under certain circumstances to marry the widow" (p. 1133).

2

Widowhood in
Other Places and Times

Myth: Families in traditional societies take care of any members with problems, and this is especially true of their care of widows.

Myth: Modernization or social development inevitably benefits all societal members, including widows.

Neither of these sets of beliefs can be supported by the realities of widow's lives in either traditional or rapidly modernizing societies, as we shall see when we look at specific countries. Yet the idealization of traditional cultures and social groups continues into current times (Coontz, 1992).

There is really no guarantee that families will take care of their members who are going through troubling times or facing problems. In fact, all indications point to serious impingement on personal safety, happiness, and all sorts of rights by members of a dependent individual's own family, in the past and present.[1] In addition, attempts to ensure such rights by modernizing governments are so lacking in power over tradition or so half-heartedly applied, that they do not offset the weakening of the protective support systems that did work in the past. We can illustrate these points with some case studies of the situations of widows in several societies experiencing different processes of social development.

Widowhood in Traditional
Times and Places: India

"For a Hindu woman, widowhood is considered a punishment for the crime committed by her in her previous life. Hence, she is looked down upon as a sinner" (Patil, 1990, preface).

The subcontinent of India is a large and very complex society in which caste, social class, religious, tribal, and urban-rural divisions form varying combinations on any theme. India was occupied by the British for about two centuries, until it won its independence under the leadership of Mahatma Ghandi in 1947. It then experienced extensive conflict between Hindus and Muslims, which resulted in an exodus of Muslims north to form a separate nation of Pakistan. India is now about 82% Hindu, only 12% Muslim, and 6% other religions (see Gujral, 1987, p. 43). As a nation, India is second only to China in population. India is still heavily rural and agricultural, although the cities are becoming some of the most populous in the world. The people are highly traditional, influenced by religion and the centuries-old caste system. Poverty and an inadequate public health system account for a high mortality rate, varied by state. To better understand the size of the population, we can turn to the U.S. Bureau of the Census (U.S. Department of Commerce, 1992a) figures on *Global Aging*. According to this source, there were almost 53 million people aged 60 and over in India in 1990, and 19% of the men but 64% of the women were widowed. Thirty-five percent of the men but only 8% of the women were literate, and a lower proportion of the elderly than of the population as a whole lived in urban areas.

The situation of women, and of widows in particular, has undergone numerous historical changes in India, their status allegedly having deteriorated from an ideal far-distant past but steadily improving in recent years. The subject of widowhood was rather neglected until recent years, and now the most available knowledge concerns the Hindu widow (Gujral, 1987; Patil, 1990). Several factors still make the life of widowed women particularly difficult, with many remaining vestiges of the worst times resisting attempts of colonial and independent governments to change their condition. This is one place where there is a clearly defined role of widow that lasts for the remainder of a woman's life.

In the first place, India is a highly patriarchal, patrilineal, and patrilocal society. Joint family residence, combined with arranged marriages of often young girls, make women highly dependent on their in-laws. Lack of education, rural poverty, and the culturally defined need for many children, especially sons, have kept women in a perpetual round of childbirth and work. Women have a definitely low status in Indian society and are socialized throughout the life course into such awareness (see Ullrich, 1988, p. 171).

In the second place, Hinduism provides support for many negative features of widowhood that are not prevalent in other societies (Patil, 1990). The belief that the death of the husband is the fault of the wife—if not due to her present sins, then to ones she committed in a prior life—justifies even extremely harsh treatment. The ideal behavior on the part of a widow was, and in some rural areas still is, *suttee,* or self-immolation on the funeral pyre of the deceased husband's body. This practice, usually limited to the higher castes because the lower castes could ill afford to lose the labor of their women, most frequently occurred in the state of Bengal, particularly near Calcutta, where 839 *satis* (suttee is the practice; sati is the woman who commits the act) were recorded in 1818. The practice was forbidden by the British colonial powers in 1829, but the rule was not strictly enforced because the conquerors tried to stay out of religious and family life. It keeps reappearing occasionally, especially in rural areas (see Patil, 1990, p. 69). In fact, a case of suttee occurred in Rajasthan when I was there in 1987 on a Fulbright fellowship. Not only did the young widow die, but a shrine sanctifying her appeared on the spot one night and flowers were frequently placed on it. Many such shrines are located in India, although the government has tried to remove them in recent years. The Hindu religion defines the act of suttee as a ritually approved sacrifice surrounded, as in a wedding, by elaborate preparations and rituals. It brings honor not only to the widow but also to her and her husband's families (Stein, 1978, 1989, p. 467). Its value in India's traditional past and current rural areas has been tied to the Hindu belief in reincarnation and the need of deceased men to be served in the afterlife. The religion contains a devaluation of women and the purdahlike custom of their isolation from men, borrowed from the Muslims. It supports a widow's loss of status and approved suttee in the past (possibly even now).

A woman who did not commit the ideal act, as few ever did, can be forced into a very miserable life, dependent on the whims of her in-laws, because ties to her own family are cut after marriage (Patil, 1990). The family of origin has rarely been able to protect the daughter, even in cases of severe mistreatment by her husband, her in-laws, or both. Widows' appearance and treatment by others are constant reminders of their low status. "A widowed woman has no right to participate in any socio-religious functions, and her presence is considered as inauspicious. . . . A Hindu widow is deprived of wearing the Tali [blouse], flowers, glass bangles, nose ring and applying 'kumkum' [the red dot on the forehead]" (Patil, 1990, pp. 20, 50).

Thus, widows have been forbidden from attending most social events because they are considered inauspicious beings, and their distinctive and unattractive appearance is aimed at discouraging men from becoming interested in them. In some areas, the widow's head is shaved. The appearance norms have weakened in much of India, but one can still see distinctive garb on widows in some rural areas. Widowhood is made relatively frequent by the fact that the husband is usually much older than the wife. There are still many sanctions against remarriage, despite the Hindu Widow's Remarriage Act of 1925 (see Patil, 1990, p. 66). Few widows actually do remarry; the strength of feelings against such unions keeps the rate extremely low even now. Widowers tend to remarry soon with the help and approval of everyone wishing more children in the patriarchal line.

The worst off in India is the widow without children—that is, without sons. This situation was very common in the past due to the presence of child brides. The marriage of very young children, the girl long before puberty, was practiced in the past so that the bride could become socialized into the groom's family, to whose household she moved after the ceremony. The frequent result was that she then became widowed before the marriage could even be consummated. The lot of the child widow was defined as worse than even that of a servant because she had no power herself in the in-law household and no protector. She had failed in two ways—by having a husband who died and by not having sons. She had to follow the exclusion norms of all widows. Better off was the widow with grown sons who inherited the father's property and whose responsibility it was to maintain the widowed mother.

The mother-son tie was considered the most loving and devoted in traditional India, because marriages were arranged by the families and love was not required (Ross, 1962). Daughters left early in life to marry, with their main obligations being toward their in-laws, not to their own mothers. A widow had the legal and social right to maintenance by whoever inherits the husband's property—traditionally, the son (see p. 195). The son must support her out of his property even if there had been no inheritance. The lucky widow was the matriarch of the family and the household, the daughter-in-law carrying forth most of the work. Most Indian women, widowed or not, cannot live alone even now because they were not socialized for independent life. Thus, "she must live with her son over whom she has no authority" (Patil, 1990, p. 37).

The Indian government has been attempting to lessen some of the worst problems faced by widows, not always successfully. For example, traditional Hindu families rushed to marry "three million little girls and two million boys" before the Sadra Act of 1929-1930 forbidding marriages of girls under age 14 and boys under 18 was implemented (see Felton, 1966, p. 168; Lopata, 1987b, p. 13). The Hindu Marriage Act of 1955 set the minimum age for girls entering marriage at 15. It has recently been raised to 18 for girls. Stories abound in the mass media of families that "sell" their daughters to men of Arab and other societies.

The laws and customs of inheritance form an important factor in a widow's life in any society. It was not until the Hindu Women's Right to Property Act of 1937 that she was legally ensured to receive shares of the couple's joint property and of the separate property of the husband. Her rights are limited, however, in that she cannot sell, mortgage, or give away any of the ancestral property, which reverts to the heirs on her death (see Patil, 1990, p. 95).

> Under the Hindu Code, when a husband dies intestate, all property acquired by the husband himself is divided equally between his widow, mother, sons and daughters, whether married or not. However, ancestral property is inherited only by sons who have equal rights to it from birth, though the widow is entitled to use the proceeds and income from the property, and to being cared for by her sons, until her death. Ancestral property, moreover, cannot be sold or otherwise disposed of by anyone in a family without the written, legal consent of all other family members. Thus, it is very infrequent that sons or other family members

actually sell land, because it is extremely rare for everyone in the family to agree. (Vlassoff, 1990, p. 8)

The distinction between property acquired by the husband and ancestral property is an important indicator of the strong lineage power. Finally, the Hindu Succession Act of 1956 gave a woman the right to inherit from the father, as well as from the husband. She gets equal shares with the son, daughter, and mother. A Hindu woman now has full power to deal with her property, including its disposal.

Ghosh (1984) summarizes all the legal change: "After about two thousand years the curse of Manu was lifted" (p. 2). The curse to which he refers was the code of Manu that dominated Indian society and deprived women of any significant rights that might provide independence from the male family line.

The benefits of the succession act do not necessarily accrue to widows, because older ones tend to be illiterate and ignorant of the laws, unable to protect themselves. Vlassoff (1990) studied widows in a small village in Maharashtra State and found that many had either signed papers relinquishing their rights to any land in favor of the son or did not even know that they owned any land. In fact, widows were often even forced out of the home and cheated of their rights by various members of the late husband's family. The widows she interviewed did not actually obtain economic benefits from the sons and had to work and provide for themselves. They valued their sons highly, however, counting on relinquishing all responsibilities to them and being provided for in old age. Sons were also valued as carriers of the family line or name. In Vlassoff's study, widows were happiest if living with sons but visited regularly by daughters. In this particular case, daughters remained nearby after marriage due to a local mate selection custom, a rarity in traditional India.

The economic problems of Indian widows without inheritance are frequent particularly if they are uneducated and in rural areas without income-paying jobs. The government of Karnataka, one of the Indian states in the South, passed a law in 1984 giving destitute resident widows without a son a pension under a social security program (see Patil, 1990, p. 69). In other locales, such as Varanasi, begging and prostitution are known to be a means of widow survival, because jobs are difficult to obtain without education. Therefore, dependence on in-laws continues until, or unless, they have adult sons who willingly take over the maintenance and care of the mother. Coresidence with married sons can have its own problems. Relations with the daughter-in-law vary according to the power each holds, supported by the male link. If the two women are in conflict and the son is "modern" and takes the wife's side, the widow may be in an awkward position, having even to cook her own meals separately.

Even at the present time, various forms of these dependencies exist for many, if not most, widowed women in different areas of India. Modernization has removed some of the previous supports, but the government has been slow in introducing changes through laws, and these are often ineffectual. As is frequently the case all over the world, national or state laws that try to rectify some of the problems are not followed locally if they go against deeply ingrained cultural norms.

An example of a new problem in the support of widows, also experienced in other urbanizing societies in which sons are still responsible for the economic maintenance of the mother, is the movement of these adult offspring from the land to the city. At first, the sons send back money to replace their labor. Later, as they become more modernized, they turn their attention to their families of procreation, their wives and children, neglecting their obligations to the elderly parents or widow (Gujral, 1987). There is no one to take their place and the women are too uneducated, in the rural areas but also often in the cities, to know about and take advantage of societally created resources.

Thus, Myth 1, at the beginning of this chapter, that traditional families take care of any members who have problems, certainly goes against realities in India. The myth is believed by Indians, as it is by members of other traditional societies, despite constant reminders in the Indian mass media of the mistreatment and even murder of women, wives, and widows.[2] At the same time, social development in urban, middle-class areas of India has not benefited many widows, because most of them and their associates were born and raised in traditional times in which women are deprived of acceptable status and social rights.

Widowhood in Transitional Times and Places

When we look at studies of the situation of widows in rapidly changing societies we find even now many vestiges of a similar patriarchal past, although each presents some unique combinations of traditional and modern features.

ISRAEL

Israel is a relatively small country, whose older population of age 60 or more tends to be proportionally smaller than that of Western Europe or America, to a great extent due to the timing and composition of immigration. The overall literacy level is relatively high, although unevenly distributed among subpopulations. At that, 76% of the older women and 88% of the older men are literate (U.S. Department of Commerce, 1992b).

Israel is also a relatively new national state, located in the Middle East, forged through a War of Independence in 1948 and frequently engaged in defensive wars or other hostile activities with its Arab neighbors. Most of Israel's residents (84%) are Jewish, the remaining being mostly Muslim Arabs (see Katz & Ben-Dor, 1987, p. 133). The Israeli population came from all over the world where Jews had previously settled. The heterogeneity is great, with even variations of religious belief and practice within Judaism. The more educated members who migrated from Europe are very different from those coming from North Africa, Iraq, Syria, Yemen, Ethiopia, and so forth. The governments in power since independence have tried to create a more homogeneous nation with the help of mass education and a variety of laws protecting citizens as new situations arise (Shamgar-Handelman, 1986). One of their problems has been the frequent contradictions between policies of the modern political state and the traditional beliefs and practices of the religious society (Lopata, 1994b; Znaniecki, 1952).

An important characteristic of Israel is the development and maintenance of numerous cooperative communities called *kibbutzim.* Two main purposes of the kibbutzim movement, which organized cooperative communities, were to defend the new nation from attacks by neighbors and to organize work as efficiently as possible. An additional aim, according to Diamont (1957), was to change the *shtetl,* or the mentality of the isolated Jewish ghetto of Eastern Europe, which tended to denigrate women and make men passive against external aggression. Even in the kibbutz, however, despite the ideology of equality, gender stratification in work roles reemerged. Whether in these communities or the society at large, the situation of women is complex and mixed, as reflected in attitudes and policies directed at widows.

In 1980, the average age of the million and a half Israeli women was a young 31.2 years (see Katz & Ben-Dor, 1987, p. 134). Only 54% were born in that country, 26% having come from Europe or America, 11% from Africa, and 10% from Asia. The older women were most likely to have come from other places, and 47% of the women were widowed, compared with only 14% of the men aged 60 and over. As in many other smaller nations going through rapid social development, this gap was due to wars and the tendency of men to marry younger women and to remarry if the wife died.

Israel's rapidly expanding population includes people, especially women, who are not always able to maintain themselves economically. This is true of many of the widows, deprived of the main breadwinner. Families are often dispersed and unable to retain traditional bonds despite a strong familial orientation and identification, partly because of the need to defend the religion and the nation. Both the religion and the society are strongly patriarchal.

One of the customs of the Jewish religion involving the newly widowed is the 7-day *shiva* or mourning period, during which friends and relatives visit the bereaved and allow for open grieving. Many observers of the effect of death on survivors consider this ritual highly advantageous. According to Gorer (1967), Western societies, such as Great Britain and the United States, have made almost a pornography of death, treating it as something indecent that ought not to interfere with normal life and cutting the ritual of mourning to an extent detrimental to the bereaved. On the other hand, the Jewish mourning rituals following the shiva are extended over considerable time and tend to isolate the widow and tie her to the past rather than providing means of creating a new life (see Katz & Ben-Dor, 1987, p. 136).

As in many patriarchally based countries, wives lose status in widowhood, some more than others depending on governmental policy that provides many benefits to only some of them (Shamgar-Handelman, 1986). Israel is a society with a high rate of marriage, wifehood being the main role favored for women. Shamgar-Handelman observes,

If marriage is seen as a woman's achievement, paralleling a man's occupational achievement, then becoming a widow may be seen as parallel to a man's loss of status when he loses his job because of the economic failure of his employer. (p. 147)

Most Israeli women live in family households with the man as head, and his death "moves the widow and her family into a marginal or deviant social category" (p. 147). She also loses the "social rewards accorded to the husband for the roles he performed in the society" (p. 148). Her benefits of money, power, and prestige were enjoyed by her vicariously and evaporate with his death. The only way a woman can regain these rewards is through remarriage. This is more likely for war widows than for many others because of their young age.

Israel has introduced considerable variations in the treatment of widows. In Hindu India, all wives are held accountable for the husband's death, regardless of its physical causes. In Israel, the manner of his death influences how the widow's social circles in her various roles —kin member, friend, and citizen—treat her (Katz & Ben-Dor, 1987; Shamgar-Handelman, 1986). Widows whose husbands died of "civilian" causes—work-related accidents, road accidents, illness, or suicide —are treated differently from "war widows." All civilian widows fall under the Social Security Laws, the funds coming from compulsory insurance of all employed persons, pension laws that do not apply to all workplaces, and the Income Maintenance Law in cases in which the husband's work history made them ineligible for Social Security (see Katz & Ben-Dor, 1987, p. 139). Civilian widows are also divided into two categories. Those whose husbands died of work-related accidents receive a dependent's pension. Those whose husbands died of illness, road accidents, and suicide are entitled to a survivor's pension. The sums, adjusted for the number of dependent children are different, but both are much lower than the average salary. "Civilian widows are entitled to one year of vocational training, but this benefit is subject to the judgement of social security officials that the widow is 'amenable to rehabilitation' " (Katz & Ben-Dor, 1987, p. 140). It is often assumed that many women are so traumatized that they are unable to take advantage of occupational training. The judgment of a widow's ability to be "rehabilitated" (an interesting concept of itself) depends on officials who are almost always without any psychological training or knowledge.

War widows—that is, women who lost their husbands in wars and similar hostile activity—receive numerous benefits and a distinct social status. These benefits are covered under two main laws, the Law of Families of Soldiers Lost in Action of 1950 and the Law of Victims of Hostile Acts of 1970. Recent hostilities have undoubtedly resulted in new laws covering specific categories of widows, and policies and benefits are modified, often in response to pressure by the widows and even by their parents. The point is that the benefits depend on the way the husband died and have nothing to do with the woman's action or needs or with those of her children.

The whole process by which the Israeli government passed the various laws to define and honor families of those who died through "hostile acts" and the arguments used in this process are deeply ingrained in the traditional religion, whose representatives, until recently, have been running the country. The Families of Soldiers Law was aimed at preventing indigence, and the beneficiaries included parents, siblings, wives, and children of the war dead. Families defined as not indigent were not covered and thus officially not recognized. In fact, aid to families suffering because of war death of a member first went to the parents because the culture made them dependent on a son. The war widows organized and demanded benefits to themselves and their offspring, and thus a category of "war widows" was finally created. Widows are removed from this category when they remarry, but new wars and skirmishes bring in new members.

War widows are seen as the responsibility of the Ministry of Defense, which provides a great deal of help as a form of honoring the families of heroes. They receive a monthly allowance, child support, and fringe benefits, regardless of income. They are exempt from income taxes and receive aid "in purchasing electrical appliances, a telephone, a car and an apartment" (Katz & Ben-Dor, 1987, p. 140). They can obtain help in finding jobs, special housing arrangements, tuition for job training and higher education, and tuition for their children up to a bachelor's degree. Their status accrues prestige above that of other widows, allowing them membership in the Widow's Association and other organizations and assemblies, access to therapy groups with trained social workers or psychologists, and access to recreational activities. They can go abroad as representatives of war widows. Many widows take advantage of these benefits, although many do not know of changes if they do not keep up contacts with each other and with the Defense Department's Rehabilitation Centers. The Rehabilitation Department provides all the services, but the requirement of periodic visits and evaluations by social workers as to present "condition" is often resented by the women. War widows are automatically defined as having "psychological" problems even more so than civilian widows, regardless of their relations with others.

Some Israeli war widows use various means of trying to preserve or regain their prewidowhood status. Although they fare better than most Indian widows or "civilian" Israeli widows, their honored status as the wives rather than widows of military men simply cannot be duplicated. The social circle of the wife of a military man changes with his death, and remaining servicemen do not continue treating the widow the same as when the husband was alive. Often, contact is severed altogether. The status as war widows erode as time goes by, especially as new wars and conflicts bring more recent survivors to whom attention is directed. "Status-strengthening devices," as Shamgar-Handelman (1986, p. 153) calls them, such as improvement in housing and lifestyle facilitated by the financial benefits, are rendered unavailable after the widow's children reach the age of 18 and the economic resources decrease. Many of the women reject the status acquired through the husband prior to widowhood or that of war widow and attempt to gain prestige and power through their own achievements. One way of doing so is through remarriage, and another is through the creation of an occupational or professional career. For several reasons, the latter effort seldom brings the same rewards as being married to a successful man. In the first place, women's occupations in Israel seldom match those of men. To get a better position means a change of specialty from female-identified jobs, which is hard to achieve, requiring new educational and job training endeavors at a later age than typical. Most widows have little formal education to begin with, and their prior work experience, if any, is not of much help in acquiring higher-level jobs. A few do achieve "independently a comparatively high status, which make[s] up for the status loss from widowhood" (Shamgar-Handelman, 1986, p. 163).

The interesting point about this discussion is that Israeli war widows, at least as presented by two social scientific studies (Katz & Ben Dor, 1987; Shamgar-Handelman, 1986), have many more alternatives than possible in a traditional society in which women are likely to be bound to family roles and the loss of wifehood means a dramatic drop in status. In modernizing societies or segments of societies, members of both genders have available alternative social roles and lifestyles. The organization of work into money-paying jobs can provide independence from the families of origin or that of the husband. The more resources that are available, the more their use depends on the personal resources of the individual, including the resource of being able to make independent decisions. The more patriarchally traditional the society is, the more likely the women are to face restrictions on certain resources that men do not experience.

In the case of Israel, as described in these studies, the restrictions on women are in terms of education, insistence on the importance of family roles to the exclusion of other roles, and occupational segregation, with women's jobs offering fewer rewards and benefits than men's. Thus, although war widows are allegedly not prevented from seeking status-enhancing jobs, there is little in the culture or the social system to facilitate such efforts. Actually, a similar situation is developing in urban India, where higher education and paid jobs are gradually being opened up to women. Remarriage in Israel is much more acceptable as an alternative lifestyle than it is in India, partly because of differences in religious views and partly because of a societal wish for children. The levirate system, described in the Bible and Koran, interpreted here as requiring that the male agnate of the deceased not only contribute to the widow's childbearing but actually marry her, has been rejected by most families.[3] The widow and the male relative must go through a ceremony, however, that releases the bond before the woman can remarry someone of her own choice. All but one of the war widows studied by Shamgar-Handelman (1986), who were relatively young, wanted to remarry. Many of them did, despite loss of sometimes considerable benefits. The supports provided by the government are an excellent example of what the society at large can do, through its agencies, to assist members experiencing crises.

KOREA

Korea provides a perfect example of the problems of the transitional era, dramatically reflected in the situation of widows (Koo, 1982, 1987). It also illustrates the consequences of wars, in terms of shortages of men in proportion to women. Korea is an Asian society with a strong Confucian philosophy of life and religion. The country was partitioned into two parts in 1945 and experienced invasions and wars that disrupted the social structure. North Korea went under communist control, and South Korea came under capitalist influence.

Koo (1982, 1987) contrasted the situation of rural widows to those who had moved to Seoul, controlling for age. She found a great mixture of traditional and modern influences, typical of transitional eras. The traditional elements of the situation included a gender-specific, lower-strata status. Most women lacked formal education and depended on patriarchal families living in complex, two-generation households. From the age of 6, girls were confined to the home, isolated completely from males, socialized to be submissive to "three lords," the parents, the husband, and the eldest son. "The affinity of family members, filial piety and chastity of women have been considered essential values" (Koo, 1987, p. 57). Marriage was arranged, and the bride had to fit into the husband's extended family. Her labor belonged to her husband's parents, not to her family of orientation. In fact, the wife could be divorced for disobedience to her parents-in-law or conflict with her sisters-in-law (see Koo, 1982, p. 72). For example, she was not to contribute to family strife by displaying jealousy of the other women in this social unit. If a divorce occurred, the woman had to leave her children with the father's family because, officially, they belonged to it. Status shifts were problematic: Although aging brought respect and the important role of grandmother, widowhood resulted in a loss of status. Remarriage was forbidden.

South Korea has experienced dramatic changes in the past three or so decades, including improvement in economic and social conditions that created a wide rural-urban gap in lifestyle. More scientific public health measures and medical care have lowered the rate of mortality, resulting in rapid population growth. The ratio of widows to widowers has increased during these years, the life expectancy for women being 7 years longer than for men (see Koo, 1982, p. 79). A large number of men have been killed during the wars, and husbands tend to be several years older than wives. Many widowers remarry, whereas widows generally do not.

The processes of social development have involved rapid urbanization, or the increasing ratio of urban to nonurban dwellers (see Koo, 1982, p. 57). Modernization has affected the family and thus the life of widows in other ways: "Industrialization and urbanization are instrumental in transforming the authoritarian, large, stable, rural family system into a more egalitarian, relatively independent but unstable nuclear family" (p. 60). By 1975, only 13.1% of the population of South Korea lived in extended families (pp. 70-71). The ones who did were mainly the widows.

The first major change in Korea directly affecting widows was the movement of sons from rural areas to the cities, much the same as in India. At first, elderly parents, and then the widows, were likely to remain on the farm. The women were usually well integrated into the village and maintained lively social interaction with neighbors and village clubs. They often found it difficult, however, to maintain the farm if all children moved away. Few jobs were available, and the women were least able to earn money to pay helpers. Mobility of the younger family, especially from rural to urban areas, cut off contact with grandchildren, a traditionally important form of contact for Korean women. Many widows therefore left the village and moved in with the son in the city. Almost all of Koo's urban respondents were living with their children, the older ones with grown sons and their families and the younger ones with unmarried children. The older respondents usually had several living children, the average number being four.

Although elder sons remained the most important persons for Korean widows, daughters began to appear rather frequently in the emotional support system of the urban women, a tendency not found in literature on the traditional family. Often, these were unmarried daughters.

Koo (1982, p. 111) found Seoul widows with a much lower level of family and kin interaction than rural ones, because the extended family still functioned actively in villages. Most of the kin with whom rural women maintained contact were not likely to be of the family of orientation. Many even lost track of brothers and sisters (p. 115). This is partly due to the custom of marrying the daughter to a distant family, based on the belief that her own family might cause conflict within the new unit. In some cases, the death of the husband could reinforce ties with the in-laws, especially the eldest brother-in-law, who was the official guardian of the widowed sister-in-law. The late husband's family, including siblings-in-law, were seldom reported as helpful, despite expectations that they would be, which resulted in expressions of hostility. The expectations came from traditional times, and the reality of life in transitional times failed to meet such expectations.

Often, relations with daughters-in-law were strained. One widow studied by Koo explained that, although the son supported her financially, the daughter-in-law had a job away from the home and the widow actually earned her keep as a housekeeper and child rearer. That life was not comfortable for many urban widows is documented by the fact that in Seoul "about 250 runaway grandmothers were under the care of the City Day Care Center each week; of them 85 percent were widowed mothers-in-law" (Koo, 1987, p. 72).

Friendship with approximate age-mates, with whom Korean women interacted informally and comfortably, appeared to be even more important than kin relations, which tended to be obligatory and very status oriented. Rural widows did not differentiate between friend and neighbor. Because friendships were gender segregated, widows continued to see married associates as often as widowed ones, a different pattern than is true, as we shall see, in societies in which friendship tends to be couple companionate. Neighbors were important in the lives of these Koreans, especially in rural areas, where people prided themselves in having harmonious relations. Several housekeeping chores, such as cleaning vegetables or washing clothes, could be carried forth in the company of neighbors at communal locations. Borrowing and lending were also traditional within neighborhoods, as was informal dropping in during the daytime and attending meetings and shopping together. Formal invitations to neighbors were not part of the culture.

The other main disadvantage for widows who followed their sons to the city, in addition to strain or conflict with the daughter-in-law, was loneliness. Accustomed to being integrated into a society of village women and organized social events such as sight-seeing tours, the women often found themselves in neighborhoods containing no one they knew outside of the son's home. Furthermore, people followed with different norms of socializing than those that they had successfully used before. Urban relationships were based on choice rather than geographical proximity (see Koo, 1982, p. 129). The amount of neighboring in which the widows were involved depended on their knowledge of each other, sometimes made difficult by heterogeneity of the area or recency of migration. Some widows, however, reported numerous informal community activities, including very popular financial pools. All members of a group called *Kae* contributed a fixed amount at regular meetings for a kitty that went to one of them enabling major purchases or travel. The widows also shared hobbies and travel clubs. Involvement in a variety of usually informal peer groups was particularly true of younger urban widows, the older ones being less active.

Some of the widows who were now living in the city earned money on their own, but the jobs they were able to take were very low paying, due to their lack of experience in the labor force. The government had instituted no social security system, and the widows usually had no funds for independent living, which was impossible anyway in view of their rural background and lack of knowledge.

In studying the backgrounds of rural and urban widows Koo (1982) found that they differed considerably in education, occupation, income, and household conveniences. Koo explained that she used private conveniences as an indication of the socioeconomic status of widows because most did not hold jobs outside of the home and did not have an income or occupation (p. 124). It is possible that her urban sample included widows who were second-generation urbanites and that the women who moved from the village had a slightly higher socioeconomic background than those who stayed.

In general, the case of widows in South Korea illustrates the fact that rapid social development and urbanization contribute to the breakdown of traditional supports without creating adequate substitutes. Societal events such as wars can also unbalance gender proportions. These changes can produce serious difficulties for members such as elderly widowed women, socialized into a less developed culture and lacking many personal resources. There are other societies in which the juxtaposition of traditional, family, and village support systems of widows are assumed to be functioning. In actuality, they are withering as transitions brought about by modernization and especially as urbanization and mobility change basic life patterns.

TURKEY

The situation of widows in Turkey exemplifies three conflicting phenomena. In the first place, it is a strongly Muslim nation whose women were deeply constrained within the Ottoman Empire. In the second place, Ataturk, a revolutionary ruler, introduced Western-type reforms of the Swiss Civil Code after the War of Independence of 1918-1923. " 'The successful emergence of the Turkish woman from the seclusion of the harem is, no doubt, one of the greatest achievements of the Ataturk Revolution' " (Eren, 1963, quoted by Heisel,

1987, p. 82). Other reforms followed so that Turkish women now have complete legal equality with men. As in other modernizing societies, these legal rights are not available to most of the women, especially the village residents and the less educated. The third phenomenon has been the rapid mobility of the population, from rural to urban locations and even to locations outside of the country.

As of 1991, Turkey had a relatively low percentage of people aged 60 years or older (11.9% compared to the United States with 24.6%), and widows form half of the females of that age group, whereas only 15% are widowers (U.S. Department of Commerce, 1992b). Remarriage is encouraged for both genders, but the statistical distributions indicate that few widows have the opportunity of doing so. Only 15% of the women, compared to 44% of the men are "economically active," meaning that they earn an income. One major reason for the lack of earnings on the part of older women is their low literacy rate (15% compared to the men's 50%). This is typical of patriarchally based developing countries that invest first in educating the male members. A high proportion of the elderly live in nonurban areas.

One of the consequences of social development in Turkey is the fact that despite the myth of traditionally large, patriarchal, extended family household, most of the people (60%) live in nuclear households. This is particularly true of the urban population (55-68%) (Heisel, 1987, pp. 84-85). Of the remaining families, 19% are patriarchal extended, 13% temporarily extended, and 8% dissolved. In most of the country, there are no women heads of households or women living alone. Despite the fluidity of households, the extended kinship system appears quite active, especially in nonurban communities.

As is true of all Muslim countries, the status of women is low compared with men. Sons are considered necessary for family welfare, and daughters are a disappointment. Girls are socialized to be obedient, dependent, and "chaste"; family honor depends on their virginity at marriage. Rural Turkey practices the custom of bride-price, as compensation for the daughter's labor, accompanying arranged marriages (see Heisel, 1987, p. 88). Bride-price marriages, however, are not as frequent as in the past and in the ideal—again showing a gap between tradition and present-day reality. In recent marriages, the groom is likely to provide a house and gold directly to the girl to protect her against divorce or widowhood. A woman's best protection in later years is the presence of sons.

Dependence on a son, so typical of traditionally patriarchal family systems, can become an even greater problem in Turkey than for widows in rural Korea or India if he migrates out of the country. Many Turkish widows have sons who have moved to Germany and other European countries for jobs (Heisel, 1987). They then either marry away from home or bring Turkish wives over to their new locale. Seldom does the widow also move, not knowing the culture and language. The sons in India can at least be visited for varying lengths of time and can return home with greater ease than can Turkish sons crossing borders. Turkish sons soon absorb the European nuclear-family-of- procreation-ideology and turn their attention to their wives and children, losing feelings of obligation to the older parents, including the widowed mother. The Turkish wife who migrates with her husband, especially to European cities, gains new rights, often in conjunction with jobs and increased economic independence. She then does not want to be subjected to control by her mother-in-law. Thus, the widow's dependence on her son in the strong patriarchal system conflicts with the increased power of the wife in the more egalitarian family. She usually loses security as modernization replaces that part of traditionalism.

The rapidity of change in Turkey accentuates class divisions. Upper-class urban women, married and widowed, have greater probability of taking advantage of the reform laws and opportunities for education, jobs, and other involvements in the public sphere. They are thus much less dependent on the family. Rural, illiterate wives and widows remain highly dependent on the male members of their families. Economic benefits in the form of social security are unevenly available, and few widows can find employment, so those who do not have a supportive family can face serious economic problems. Social integration of all women, including widows, consists of a local and informal female network of relatives and neighbors. Turkey, unlike Korea, does not contain a network of more or less organized social groups. More urbanized centers display class-segregated patterns of visiting, and couple-companionate relations have sprung up on weekends and evenings (see Heisel, 1987, p. 95). Widowhood often brings more time for social interaction.

Despite the failure of the modern legal system to grant choices to women and the traditional restrictions of Islamic religion, the life of many widows is embedded in support systems. They manage to develop a female network of friends and relatives, while depending on male family members for economic support. Their lives vary considerably by social class, education, and location of residence. Turkish regions differ considerably in social development, ranging from the west with high dependence of widows on traditional supports, to Istanbul in which high-status women live quite independent and multidimensional lives. For individual widows, personal resources and location are the most important factors influencing lifestyle. The older, traditional widow whose community, relatives, or both have moved socially and psychologically into a more modern lifestyle is the worst off, because she has few alternatives available to her.

GLIMPSES OF ELSEWHERE

Two phenomena appear frequently in anthropological studies of widowhood the world over: (a) the presence of many myths about old women in general, and widows in particular, and (b) myths concerning whether women gain or lose status, or at least independence, in widowhood. Part of the problem inherent in the contradictions in that statement comes from the bias of the observer. In the past, many of the anthropologists were men. They did not have access to the women's world and who were more concerned with learning about men's activities (see Cool & McCabe, 1983, p. 57). There is, however, also a realistic aspect to status changes: Whether women lose or gain status in old age or widowhood depends on their control over societal resources. In slowly changing societies, such as the Niolo of central Corsica (p. 95), the older widows can exert a great deal of influence as advisers to young women and organizers of gossip affecting the reputation of people. In other societies, widows are seen as having invisible power, summarized in the image of "witch." Although witches can have either positive or negative power, the usual imagery is negative and antagonistic (p. 61).

Summary

The case studies contained in this chapter dispel both the myth of inevitable family support systems in traditional societies and the myth that modernization, or social development of complexity, inevitably benefits all societal members. Even movement toward democratization can result in the withering of traditional support systems without accompanying socialization of all members into voluntaristic social engagement. This is particularly true of both men and women of the lower classes and even of women of the upper classes if there is any carryover of concern with "biological purity" and the ideology of two spheres. In sum, what happens to widowed women in more traditional or in rapidly modernizing societies or their segments is symbolic of the complexity of the situation so camouflaged by the myths idealizing and generalizing either extreme.

The situation of a wife thus depends on what a woman gains from being married and from the social characteristics of the husband—his position in society and various roles. The situation of a widowed woman, then, depends on the status that she can achieve or that is relegated to her after his death and her becoming a widow, if there is such a role. We have seen many variations of situations, depending on combinations of these and related factors. The latter statement is certainly demonstrated in Israel where even the method by which a husband dies has serious repercussions not only on his widow's status but also on her whole lifestyle.

One reason that widows may have problems, such as poverty, may be the societal assumption, carried into public policy, concerning their support systems. Sanchez (1989) points out that filial responsibility is a highly valued part of Puerto Rican culture but that this fact "may color official perception of needs for services":

> The notion that the family cares for its elderly members is a double-edged sword when planning long-term care services or institutionalization for the elderly. This assumption can be used to justify not providing services that the aging women need to continue functioning adequately in the community. (p. 275)

The idealization of filial responsibility to the neglect of other support systems does not help widows who have no children, as did 44% of the widows in Sanchez's sample. Although the assumption that those widows had extensive extended families was true of the past, families now are getting smaller, and many relatives had migrated to the mainland United States. Such family members often neglect continued economic support, as we saw in the cases of Turkey and Korea. Thus, of the effects of modernization has been a decrease of the feelings of filial responsibility as men turn their attention away from the family of orientation toward the family of procreation.

Notes

1. There is voluminous literature on infanticide, child and wife abuse, and mistreatment of the elderly in books on social problems, the family, and aging as well as in publications devoted to these specific cruelties to dependent family members.

2. An indication of problems created by the Indian family system is the case of "kitchen fires" killing young Indian wives. According to the media, and documented by several studies by social scientists, the dowry system—by which the bride brings to the husband's family a sum of money, goods, or both, negotiated by both families—is at the bottom of this practice. The husband's family may increase its demands, or the bride's family may not meet its agreed-on obligations with the result that the bride "accidentally" dies when her sari catches fire while she is cooking. The groom's family can then obtain another dowry from another family, because widowers can remarry with ease, whereas remarriage of widows is deeply frowned on and rare among the middle- and upper-castes and classes (Lopata, 1987b; Stein, 1989).

3. Bohannan (1963) claims that widow remarriage is *not* part of the levirate system, but it appears to be so in Israel.

3

Widowhood in America

Myth: The United States of America is a modern society, and most
        of its members, including widowed women, display modern
        ways of thinking and lifestyles.
Myth: Widows in American society lead very restricted, isolated, or
        dependent lifestyles in a limited social life space.

An aspect of modernization, as explained in Chapter 1, is a slow
process of social development from more stable social roles and
relations within family systems and local communities to rapidly
changing and multidimensional roles and relations within social
groups of a variety of complexity in ever-expanding arenas. The rate
of change in America within past decades has been enormous, accelerated by technological innovation, disseminated by the powerful mass
media, and underpinned or overlaid by ideologies emanating from
many different, often contradictory sources. According to the modernization literature (see Inkeles, 1983; Inkeles & Smith, 1974;
Lopata, 1994a), members of modern societies have left behind the
restrictive *gemeinschaft* world for complex social settings in which
they function individualistically with role flexibility.

Social change, however, is not systematic. It affects geographic and
social areas differentially, technology sometimes moving faster than
ideology, whereas at other times social movements outdistance technology. Urban centers develop asymmetrically but usually faster than
rural regions. As a result, members of societies do not have the
elements of social development, such as extensive mass education,

experience in bureaucratic organizations, and community resources assisting individual modernization available to them to the same extent and throughout their life span. This is particularly true of Americans living in a variety of settings in a vast, rapidly and unevenly changing society. Many of them were born and socialized in other parts of the world or in ethnic communities that modify both immigrant and host cultures. Their life patterns and identities vary by urban, small town, or rural settings; social class neighborhoods; and racial, ethnic, and religious environments. There is no "American" individual type whose social relationships, involvements, and behavior patterns can be predicted. Modern, transitional, and traditional features appear in most marriages, child-rearing methods, and the movement of the family in and out of private and public spheres.

The effects of uneven social change are visible in the lifestyles and identities of all American men and women, but they are particularly evident among this society's widowed women. Older widows were brought up in the patriarchally based dominant culture and its social institutions or in various subcommunities with even greater male-dominated cultures. Many older widows have not gone through the identity- and arena-opening experience of extensive, formal education. Few participated in complex organizations requiring constant change of abilities and reality construction. This portrayal obviously does not apply to all older widows, in that some lived complex lives throughout their adult years.

By the time we reach middle-aged widows of the 1990s, we find two cohorts, one born between the mid-1920s and the mid-1940s. The second cohort, labeled "baby boomers," was born between World War II and the mid-1960s. This latter cohort obtained much more education, often by returning to school as adults, and lived in a variety of places. Members of this cohort created mainly a transitional type of family, subject to many societal changes.

Widowhood in most of current America is not identifiable beyond the immediate circles of people who know a woman personally. There are no appearance indicators, and people enter social roles and organizations on the basis of social person characteristics related to the purpose of such sets of relations. Seldom are these related to widowhood—after the rituals of the funeral are over. Widowhood is experienced personally, not socially, except among those subcultures within which it is an important identity. Becoming and being widowed in America, however, can affect previously established social roles and relations, as we shall see in this chapter.

To dramatize the different ways widowhood can affect American women, I have chosen several settings studied by social scientists: the historical past, including the American Southwest; a small, stable working-class community with a relatively immobile population; a middle-class area of a middle-size city; and a retirement community to which older couples are drawn. In addition, I have found interesting studies of lower-income California widows known to the formal support system, widowed women in several urban subcommunities of African Americans, and those scattered in a variety of locales in one major metropolitan center.[1]

Just to give the reader a brief glimpse of the characteristics of the widowed American women, let me cite a few figures. As of 1992, there were 96,599,000 women in the United States, and 11,325,000 of them were widowed. They thus formed 11.7% of the female population. Most of these were older women: 36% of the widows were between the ages of 65 and 74, and another 65% were 75 years of age or older (U.S. Department of Commerce, 1993, Table 63). Of the widows, 92% were the householder, or the person "in whose name the housing unit is owned or rented" (U.S. Department of Commerce, 1993, Table 64). Most of these lived alone, some with relatives, and relatively few with nonrelated persons.[2]

Widowhood in America's Past

Widows are rather invisible in American history, except for a few who became event heroines. Absence of research on old women and widows by historians is commented on in the *Journal of Family History* (Blom, 1991). Information about them appears tangentially in various studies, and much of it is anecdotal, with multiple types of myths. Blom (1991, p. 192) explains the neglect of widowhood by historians to their emphasis on other stages of the life cycle, especially childhood, marriage, and fertility. Luckily, both sociologists and anthropologists have increasingly drawn our attention to the situation of American husbandless women, including widows (Chandler, 1991; Hart, 1976; Scandron, 1988; Simon, 1987; see also many Lopata publications).

Several myths surround the situation of widows in Colonial New England. Murstein (1974) commented on the assumed low status of widows at that time, due to the "used goods" attitudes and religious stress on perpetual marriage. He found this not to be true: "Widows were quite popular, even those with children. One reason was their economic status. The European custom of leaving the major portion of an estate to the eldest son did not survive in the colonies" (p. 300). Benjamin Franklin's statement that " 'a rich widow is the only kind of second-hand goods that will always sell at prime cost' " (quoted in Murstein, 1974, p. 300) leaves a lot to be desired as proof of high status, but it certainly indicated desirability contrary to the prevailing myth Murstein found in the literature of that time.

There is some disagreement among historians and social scientists concerning the residential arrangements of older widowed women. Keyssar (1974) found Massachusetts widows not so "rich" and often unable to maintain the farm they and their late husbands owned, due to the shortage of male workers. They then had to turn the farms over to the adult children and become dependent on them. This fact leads to the frequent assumption that older mothers of America's past lived with their married children. Heaton and Hoppe (1987), however, agreed with Peter Laslett (1976) that three-generational households were infrequent in preindustrial times. The inconsistency between the assumed need of widows to live with their married children and the infrequency of three-generational households can be explained through statistics. In those times, the short life span of most people, especially women, meant that there were relatively few of them. Those who survived were the most likely to be coresidents, due to "economic necessity, poor health or other adversities" (Heaton & Hoppe, 1987, p. 263). Whenever possible, they tried to retain their own place, adult children either remaining or returning to it. Those widows who were unable to remain heads of households or who did not move in with married children, tended to live close by (see also Laslett, 1976, on England). Heaton and Hope (1987, p. 263) found that 34% of women aged 65 and over lived as "parent of head," and only 11% lived alone in the United States in 1900. Most of the remaining older women lived with their husbands.

Keyssar (1974) supported Murstein (1974) in reporting that remarriage of both widows and widowers was frequent in Colonial Massachusetts. Life expectancy was short, so marriages were frequently broken by death, and remarriage occurred due to the survival need for two household maintainers and parents.

Some of the Colonial widows were powerful and wealthy, able to run estates or businesses (Blom, 1991). The problem was the Anglo-American legal system that left the wife a legal minor, so her share of the inheritance was often restricted by adult children. Even under that system, all widows were able to retain the dower or one third of the husband's estate, and widows with dependent children could control all of the property. It was not until the Married Women's Property Act, passed by individual states from 1860 to 1897, that widows gained the right to dispose of the dower as they wished.

Widows who did not remarry or inherit sufficient sources of income had to support themselves through various means (Blom, 1991). In preindustrial and early industrial communities, they took in sewing, knitting, and washing; hawked or traded goods; created products for sale; or took in lodgers and boarders (see Blom, 1991, p. 197). They also worked as midwives, nurses, or teachers, with minimal education. Children contributed their wages to the family income.

According to most historical accounts of the waged work of women, occupational opportunities narrowed in the 19th and early 20th centuries (Blom, 1991; Lopata, Miller, & Barnewolt, 1986). This was especially true of widows, many of whom had minimal education. Thus, they became increasingly dependent on their children or, in extreme cases of poverty, on the parish or community. American society and its individual states provided assistance to war widows in the form of Civil War pensions if they did not remarry, much as currently experienced by Israeli war widows (see Vinovskis, 1990, p. 116). The late 19th century found many widows deprived of their children by governmental agencies or "charitable societies" on the assumption that the women could not take care of their children properly while simultaneously earning the family income (Lopata & Brehm, 1986). Only after a White House Conference on the Care of Dependent Children in 1909 did individual states start providing mother's pensions to enable widows and other husbandless women to care for their children at home. Not until 1939 were widows and children dependent on a social security-earning man covered by Social Security benefits (Lopata & Brehm, 1986).

Arlene Scandron (1988) edited an interesting analysis of husband-less women in America's past. *On Their Own: Widows and Widow-hood in the American Southwest, 1848-1939)* dispels many of the myths of women's dependency on the husband created from generalized descriptions of Colonial America and other patriarchal societies. The studies indicated the independence of Native American women of several tribes, such as the Pueblo Indians. These groups maintained a matriarchal, matrilineal, and matrilocal residence family structure that provided continued support to its women, even in widowhood (Nelson, 1988). Women controlled their own property. "Their assets are never merged with their husbands' as joint property, and cash women earn in any way is considered to be entirely theirs, to dispose of as they wish" (Nelson, 1988, p. 28). These groups formed an exception to Bohannan's (1963) conclusion concerning the rights that men generally acquire over women after marriage (see Chapter 1). The daughters remained in the extended household or camp throughout their mother's and then their own lives. A similar family system was typical of the Navaho and Zuni tribes.

In such communities, the life and relations of a woman were not heavily disorganized with the death of her husband, because he was the outsider and she continued to dwell with her family. Some problems did emerge with widowhood, however, such as the need to replace male labor, sexual involvement, parenting, and participation in the kinship groups established by the marriage. The labor could be carried forth by other available males, the widow's father, brothers, sons, or sons-in-law. Remarriage was also possible. The freedom a widow had to engage in sexual relations varied by group. The concern over biological paternity, so strong among patriarchal systems, was minimal among matriarchal ones, so there tended to be much less control over the woman's sexual behavior. The children belonged to their mother's lineage (see Nelson, 1988, p. 36).

Schlegel (1988) also pointed to the extremely supportive extended kin network of traditional Hopi society. Even if not contained in the same household, the unit contributed to all four support systems of its widows: economic, service, social, and emotional. The family operated as a work group, providing economic and service supports, and was continuously available for social interaction with the widow and her children. The loss of a spouse did not carry a drop in status for either men or women, and marriage did not involve the depth of emotional dependence that it does in modern urban communities. It was undertaken for practical reasons, and emotional supports came, especially for the women, from the matrilineal unit. The Hopis maintained themselves in their own world, organized into matrilocal residences headed by women and inherited by daughters as late as the 1860s.

Families were organized into clans that owned rituals, political offices, and farmland. The men—husbands, unmarried sons, and sons-in-law—farmed the land that was allotted to a house. A man had three locales for his responsibilities and identities: his marital household with ties to his wife and children, his sister's household in which he also had duties to her and responsibility for training her children, and his ceremonial peer clubhouse. The relation between brother and sister was considered the most important, husband-wife relations being of lesser significance and not expected to provide emotional supports until much later in life. A widowed sister could count on help with the children from her brother, who was responsible for them even when the father was alive. It is not surprising that the marital unit was not of the same primary importance to the man because of his multiple identities, or to his wife who was bound to her kin group, as it was to transitional and modern "Anglo-American" couples (see Schlegel, 1988, p. 50). Remarriage by both women and men was encouraged. The larger the household, the safer were its members from economic deprivation, because there were so many workers contributing to its welfare.

After the turn of the century, American Indian widows of the Southwest could contribute to the family economy through production of pottery and baskets sold to tourists. Sons continued to provide meat from hunting and herding and cash for the purchase of consumer products. Other relatives continued to provide economic goods and services.

Widowhood in America's Present

According to Hacker (1983, p. 115), the 1980 census showed that 68% of American widows were aged 65 or over, 20% were between the ages of 55 and 64, and 12% were under the age of 55. A surprising finding is that one third of all women who are widowed became so while still under the age of 40.

Widowhood in Relatively
Homogeneous Communities

A community is generally defined as a group of people who occupy a certain territory and share a *consciousness of kind*—that is, a feeling of being alike, a web of relations, and a culture (Lopata, 1994a). In modern societies, the ties between members of communities are through both informal and at least somewhat formal organization and include recognition of membership, social roles, and identities. Communities can be strictly local, clearly bounded from neighboring communities, or the members can be dispersed geographically or in clusters. In the latter case, members of other communities live nearby but do not share their culture, social ties, or consciousness of kind. Thus, we can speak of professional or ethnic communities, as well as local communities that share major institutions (Hunter, 1974; Lopata, 1994a).

This broad definition of community can enable us to speak of a community of widows in settings where there is such a phenomenon. I will use here three such communities studied by social scientists: Momence, Illinois; Columbus, Ohio; and a unnamed retirement community in Florida.

MOMENCE, ILLINOIS

Momence is a small town in Illinois at a sufficient distance from Chicago to be socially independent. It is small enough for people to know the identities of "the majority of the cast of characters," if not to know them personally (see Fry & Gavrin, 1987, p. 41). Its population is working class with middle-class aspirations but without access to resources enabling such lifestyles. This means that mobility is relatively low; children and grandchildren do not have access to quality educations with which to gain jobs in larger, urban communities. The economic leaders are small businessmen and bankers, many catering to the surrounding farm areas (Fry & Gavrin, 1987). The public life of organizations and social events, however, are run by the women, many of whom are widows.

As part of a cross-cultural study of aging, Fry and Gavrin (1987) concluded that widowhood in Momence is not a major life course marker, in that social transition into it is rather easy, once the traumatic events surrounding the death are over. Life course transitions involving children are of greater significance. Gender differentiation is high, and older women, who are most apt to experience widowhood, are already involved in public social life. The loss of husband does not affect their working-class lives as much as it does middle-class women in, for example, metropolitan Chicago, where women are much more dependent on being married, having a husband, and having a particular husband.

Thus, the community of widows in Momence is traditional and socially active. The situation of its widows is very different from that in larger metropolitan settings of transitional and modern times:

> The culture of widows is by and large a peer culture bonded by homophyly in gender, widowhood, and common experiences built around long-term participation in community life. The informal basis of this peer culture can be seen in card playing, eating in the local restaurants, and, for those who can afford it, travel to exotic places. (Fry & Gavrin, 1987, p. 43)

Formal organizations of women exist and integrate both the married and the widowed. Social integration is also a consequence of the previously mentioned low mobility rate, which leaves children and even grandchildren within easy contact distance. As in many stable communities, location on the social map depends on location in a kinship network. The service and social support systems are informal, rather than state supported (see Fry & Gavrin, 1987, p. 45). In addition, there are no community continuing-care facilities, the elderly living and often dying in their own homes.

The strong continuity of life and life term arenas envelops all members, with the disadvantage of known personal history and reputation, which may be hard to live down (see Fry & Gavrin, 1987, p. 47). This is unlike the situation of widows in cities, where the past and such identities as widowhood can easily be lost in public arenas.

COLUMBUS, OHIO

Shirley O'Bryant and her associates have extensively studied older white widows who are home owners in a metropolitan community. Columbus is known as the "biggest small city" in America and is considered a most typical environment for Americans (see O'Bryant,

1987, p. 49). The general theme of the studies has been aging, and analyses focused on several circumstances of widowhood, including the effects of caretaking of the husband during the latter's fatal illness (including Alzheimer's) versus sudden death, the effects of staying in the home after widowhood versus moving, and so forth.

The Columbus widows in the O'Bryant studies were racially identified as white, because too few women of color fell into the various samples. Most had been born in Ohio and had lived in their homes for a long period of time, which means that both they and their homes were old. The majority of the women were healthy and had either low or medium incomes, but they were not destitute. Most of the women were part of support networks. Those lacking such networks were likely to be fairly isolated, lonely, and with low life satisfaction. Living alone was not the source of such feelings, but lacking a support network was. This is an important point: O'Bryant (1991b) concluded that people need to be interdependent, even in a society that idealizes independence.

The study of residential retention in widowhood addressed several questions rising out of the fact that from the point of view of efficiency-oriented outsiders, the women were "overhoused," the space and facilities being larger than needed for a single person. The questions were these: What are the sources of attachment to the home? What are the advantages and disadvantages of remaining in one's home during widowhood? Who provides a widow with necessary supports that enable her to maintain her home? What is the relationship between the supports supplied by neighbors, friends, children, and siblings, analyzed by their availability and gender (O'Bryant, 1988a, 1988b)? What are the differences between women who stayed in their homes and those who relocated (O'Bryant & McGloshen, 1987; O'Bryant & Murray, 1986)?

O'Bryant found four components of attachment to the home for older persons: (a) traditional family orientation, (b) competence in a familiar environment, (c) the status value of home ownership, and (d) a cost versus comfort trade-off—that is, uncomfortable homes were acceptable when they were relatively inexpensive (see O'Bryant & Murray, 1986, p. 59).

Thus, in the established community of Columbus, the widows felt that owning a home and living in it provided a source of social status and that it was physically and psychologically more comfortable and supportive than a new environment would be. Those who moved differed from the "stayers" in (a) not having siblings, (b) in believing that their homes cost more than they were worth, and (c) in not identifying the home with family tradition. Those who stayed were able to maintain themselves and the home with the help of a variety of people, with sons and sons-in-law as well as brothers taking over the jobs previously done by the late husband. Paid workers were also hired. We will come back to the subject of attachment to homes in a later chapter.

RETIREMENT COMMUNITIES

Communities usually contain people of all ages and marital roles, enabled to live within their confines with the help of varying degrees of institutional completeness (Breton, 1964). Technically speaking, people can be born, grow up, and spend the rest of their lives in a community, having all basic needs met locally. Of course, few local communities of modern times have such institutional completeness in that their economic, familial, educational, political, religious, and recreational areas of life are self-sufficient and geographically bounded, not dependent on the larger society.

An interesting phenomenon in current America is the development and rapid expansion of age-segregated local communities. These tend to be identified and organized as "retirement" or old-age communities. Some of these communities are purposely designed as such. Others come about in consequence of events that draw people of certain ages together or that push people of other ages away. During the years of rapid urbanization and industrialization, including industrialization of agriculture, many small American towns ended up with a disproportionately high number of elderly people. Public housing for seniors is age and income segregated, because only the poor elderly can acquire rooms or apartments in it. Hotels in urban centers have been converted into retirement housing, offering rooms with baths, cleaning services, congregate eating, and complex social programs.[3]

Housing developers have purposely created whole new retirement communities open to residents no younger than a defined age, be it 65, 60, or 55. These tend to draw middle-income people, especially if the communities are located in the Sunbelt, which attracts residents from climatically less desirable settings or from age-integrated settings in the same region. States such as Florida, Arizona, and California abound with these ever-expanding communities. The graying of America, cultural phenomena such as retirement, and financial support from the Old Age, Survivors and Disability Insurance Program or Social Security make such lifestyles possible (Neale, 1987). The concept of retirement grew out of the prior organization of much work into salaried or wage-paying jobs in employing organizations. Various societal events, including a program initiated in Germany, resulted in the creation of an age ceiling, or retirement age, on jobs. During the Great Depression, American society finally adopted a social security system in 1935. This program provides insured workers with regular paychecks in retirement, based on earning history. In 1939, wives, widows, and dependent children were added to the system, with varying qualifications for benefits (Lopata & Brehm, 1986).

The Protestant work ethic (Weber, 1904/1958), which idealized hard work and economic success and thus assigned people not earning an income less prestige than the earners, has gradually given way to an increasing interest in leisure. Thus, retirement has become redefined from rejection by the economic institution to opportunity for spending the remaining years in pleasurable activity. This, then, has given encouragement to retirement communities built around the concept of vacation and fun (van den Hoonaard, 1992). These communities frequently have included golf courses, swimming pools, and recreational centers. A variety of conveniences, such as air-conditioning, garbage disposals, and dishwashers, are contained in each apartment condominium or home, and services often include building and grounds maintenance, security patrols, cable television, and transportation to nearby facilities. Organizations of residents usually take over management from the builder and offer a multitude of activities from card playing to hobbies, entertainment, lectures, and travel (Neale, 1987; van den Hoonaard, 1992).

Most of the retirement communities draw to them married couples, and these tend to come from similar areas of the country and even from ethnically, religiously, or socioeconomically similar groups. As far as I know, there are no racially integrated retirement communities, although there may be a few residents who do not match the majority, either at the beginning, before the composition becomes evident, or later on, as second and third cohorts of owners move in.

Thus, the homogeneity of the population along many lines is strong, and leads, according to most observers, to ease of contact, informal interaction, and organizational participation, preventing one of the major problems of old age: loneliness. That is a main advantage of retirement communities: the ease of interaction and potential for making friends. The other advantage is freedom from the annoyances of children and young people. On the other hand, some residents report that they miss age-integrated housing. One solution is part-time residence, as undertaken by "snowbirds." Some snowbirds come to the Sunbelt retirement communities only during the season when snow is likely to cover the areas back home. Others may settle in such communities but leave during the hot summer months to stay in some form of private housing or with relatives in the North.

One major problem with such traditional retirement communities is that deviation from the norm can result in social isolation. Van den Hoonaard (1994) reports that the deviants include those of different ethnic background, the widowed and, to some extent, the snowbirds. Newcomers of different backgrounds usually move out fairly soon, never developing satisfactory relations with the members of the dominant group.

Newcomers to old neighborhoods also have difficulties in integration unless they have special characteristics, such as interests or abilities desired by the oldtimers. The snowbirds become limited to such activities that do not require year-round presence, such as card clubs or management of the community and its continued activities. For example, in one Florida community of primarily Jewish residents, the snowbird migration is dependent on Jewish holidays (see van den Hoonaard, 1992, p. 154). In this particular locale, most residents spend most of the year within the community, making snowbirds marginal and seen as insufficiently committed to local life. The part-timers, on the other hand, often do not have the patience to understand all the intricacies of this local life.

The situation of women who had been integrated in the retirement community as members of a couple and who then become deviant as a result of widowhood leads to many complications unless widowhood becomes the norm, as in Hochschild's (1973) *The Unexpected Community*. The whole life of most developer-created retirement communities revolves around couples, although there can be gender-segregated activities during the day. Serious illness and death are threatening to a population that is so close in age to the possibility of experiencing these. Rituals surrounding death are observed, but then the presence of the widow creates awkwardness, a problem often avoided by simply avoiding her.

At Eldorado, the community (name changed) studied by van den Hoonaard (1992, 1994), the percentage of the houses occupied by single people—meaning the widowed, of which 75% were women— increased from 9 to 29 between 1980 and 1990. The residents were mainly Jewish, so *shiva* (1 week of heavy grieving) was observed:

> Once the week of intense mourning was complete, the widow or widower could reasonably expect only the closest friends to continue to pay attention to them. Widows, in particular, expressed great surprise and disappointment with the response of people who they considered friends, for most of them ceased to show concern from this point on. (van den Hoonaard, 1992, p. 165)

The couple-companionate interaction continued, and the no-longer-coupled women did not fit in, their status lowered by widowhood. The researcher found no singles' groups, and her informants stated that there never would be one. The clubhouse, open to all residents, was used mainly by couples. In fact, the couples suggested that widowed people would be "happier" in other communities. Couples who included widows in their evening outings—for example, for dinner in a restaurant—found the whole experience embarrassing, especially around bill-paying time. The norm of independent or split bill paying by women is simply absent in this population of older, currently or previously married people. The marginality of widowhood was felt by the women in many situations, often leading to social isolation. This was sometimes increased by the failure of the newly widowed to make overtures to former associates, due to a lack of norms and experience and to the fear of rejection. Widows were often dependent on others for transportation, because so many women of their life history had not driven a car much, if at all.

Van den Hoonaard (see 1992, p. 172), however, found widowers even worse off, because they did not know how to take care of themselves and because the men in the community did not interact informally or do as many things together as women did. If they did not play golf, their days, weekends, and evenings became empty of associates. Widowers had a much higher rate of remarriage than did widows, partly due to the gender distribution, partly due to feelings of incompetence over living alone. Many of the widows did not want to remarry and go through the same experience with the death of another husband. In addition, they did not want to give up their freedom and economic benefits, a sentiment found also to be strong in other settings (see Lopata, 1973d, 1979). Some of the no-longer-marrieds developed semipermanent cohabitation arrangements that removed some of the stigma of widowhood and were not disapproved of by the community as long as they had begun in what was considered too short a time after the death of the spouse (see van den Hoonaard, 1992, p. 174).

ETHNIC COMMUNITIES

Widows who do not live in small communities in which they form a viable network or in specially designed retirement or elderly housing can reside in areas in which they have several ties besides widowhood that form additional connecting links. Two such settings are ethnic and racial communities. Widows can be dispersed among people with different age, gender, and marital status in larger communities.

America encompasses many ethnic communities, varying considerably by time of formation, growth and size, locations and manner of settlement, institutional complexity, and relation to the rest of society as well as to the home country. Consciousness of kind and social networks tie each ethnic community together and make it possible for members to actually live among members of other ethnic communities or ethnically unaffiliated residents and still interact with one another, sharing consciousness of kind. Members find each other across space, ignoring people of other identities (Lopata, 1994a).

What makes ethnic communities different from other local settlements is their shared subculture, social organization, and the uniqueness of their consciousness of kind. The formal organizations and ethnic media hold the communities together, despite the fact that most are spread out in many localities. The glue is the ethnic identity, forged out of a modified combination of home country culture at various levels and host country culture. Ethnic leaders, with the help of these associations, the church, the school, and business and professional subcommunities, try to develop, crystallize, and maintain ethnic identity and solidarity. Not all eligible "ethnics" identify with the community, nor are all they involved in its organizational structure and activity. The participation varies by the person and the local community and can extend to multiorganizational and multiterritorial arenas.

In the United States, ethnic community members vary by generation, reasons for migration, age, race, religion, and socioeconomic status. The longer the ethnic group has resided in this country, the more likely it is to be dispersed, with some concentration remaining in the areas of original or secondary settlement. Widows are present in such communities through the death of the partner with which they came to this country or whom they married here or by being brought over by adult immigrant children. In the case of European ethnic minorities, they are likely to be of the second or third generation brought up in an ethnic community. Many of the older ones, and their very old mothers of the first immigrant generation, have become either relatively isolated or dependent on their children due to a lack of knowledge of English and American urban life. Older ethnic widows can often be found in the old neighborhoods, not being able to sell their homes for enough money to guarantee purchase in a newer area (Gans, 1962; Lopata, 1994a). The neighborhood is likely to have changed, with only a few of their friends remaining. New immigrant groups take the place of their conationals and of institutions supplying their needs, such as churches and voluntary associations. The latter have moved to areas of secondary settlement, following the new generations, or they have simply died off. Thus, ethnic widows usually have two main directions of social involvement: their children and their community. The direction and strength of involvement depend on the person and the ethnic community.

In Polonia, the Polish American community that I studied, there is a surprising amount of ethnic consciousness and social involvement, even by the different generations of widowed women. The degree and forms of participation really depend on a woman's location within Polonia (Lopata, 1976a, 1977, 1994b). The community is complex, highly organized, status competitive, and heterogeneous in ethnic subidentities. The first generation of the first cohort of Polish immigrant women has already died off, having arrived in America between 1880 and the 1920s. The older widows are either their daughters or second-cohort immigrants who came after World War II. There are some, but not many, widows of the third cohort that emigrated from communist or newly independent Poland.

The older, second-generation Polonian widows tend to be first-generation urbanites, because their parents were likely to have been born in villages of Poland.[4] Their late husbands were more apt to have been born in Poland than they are, being older and part of the large influx of men who were displaced by World War II, unwilling to return to the homeland after the communist takeover. The very old women are likely to be "urban villagers," as Gans (1962) labeled the Italians he studied in Boston. They do not have a mental map of the city, being familiar only with the neighborhood within which they have spent most of their lives. They had been affiliated with a church and its numerous clubs and organizations throughout their lives.[5] Most of such groups are now gone from the oldest neighborhoods. Agencies such as the Polish Welfare Association of Chicago try to reach these women, many of whom are not comfortable in the English- or Spanish-speaking world by which they are now surrounded (Polish Welfare Association, 1991). The women underuse the formal resources of this voluntaristic urban center, having been dependent on the Polish organizations for most of such services.

The education that older widows obtained in childhood was usually very limited both in the number of years and in terms of breadth of perspectives. If they gained it in the United States, it was almost always in Catholic schools with nuns, many of whom had been trained in Poland or in the expanding Polish language sisterhoods in this country. Polish peasant culture discouraged formal education, especially for women, who were to obtain what they needed to know from home. Greeley and Rossi (1968) found Polish Catholics religiously and culturally rather ill-informed, not knowing much of either American or Polish national culture. Although many were employed until marriage, few returned to the labor force after their children grew up. Thus, their experience in the urban world in which these women now live is very limited.

Of major importance in the lives of the oldest Polonian widowed women are their children. Married children often have moved to outlying areas of the city and the suburbs. A higher proportion of Polish American widows than of nonethnically identified women live with an adult child. Usually, such children are single or divorced and live in the mother's home. The dwellings often lack sufficient conveniences typical of more modern residences. The household-sharing children provide most of the service and social supports. Often, the mothers are of poor health and unable to function alone. Their lives have been difficult, with many deaths and much hard work.

Although the marriages of many lower-class Polish American widows were full of tribulations, the subculture and possibly the current life restrictions require idealization of the late husband to the point of sanctification. The scale I finally developed to determine the degree of sanctification expressed by different women contained, as the bottom line, the statement, "My husband had no irritating habits!" Polish American widows of the lower and lower-middle classes were more likely than more educated widows to agree with even that statement, although other items in the interview brought forth more negative feelings. The more isolated and never socially involved women were particularly hostile toward their past and their environment. One of the reasons is the failure of support systems that they assumed existed automatically and without initiative on their part.

These women, however, no longer represent the Polish American population, because many members of their generation have already died off and the new Polonia women are very different. The presence of the three cohorts of immigrants and upward social mobility indicates a greater heterogeneity of Polish American widows than suggested earlier. The second-immigration cohort and the third generation of the first cohort obtained more education and more white-collar jobs and benefited from Polonia's complex social organizational structure. The women who retained identification with the community generally remain active in older age and widowhood. A highly developed status competition provides opportunities for individual accomplishment, made easy by the proliferation of voluntary associations. Such groups still abound around the Polish parishes, some of which again hold masses in that language. Nationalistic, occupational, artistic, and "polka world" groups are available even in smaller locales, although the interorganizational groups are headquartered in larger cities, such as New York or Chicago.

Events in Poland have been of interest to Polonia, especially at times of world attention and as Polish political leaders moved back and forth across the Atlantic. Emergencies of wars or revolutions have drawn considerable financial and supply supports from here.

The newest immigration cohort in Polonia obtained much more education than the earlier ones, usually in Poland. This cohort and younger generations of former cohorts have moved into middle-class social life space, although retaining some of the cultural forms of social relations and family norms. In all, widows of this ethnic community who are in any but the oldest age group are, or have been, surprisingly active in the community. This makes them quite different from, for example, Italian American women of comparable age and marital status (di Leonardo, 1984).

Polonia's life also varies by local community. Polish Americans in Los Angeles, California, are quite different from those of Buffalo, New York. In sum, Polonia is a total ethnic community tied together by consciousness of kind, a complex organizational structure, and a mass communication system. It includes many local groups and neighborhoods within which a variety of lifestyles and identities are available to widows. Of course, only some of the millions of people in the United States who can trace a Polish background identify with, and are active in, the Polonian community. Despite the influx of the third cohort, the graying of Polonia is apparent among the established community groups. For example, most members of the Legion Mlodych Polek (Legion of Young Polish Women), which holds the annual White and Red Debutante Ball in Chicago, are older widows.

Widows of other ethnic groups display varying patterns of life. The Italian community has a much stronger kinship support system and a weaker organizational involvement by women than is true of the Polish Americans. Sibling solidarity and interdependence are of special importance among the Italian American elderly (see Squier & Quadagno, 1988, p. 129). Many Mexicans in the United States are recent immigrants and retain close ties with the mother country, the elderly widows remaining in the village or being brought north to help care for the family (Becerra, 1988). Asian ethnic communities tend to be smaller and of more recent arrival in America. As we saw in Chapter 1, widows in Korean families tend to live with their sons and their families. This pattern is continued in America. Naturalized sons tend to bring their parents over to the United States, thanks to the Immigration Act of 1965. Only 19% of the Korean American elderly live alone. Widows who do not live with their first son or another adult child can sometimes be found in centers of similar people (see Min, 1988, p. 223).

AFRICAN AMERICAN COMMUNITIES

It appears from current literature that the African American communities within American society are not as tightly tied to each other as are other ethnic communities. Original cultures were different, and slavery a number of generations ago did not form a bond that carried into an organization and identification structure pulling members together. That is not to say that there are no multiorganizational units and a growing consciousness of kind of more than minority status. Starting with the 1960s and the "black is beautiful" movement, there has been an increasing attempt to build a community feeling and activity throughout the United States. From this point of view, there is a similarity between ethnic communities whose members have a background in specific European, Asian, Central and South American, Middle Eastern, or African national culture societies and the African American community. It is not the purpose of this book to dwell on the differences, only to report the results of studies of African American widowed women.

As McDonald (1987, p. 139) explained, older American black widows have three strikes against them: they are widowed, they are elderly, and they are black. We must keep in mind that for many reasons—history, prejudice and discrimination being main ones—a high proportion of African Americans are still in the lower class, although they are now much more urban than in the past. One of the myths that exists in America concerning African Americans is that they live in extended-family households. In fact, large numbers of them live alone—as I (Lopata, 1973d) found among African American widows in Chicago, and McDonald (1987) found in Detroit, Indianapolis, Los Angeles, and Washington, D. C. One difference between them and white American widows is the fluidity of housing arrangements. In other words, the woman may have children, siblings, and even more distant relatives, moving in and out of her household, or she may be moving in and out of theirs, as life events make independent living difficult. Such events tend to occur more often in black American families than in white American families, partly because of the frequency of marginal existence and partly due to customary support systems (Lopata, 1973c; Stack, 1974). Unemployment among lower-class black males makes the support of a family very difficult, if not impossible. Even among whites, recent studies indicate an increasing frequency of the "empty nest" being refilled temporarily as adult children cannot afford their own homes or experience divorce or widowhood.

Stack (1981) identified ghetto life as adaptive to disorganizing events through "patterns of co-residence, elastic household boundaries, lifelong if intermittent bonds to three generation households, social constraints on the role of the husband-father within the mother's domestic group, and the domestic authority of women" (p. 369). As the reader probably knows, the number of stereotypes about the African American woman are also legendary. On one side, she is presented as strong, needing this strength to pull together and maintain a fatherless family despite enormous economic and neighborhood problems. On the other hand, she is seen as too powerful a matriarch who emasculates men, including her sons. The latter image drew a great deal of attention in the 1960s as a result of the Moynihan Report (Moynihan, 1963). Both extremes of these stereotypes are of underclass women, because middle-class women appear indistinguishable from their white counterparts in their lifestyles, except that they are likely to have more egalitarian marriages (Willie, 1976).

The older African American woman, regardless of her marital status, is often portrayed as the grandmother who takes care of her grandchildren if the mother cannot do so for any of a variety of reasons. Cherlin and Furstenberg (1986) found this image at least partially correct in that black grandparents were different from white ones:

> Black grandparents were much more likely to take on a parentlike role with their grandchildren. . . . These grandparents saw themselves as protectors of the family, bulwarks against the forces of separation, divorce, drugs, crime—all of the ills low-income black youth can fall prey to. (pp. 127, 129)

All the reports of grandparenting quoted by these authors involved older women. The two grandfathers at the center where Cherlin and Furstenberg conducted their research "had little to say" (p. 130). The proportion of widows to women of other marital situations is lower among African Americans than among whites, simply because so many do not have husbands for other reasons, never marrying or having divorced and not taking the identification of widow even after the death of the ex-husband. In fact, there has been a dramatically decreasing tendency of black women to enter marriage since World War II (see Cherlin, 1981, p. 108). This is particularly true of the women with minimal formal education—that is, with less than a high school degree.

In fact, disadvantaged black women have became more disadvantaged and more dissimilar from white women in recent decades. As of

1982, over 29% of African American females were single, and less than half were married (see McDonald, 1987, p. 143). Most black women who head households live near the poverty level, especially if they are widowed. The shortage of men at all ages means that few widows can remarry. This shortage is due partly to violence, especially among young adults; incarceration; and poverty-associated unhealthy living habits (Wilson, 1978, 1987). Thus, marriage is less central in the lives of lower- and underclass black women than among white women, partially due to the impossibility of maintaining it over time and partially due to the strength of the kin network. This means that widowhood may be less traumatizing in the African American community. On the other hand, those marriages that do survive into widowhood may be even more significant for the woman in such an environment and thus may be even more devastating than if the marriage is taken for granted. Widowhood for African American women of the middle class would be socially disorganizing to the extent that the social network depended on marriage and that particular husband. Widowhood would be personally disorganizing to the extent that emotional supports and identities were tied into the marriage and that particular husband. This same set of circumstances affects middle-class white women.

McDonald (1987, pp. 149-150) found that the older widows in her samples, living in the black communities of the large American cities, were more likely to have lower educational and income levels than the black married women. Few lived in nuclear families. Those widows not living independently usually resided in extended-family households. Only 9% of the widows lived with a parent. The widows underused the health system, seldom visiting a physician or the hospital even when ill, because of a fear of being sent to a nursing home. Most of the African American widows were really strapped for income. Half were retired and few obtained any benefits from the work their husbands had done when they were alive. Despite this, they did not report economic support from families. They expressed very negative attitudes toward remarriage as a resource for support systems. The widows in McDonald's (1987) samples, as well as the African American widows in my (Lopata, 1973d, 1979) Chicago studies found much emotional and social support from religion and the church. This reinforces the conclusion of other studies as to the importance of religious institutions in the black community.

In addition, the African American widowed women of various cities reported being able to draw emotional strength from their own selves, feeling competent and strong (see McDonald, 1987, pp. 153-155). The widows, more often than the wives, believed that "black women are stronger than white women" (67% vs. 38%, respectively). The widows, more often than the wives, hold mixed emotions, feeling depressed when alone (38% vs. 7%) and yet agreeing strongly that "everything happens for the best" (58% vs. 38%) and that "most black women are jealous of me" (because they see themselves as better off than other women of their group; 35% vs. 7%). An interesting difference appeared when both groups were asked whether they could depend on their families if they needed help. Widows were less likely to define themselves as getting support than were wives, possibly because such help is more likely to come from household-sharing nuclear families, including a husband.

Scattered Locations

Most widows are not located in small or culturally relatively homogeneous communities in which they form a significant proportion, either by attrition of other residents or by purposeful selection. This means that they are scattered, although not completely at random, throughout age- and marital-status-integrated communities. Although there might be a small clustering of widows because of stability over time or some feature of the environment that draws husbandless women, there is no prearranged pattern. Widows can form or belong to social groups especially devoted to women in their marital status, such as the Widow-to-Widow or Spares clubs. Membership in such organizations is usually transitory because their purpose is to help women go through grief and because there is no role of widow in our society that would carry a set of purposes and a social circle. Widows in the community thus tend to be involved in similar activities as other women of the same age, interest, and social class. They are unique, however, in not continuing membership in groups that are auxiliaries of men's associations, such as Eastern Star or Rotary Anne, once the connecting link of the husband is gone. The main association they share with married couples is the church, and even here most special-interest groups are gender segregated.

CHICAGO

Many characteristics of metropolitan Chicago complicate the situation of widows. It is a large, relatively young and rapidly expanded city, located near the center of the United States, with a heterogeneous population, many members of which are only second- or third-generation urbanites and Americans. Chicago is the most racially and ethnically segregated city in this country (Lieberson, 1963). It has drawn a large number of African Americans, mainly from the American South, starting with World War II. These blacks form a large inner-city underclass referred to earlier plus an increasing middle class living at the periphery of the city and in some of the suburbs. As late as 1930, its population consisted of 25% foreign-born and 40% of mixed parentage in that one or both parents were foreign-born. This left only 35% native-born residents of native-born (but not necessarily Chicago-born) parents (see Lopata, 1979, p. 48). It still has the largest number of people with a Polish background outside of Warsaw, Poland. Other European ethnically identified Chicagoans include Germans, Russians (especially Russian Jews), Italians, and Swedes. There is now a large number of Hispanics who will soon outnumber both whites and blacks in the city and a newly significant number of Asians. In fact, immigrants coming into Chicago from Asia now outnumber those from Europe and the city's population is changing from white to multicolored, evidenced especially in the schools. "White flight" is a clear and strong movement into suburbs and, in recent years, exurbs. With the exception of these new arrivals, the city proper is aging, whereas the surrounding communities are mushrooming with new buildings and new families. Chicago's population is much more likely to be located in single-family dwellings, two flats, or town houses than is, for example, the population of New York. There is no equivalent to Manhattan in Chicago, although some new housing is being built near the commercial and office "Loop" or center.

The city is also changing in its economic base, from a strongly "smoke stack" manufacturing and industrial base to a more scattered service and small telecommunication and business base. Jobs have moved away from the center or, at least, have not expanded as fast in the center as has the population so that a smaller and smaller proportion of employed workers comes into the center from the outskirts. The superhighways, once the arteries enabling life in the bustling city, are now clogged at many times of the day, with almost as many workers going to the suburbs for jobs as coming in from these areas. With very few exceptions, the suburbs are socioeconomically and racially segregated.

How does the heterogeneity and mobility of metropolitan Chicago affect the lives of its women in widowhood? It affects them differently for different kinds of widows. Ethnicity, religion, racial background, number of years or generations in the city, education, occupation of husband (and increasingly of the wife), socioeconomic status and its accompanying resources, age at widowhood, parental status, location, and personal "modernization" are all factors influencing the social life space, social roles, relationships, and identities of each widow. There are pockets of ethnic widows with support networks of varied complexity and both an in- and an outflow of supports. There are extremely isolated widows and those dependent on a very limited number of persons, usually a daughter. Some widows specialize in neighboring to the exclusion of other sources of contact. There are widows who are involved in complex social systems of voluntary and occupational groups. Chicago even contains urbanite women whose networks extend throughout the city and its environs as well as cosmopolitan widows who interact directly or indirectly in a global arena. For some women, a pervasive identity of widow clings in a traditional style; for others, it is a very personal aspect of the self. The life spaces of some become restricted with the death of the connecting link between them and the outside world. For others, the life spaces expand as past restrictions are lifted or new abilities are developed and new ventures undertaken.

In general, the Chicago-area widows who fell into our samples (Lopata & Brehm, 1986) of current or former beneficiaries of Social Security suffered a financial loss following the death of the husband and remained poorer than in the past unless they remarried. These women were better off, however, than many other widows, having a higher average education and income than widows with no present or prior connection with Social Security. Thus, the poorest were women whose own, or husbands', work histories were not covered by the Social Security program. In addition, widows who did not have children receiving benefits and who were not old enough to get them as former employees or widows of insured men fell into what the Social Security Administration calls a "gray" period of ineligibility for benefits (Lopata & Brehm, 1986).

Half of the metropolitan Chicago widows were living in the same housing unit as before the death of the husband. Thus, the assumption that all urban widows must sell their homes and move to cheaper quarters or move to be near to their children was not reflective of half of our women. Hardly any of the women moved to the Chicago area after widowhood. The home, as indicated in the discussion of Columbus, Ohio, widows, is a symbol of independence and status, and 53% of the Chicago women owned their dwelling, a drop of only 6% since widowhood. In fact, 80% of the women were heads of their own households; the remarrieds tended to list the new husband as head. Forty-three percent lived alone, and 24% shared a two-person household. Two thirds of the dwellings were in residential areas within the city or its suburbs. The judgment of their areas by interviewers indicated an absence of the extremes of wealth or poverty.

Summary

Widows, as other Americans, live in a variety of surroundings, occasionally near each other, not by design but by attrition or socioeconomic condition. Thus, in small towns, ethnic communities, or retirement communities, they become the remainders of couples that stayed or moved together. In cities, they reside where they and their marital partners selected family housing, depending on income; size of family and the ages of their members; preferences of area and type of unit; familiarity with the neighborhood or people in it, such as relatives and friends; perceived advantages of facilities and institutions, especially schools and churches; and so forth. Older couples move for a variety of reasons. Some define the housing or area as no longer desirable or necessary; others are attracted to other places by leisure time attractions or the presence of children. There the widows remain, or they return to the old community, not having developed roots in the new location. Some move into public housing for the elderly, with the help of friends who have already done so or of social service agencies.

American communities differ considerably in the resources they do or do not provide people at different stages of the life course. Not everyone can move to take advantage of these or to get away from problems and disadvantages. In fact, many people do not know of other resources and how to reach out to them, so they are stuck with little choice. The more traditional and less modern the woman, the less likely she is to be located in a community on the basis of rational selection, being dependent in such decisions on others or remaining where she had resided in the past.

I was once on a university platform with fellow sociologists who had been studying the elderly in small towns of Missouri while I was studying widowhood in the Chicago area. At the end of our presentations about the situation of widows, someone in the audience asked whether life was better for widows in small towns or in large cities. Our answers had to be given in terms of the relative advantages of each type of location. Small towns provide continuity of identity. For example, Mary Jones of the Herbert Jones family marries and becomes Mrs. Thomas Hardy whose husband is the town's (pastor, baker, drunkard). This identity she carries into widowhood. She continues to belong to the same church, joins the society of widows and its activities, and continues life with relatively little need or opportunity for change. Thus, she is constrained by her own and even the family's past and by limited resources for entering new social roles or relationships.

If Mary Jones grows up in the city, her family background may not be known if the family changes school districts. Her married life and her widowhood identity may be known only to a limited number of people. Her employer is certainly unlikely to know her father's and then her husband's occupation. She may live in a neighborhood that has institutionalized minimal neighboring, and she may select friendships from a wide variety of contacts. Her married identity can be a relatively segregated part of her interactive self and can be put aside with widowhood. She may try a variety of new occupational, associational, friendship, and even appearance paths and identities. She is less likely, however, to have a continuing support network whether she wants one or not due to the rate of mobility of associates and social groups. There are no norms forbidding remarriage, although there are conventions regarding its timing and the characteristics of a new mate. The matching norms are similar to those of a first marriage. Modern societies, however, necessitate a great deal of self-confidence, knowledge, and flexibility of resources to voluntaristically engage in the urban life in many of its forms.

On the other hand, the city presents many problems to widows, especially older ones. These include crime (even more important, fear of crime); transportation difficulties; crowding; pollution; rate of mobility and the disintegration of community areas; racial tension and conflict; ethnic and religious hostility; a poor schooling system that sends adult children into the suburbs, making contact with grandchildren difficult; social class and other segregation; increasing demand for increasing education for even mediocre jobs; and gender harassment.

The myth that American society is "modern" or "socially developed" to a large scale contradicts the realities of life in its various locations and among many of its members. Traditional and transitional lifestyles abound, often in pockets of highly urbanized areas or in neighborhoods throughout the country. Widowed women not only live in these unevenly developed areas but also develop a wide range of social life spaces. Many of the older ones were socialized into a two-sphere worldview, being limited to the private sphere and unable to use the societal resources for more flexible and complex social life spaces. Because so many are old and limited in their ability to take advantage of the more modern aspects of America, the majority of myths about widows generalize to all of them. The picture is not of modern women; quite the contrary, it is of very old, very restricted, and dependent persons. This view is untrue of an increasing proportion of widows, including the middle-class, more educated ones among the very old, and the untold numbers of the aging younger ones. We will examine some of the variations on these themes in the chapters that follow.

Notes

1. We are, of course, dependent on the studies by social scientists whose descriptions and samples of widows reflect their theoretical and practical interests. This means that we do not have comparable data, being well supplied as to some areas of the women's lives and lacking knowledge of other areas.

2. Although the number of widows in America has risen dramatically over the decades, because the U.S. population has expanded with births and immigration, the proportion of widows has actually decreased since 1970 from a high of 13.9%, as has the proportion of married women, mainly due to an increase in the percentage of single and divorced women. In fact, Cherlin (1981) notes that in the mid-19th century, most of the dissolutions [of marriages] in a given year were caused by the death of one spouse, but by the mid-1970s, for the first time in our nation's history, more marriages ended every year in divorce than in death. (p. 25).

Mortality rates have decreased considerably even in the past decades, and widowhood has come at a later age for both men and women. In addition, the proportion of remarriages to first marriages had increased until the 1980s due to the continued increase in the divorce rate. After that, the remarriage rate fell and stabilized due to the increase in cohabitation without marriage (Cherlin, 1981, p. 27).

3. At the age of 80, my mother moved into Chelsea House in Chicago, a self-contained retirement hotel housing 320 active people. She enjoyed it for 9 years, participating in community activities, including a speaker's bureau. People running for political office made sure to present themselves to these voters. A conference of social gerontologists was even held in this locale, with Robert Havinghurst, Clark Tibbits, and Vivian Woods, for example, as major speakers. Some of the residents also took part in city events, such as concerts and shopping in the Loop. Thus, by remaining in Chicago, these residents were not isolated from family and modern life as much as are the residents of most leisure village communities of the Sunbelt.

4. My comments throughout this book about Chicago-area widows are based on two extensive surveys and the use of a variety of other methods, including participant observation, research into primary and secondary sources, census figures and interviews. The first study, conducted in the early 1970s and funded by the Administration on Aging and Roosevelt University, focused on changes in social roles and role clusters and involved a sample of 300 widows in metropolitan Chicago. The second, again preceded by qualitative immersion in the subject, used a weighted sample, drawn by the U.S. Social Security Administration statisticians, of 82,077 widows who fell into five categories of beneficiaries: recipients of old-age benefits, mothers of eligible children, women who received only lump sum payments to help with funeral expenses, and former beneficiaries who remarried or whose children grew beyond entitlement age. That study used the support systems framework.

5. Thomas and Znaniecki (1918-1920/1958) found in their study of *The Polish Peasant in Europe and America* 70 organizations in one parish, Saint Stanislaw Kostki.

4

Wife Into Widow

<table>
<tr><td>Myth:</td><td>Sudden death is much harder for the survivor than prolonged dying.</td></tr>
<tr><td>Myth:</td><td>Prolonged dying is much harder for the survivor than sudden death.</td></tr>
</table>

The debate as to which type of death of a significant other is harder to take for the survivor has been carried out in the mass media, scientific literature, and personal conversation (DeSpelder & Strickland, 1992; Stroebe, Stroebe, & Hansson, 1993). In short, the argument on the one side states that sudden death of the other is traumatic because of its very suddenness and the possibility that it leaves a lot of "unfinished business" (Blauner, 1966). At the same time, it saves the often deteriorating experience of caring for a slowly dying person. Prolonged dying enables the working out of the personal relationship between spouses but provides many problems of care and can be socially isolating if other care providers and former associates withdraw. In calling both statements myths, I am making the point that the experiences are so different as not be comparable in terms of the degree of problem for survivors. Many factors influence both situations, including cause of death and the age of the husband and of the wife at that event. Other important factors are the significance of the marriage to the woman and her emotional involvement with her husband throughout the marriage (Stroebe & Stroebe, 1993b). The circumstances surrounding the death leave an indelible imprint on the memory and affect the whole social life space of the widowed woman. The consequences of widowhood vary also by many other factors and their combinations, including religion, ethnicity, race, education, socioeconomic status, health, household composition, and lifestyle. We will examine these and other factors in greater detail in the forthcoming chapters.

Death and the Survivor

Various changes in American society have built marriage into an extremely important personal relationship, allegedly meeting all the emotional, social, service, and economic needs of each partner. Much research indicates that marriage is even more important for the wife than for the husband, especially in transitional times during which many of their other relationships are pushed into the background with the ascendance of the nuclear family (Lopata, 1993a, 1993b). The ideology of love and sexual satisfaction within marriage for both partners, companionship to the point of comradeship, confidant and even friendship interaction, and a joint construction of reality, added to the traditional mutual interdependence of supports, makes this a heavily imbued dyadic relationship. The availability of relatively easy divorce leads to the conclusion that the death of a spouse in a continuing relationship must be personally as well as socially traumatic. Only the death of a child, especially a relatively young child, is deemed more emotionally traumatic (Rubin, 1993). There are two expected consequences of a death of a spouse: personal-emotional and social-economic. Many myths and stereotypes, however, surround the circumstances and consequences of conjugal bereavement.

SUDDEN DEATH

Despite all the images of death at the end of a satisfying and productive life, even in America people die "off time," before anyone has rehearsed, through anticipatory socialization, for that death (Neugarten & Hagestad, 1976). Accidents, heart attacks, natural disasters, murders, and suicides catch survivors unprepared and often leave them very angry (Glick, Weiss, & Parkes, 1974). Death of young people is allegedly most disturbing to the society at large and to people in primary relationships. Americans are very uncomfortable with any death, especially with the death of a person who should live until old age, as evidenced by the lack of formal supports and the awkwardness felt by personal associates. Sudden death of a young husband can produce a great deal of personal, emotional, social, and economic trauma and disorganization. The widow can be left with small children, frequently without adequate insurance or other means of supporting the family. She is deprived of all the supports of a husband and father for her children. In past decades, the wife was not apt to have been employed or at least not earning enough to maintain the household and family by herself. Such an off-time event can leave the woman enraged with the cause of the death, asking "Why me?" while everyone around her in the same age cohort is continuing her or his normal life. Of course, a similar set of sentiments and emotions, although allegedly less traumatic, can be experienced by older survivors of sudden death (Parkes, 1972).

Sudden death leaves the survivors with varying degrees of "unfinished business," as mentioned earlier. Relational problems remain hanging, unresolved. Arrangements easing the consequences of the death for the survivors cannot be made. The wife, for example, may not know anything about the couple's financial situation because husbands traditionally handle that part of family life. Both the husband and the wife could make necessary arrangements, if imminent death is known beforehand. The fact that everyone will die someday does not necessarily result in adequate preparation while people are feeling well and death appears far away. Kalish (1981, p. 190) makes a list of the kinds of things people can do when death is close, releasing the feelings of anxiety that problems will never be resolved. Sudden death prevents anyone from closing off that chapter of the deceased's life. The suddenness also forces the whole event into a shorter period of time than most people are able to absorb (see Stroebe & Stroebe, 1987, p. 204). Too many things happen too fast, leaving a feeling of helplessness. The future may look blank, with all plans from the past no longer relevant (Lerner, 1978). In general, survivors of sudden death tend to have been healthier before the event than survivors of expected bereavement, mainly because of age and the fact that husbands with long-term illnesses tend to have somewhat unhealthy wives. Widows of sudden death, however, tend to suffer a higher rate of psychiatric ailments, to be more depressed, and to have the depression last longer (see Stroebe & Stroebe, 1987, pp. 206-208).

There have been many studies of the importance of "anticipatory grief" or the consequences of forewarning of the death of a significant other on the psychological adjustment of the survivor (Roach & Kitson, 1989). Of course, as with all research, the results are affected by the definition of forewarning and the timing cutoff, some researchers restricting sudden death to immediate knowledge, others defining it as such if it took place within 1 day, 5 days, or even almost 2 weeks. The connection with age and forewarning was assumed by them, on the basis of other studies, to be significant in influencing its effect, although with complications to this association (Roach & Kitson, 1989). Forewarning itself is varied by the depth of the certainty of the coming death. Roach and Kitson used both "length of time between the start of illness and the death of the spouse . . . and length of time between knowledge of the seriousness of the illness and death of the spouse" (pp. 188-189). They also measured forewarning by the number and types of preparation for the death undertaken by the wife. These were very practical activities, such as changing appearance, going back to school, getting a job or changing one, learning about legal rights, and so forth. The researchers measured psychological stress using a brief symptom inventory and a self-rating depression scale (p. 190). Their conclusion, different from that of many other researchers, was that there is no significant effect on psychological distress of forewarning or length of husband's illness. Roach and Kitson explain this in terms of hope held onto until the moment of death, the reality of the impending death not really grasped from a simple awareness of the seriousness of the illness. The authors concluded that women who had actively prepared for widowhood fared better in terms of psychological distress after the death than did women who had not prepared. Roach and Kitson stress the importance of women's learning to be independent even in marriage, in case that relationship ceases through death or divorce.

The explanation of the differences in the findings of Roach and Kitson and those of other researchers focusing on the effects of forewarning may lie in the degree to which the forewarning results in a passive acceptance versus an active response. Women may know the husband is ill but may not really absorb the consequences of that fact until the death actually takes place. They are thus similar to the women who are not aware of this possibility. They report that "death at a young age is more distressing than death in later years" (Roach & Kitson, 1989, p. 196).[1] Such a statement is supported by Neugarten and Hagestad (1976) who found that the older the woman, the more likely she is to have "rehearsed" widowhood, not being surprised even by sudden death not preceded by a definite dying process. On the other hand, older wives may be more dependent on the husband than are younger ones, so age by itself appears not to be the determining factor as to the strength of the grief reactions.

Suicide is one form of death, usually sudden, that varies in its effect by societal attitudes, cause, and method. Durkheim (1951) classified suicides into four types. *Altruistic* suicide can occur when the society or another social unit is so strong that the person is willing to give up his or her life for the perceived benefit to others. *Egoistic* suicide occurs when the person has lost ties with society, often as a result of a dramatic movement up or down the socioeconomic scale. The *fatalistic* suicide does not see any future for the self. *Anomic* suicide occurs when cultural norms and community identification lose their meaning and significance for the person. Some societies, such as traditional Japan, have encouraged altruistic and even egoistic suicides in cases of war or loss of face. Despite psychological commentary on the traumatic effects of suicide on the survivors, none of the analyses I have seen are based on the Durkheimian model (see Backer, Hannon, & Russell, 1994, pp. 248-250).

The Catholic Church considers suicide a sin, and American society in general defines it as immoral. In fact, there are laws against it, and insurance companies are allowed to restrict payments to survivors of suicide. In recent years, the morality and legality of doctor-assisted suicide has been a subject of strongly felt debate by the mass media and the public at large. The state of Michigan has defined this as a criminal act and arrested Dr. Jack Kevorkian, who has already assisted a number of terminally ill patients (Backer et al., 1994). The legal situation there is not clear, and other states are experimenting with laws allowing or forbidding assisted suicide.

In consequence of the combination of feelings in this society toward suicide and the emotions raised by this act in individual cases, surviving spouses (also parents and children) are found by counselors to be very disturbed. Feelings of guilt of having contributed to the depression, if not caused it, are inevitable even when the suicide note does not blame the family. In the case of the widow, there is also anger at the husband for having committed suicide, deserting the family, depriving it of a normal life, and causing embarrassment and stigma. Fear of reinvestment in intimate relationships can result, especially when feelings of guilt pervade. According to psychiatrists, the interweave of feelings is fluid and does not have a rational base (see Cain, 1977, p. 230). It includes all forms of guilt, identification with the suicide, depression and even self-destructiveness, search for meaning, and incomplete mourning through avoidance.

The self-concept can be affected by "a sense of shame, dishonor, and stigma; of having been cast away, abandoned, unwanted; of being worthless, unloved if not bad or rotten, of being helpless, vulnerable; of being internally unsure of self or others" (Cain, 1977, p. 230). The social aspects of survivorship in the case of the suicide of a partner can also be highly disorganizing and liable to lead toward negative reactions. Some situations, such as painful and untreatable disease, are sometimes privately accepted causes for self-destruction. Others are met with stigma and may even lead to avoidance of the survivor. Whole families are deeply affected by the suicide of one of their members, often resulting in conflict over blame. In-laws and friends of the deceased may be most likely to make life difficult for the widow or avoid her entirely, regardless of her needs. Behavior may be demanded of her that is difficult to carry out:

> Facing an inquest, reading accounts of one's own very personal troubles in the public press, the stigma attached to suicide, and dealing with such matters as life insurance policies, which the suicide has put into jeopardy, are all additionally stressful, and may often have to be handled with little support from others. (Stroebe & Stroebe, 1987, p. 212)

On the other hand, prolonged dying can have strong negative effects on the survivors, especially if they are directly involved in the dying process. Again, this effect depends on the degree of illness and disability and the type and length of care.

CAREGIVING IN PROLONGED DYING

> **Myth:** Most people in American society now die in hospitals, so families are no longer involved in their long-term or immediate predeath care.

Most people wish to die at home, but relatively few do so. In fact, "The present pattern of death in our society is such that, regardless of

age, about 80 percent of all persons die in an institutional setting—
hospitals, nursing or convalescent facility, or retirement home providing care for the aged" (DeSpelder & Strickland, 1992, p. 19).

In reality, people who end up in medical settings in the final days
of their lives have usually been cared for by their families at home.
Care of the ill is still usually carried on at home for the duration of
the illness or until the caregiver reaches the end of resources. Most
people who are located in long-term medical facilities are likely to lack
close families; widows and childless patients outnumber those with
still-living families of procreation. Ill men tend to be cared for by their
wives, who then become widowed and are apt to spend their last days
in institutional locations. In fact, there is a recent movement of
bringing dying patients back home, if they had been previously institutionalized, with the help of the hospice program. This program,
instituted by a British physician, has spread to the United States and
is available in many communities, some of which have hospice centers
where dying patients can temporarily reside. More frequent in America is the program of help to the patient and the family carried forth
in the home. The purpose of the program is to help the patient to "die
with dignity" and to serve as a support system for his or her family
when it has decided that further cure-directed medicalization is no
longer desirable (see Backer et al., 1994, chap. 5).

According to the National Cancer Institute, the hospice program's
goals are the following:

1. To ease the physical discomfort of the terminal cancer patient by
   employing pharmaceutical and advanced clinical techniques for effective
   symptom control
2. To ease the psychological discomfort of the terminal cancer patient
   through programs allowing for active participation in scheduled activities or periods of peaceful withdrawal as determined by the patient
3. To aid in maintaining the emotional equilibrium of the patient and the
   family as they go through the traumatic life experience of progressive
   disease and ultimately the final separation of death (Cohen, quoted in
   Shanis, 1985, p. 374)

The services that most directly affect the spouse include skilled nursing
care, social services, paid control and symptom management, short-
term inpatient respite and acute-episode care, homemaker services,
constant availability on call, volunteer support and respite for families,

and bereavement services. The program is thus of great assistance to the primary caregiver and contributes to her (or his) feeling that she (or he) and the patient form part of a larger community-based team. Hospice also tries to pull in other family members but does not depend on these unless they are defined as the primary caregivers.

The hospice program involves a professional interdisciplinary team working with an "attending physician," trained volunteers and nurses who provide advice, pain containment medicines, and whatever physical equipment is necessary to care for the patient at home (Backer et al., 1994; Kastenbaum, 1991). Family members are trained to deal with various problems, and they also receive bereavement follow-up support. The volunteers provide services such as companionship for the patient and respite for the caregivers, transportation, shopping, and other supports.

Regardless of the general support system provided to the main caregiver—and many spouses report it to be very inadequate at the most important times—the processes of dying and of caring for a dying patient are obviously traumatic, in both physical and emotional terms. The dying patient is himself going through grief over the changing and terminal self, grief that he often finds it hard to express directly. Loss of control over the self and the environment as well as changes in physical appearance are experienced as a loss (see Parkes, 1993, p. 97). Kübler-Ross (1969) found patients going through "stages of dying," including, but not necessarily in the same order, denial, bargaining, anger, despair, resignation, and acceptance. The anger is expressed toward the closest people around for their failure to stop the dying and all that is experienced with it. Loss of energy by the patient is accompanied by irritation, dependence on others, and attempts to do things that the body can no longer do.

For example, the husband of historian Gerda Lerner (1978) died of cancer in their home, although he had been hospitalized for extensive periods of time before that. The wife's helplessness in not being able to alleviate her husband's fears and pain, combined with the husband's avoidance and helplessness over not being his usual self and not being able to support her, turned a year and a half into a draining experience. Lerner found that both she and her husband had to learn the importance of breaking down the barriers that prevented full communication and empathetic understanding, difficult under such conditions. Lerner also detailed, in *A Death of One's Own*, the exhausting scheduling of care for her husband even when he was hospitalized, including synchronization of the efforts of all friends and relatives on the outside.

Autobiographical and ethnographic studies of the pain experienced by the person whose significant other is dying draw our attention not only to the personal grief but also to the problems of responding to the changes in the patient. The wife must respond, or cannot prevent herself from responding, emotionally to what is happening to the husband. She can be the major recipient of her husband's anger, depression, or resignation without having the resources with which to make the dying any easier. She also has to meet the needs of other people, such as the children, who are not as directly involved in the death but who are suffering from it.

My review of 20 years of research on the emotional and physical consequences of caregiver stress discovered certain general patterns, although there is a great deal of inconsistency in findings of different researchers, depending on measures used.

> Chronic illness in a close relative leads to the caregiver role; caregiving demands lead to stress, stress and situation-specific factors combine and lead to dysphoria [a general feeling of anxiety, depression, and restlessness]. Dysphoria can, in some cases, lead to ineffective coping and, in vulnerable individuals, to depression. Depression may compromise the immune system, depression and an impaired immune system lead to adverse health consequences. This chain of events can be interrupted if caregivers cope effectively, and have support and better than average resources. In addition, caregivers must seek adequate health care for themselves, which many apparently do not. (Wright, Clipp, & George, 1993, p. 189)

Psychologists and related health care specialists recommend that it is necessary for the caregiver to receive some respite and other forms of support, because the whole experience is very difficult and can result in serious physical and mental health damage.

A different care and emotional situation exists when a spouse becomes so incapacitated as to require institutionalization. At any one time in present-day America, the number of elderly in long-term institutions does not exceed 5%, but many more people go through such places in the final stages of life, as indicated earlier. The very decision to institutionalize the husband is emotionally draining and full of ambivalence (see DeSpelder & Strickland, 1992, p. 340). There is sadness, guilt, and loneliness, accompanied, however, by relief over placement in a good care facility and not having to personally provide physical, medical, and emotional care 24 hours a day. Gladstone (1993) reported stress on the part of the community-residing spouse over the type of care being provided to the institutionalized spouse, tension with staff, and the difficulties experienced with the visiting situation. Some wives also felt a loss of purpose that the care had provided to their lives. The care had been so intensive as to overshadow all other concerns and relationships, creating a vacuum when it was no longer needed. Benefits to the self from the reduction of care, however, can lower the distress produced by all the other aspects of the situation. An interesting insight came from Gladstone's study: The community-based spouses described their marriages as a memory of something already finished, as in a limbo position, or as changed to the extent of resembling more a parent-child than a wife-husband relationship.

Any of these responses were followed by the statement that the marriage still demanded loyalty and unchanged continuity of behavior. The institutionalized spouses tended to idealize the marriage or to describe it in mixed or only currently changed terms. Of course, the perceived change in the marriage may have occurred much earlier for the women than for the men.

Charmaz (1980) found one of the major problems of dying in an institution to be the fact that the environment encourages social death before the physical death. Hospital staffs tend to treat the patient as a dying body rather than as a person. This is not only demoralizing to the patient but can also create anger among the survivors or push them into the same kind of withdrawal. Visiting in a hospital is made difficult by its strangeness, rules, and regulations; the frequently hostile attitudes of staff members; and the sight of other suffering people. The whole situation can make awkward the interaction between the patient and the wife, adding to guilt and sadness. Emergency incidents can create tension in relations with other family members, who may be called together and then have to leave if death does not come when anticipated. There is an additional emotional problem that wives (and other relatives to varying degrees) experience, and that is the psychological refusal to think of the future. From one point of view, this refusal may be an advantage because it prevents premature grief work, through which the survivor begins to withdraw from the dying person before the death. Prolonged, day-by-day waiting can have many mental and physical effects. All in all, the wife can feel completely helpless in the face of death, even when it takes place at home but especially when it comes in the foreign territory of the hospital.

Many of these problems are consequences of the fact that the time of death is usually uncertain. Death is always a possibility, but awareness of imminent death brings it to the fore, albeit rarely in definite terms. Glaser and Strauss (1965) devoted a whole book to *Awareness of Dying* in the hospital setting (see also their 1968 *Time for Dying*). A whole circle of people are involved with the seriously ill patient in a hospital: doctors, nurses of various levels, families, and other patients. Even the medical staff may be uncertain as to the time frame of the patient's death. Glaser and Strauss (1965) model three situations: " '(1) sudden or unexpected death, (2) certain death but uncertain timing, and (3) certain, timed death' " (quoted in Lopata, 1986b, p. 696). Awareness of approaching death rarely leads even the medical experts to predictions of exact time. In addition, the awareness may not be shared with everyone in the circle of the patient. In the past, and in many hospital settings even now, the staff is often hesitant about telling the patient his or her prognosis, fearing depression, unpredictable behavior, or both. Kübler-Ross (1969) had a difficult time convincing physicians, even more so than nurses, that open awareness by everyone of impending death is necessary and beneficial. Not every hospital is able to accept such a context. Even families are often kept unaware for fear that they might disturb the patient, make inconvenient demands, or express themselves in ways that will disturb other patients and their families. Families, often including the future widow, may not want to share their awareness with the patient, thinking that there is no need to upset him or her.

Relocation in a long-term institution does not end the relationship, especially if the patient is *compus mentis,* or aware of what is going on around him (Gladstone, 1993; Miller, 1987; Miller & Kaufman, 1993). The staff performs most of the medical and physical care functions, but the spouse continues emotional and social supports. In fact, some physical care is also carried forth, in addition to, or in support of, professional care. Service supports, in the form of provisions of personal items, sometimes even of foods, or organizing events are also possible. The institutionalized husband can do little for the wife, except on the emotional level.

Gladstone (1993) points out, referring back to other studies, that one of the main supports that spouses can provide each other through transitional times such as approaching death may be the feelings of external and internal continuity. It is one of the possible contributions of significant others to the patient to help in the process of "life review" that pulls together memories to give a meaningful continuity to existence (Butler, 1963). The wife can remind the husband of pleasant events, helping to construct his life as worthwhile. This is the time for some of their unfinished business to be completed; the dying patient can make amends and patch up things with other people. Even the wife can benefit from this process, giving herself some of the credit for the positive side of the past.

On the other hand, the caregiving role can contribute to women's self-development, according to O'Bryant, Straw, and Meddaugh (1990). In terms of my role theory, the process by which the husband enters the sick role provides the wife opportunities to orchestrate a social circle, granting her certain rights and responding to her duties as his caregiver. One of her rights is that of taking over multiple responsibilities previously falling within the province of the husband. The wife can thus gain a feeling of mastery because she proves her competence to herself and, as O'Bryant and her associates suggest, to others who treat her as a competent person. The feeling is especially evident among currently older widows, who had previously developed specialization in female-specific tasks. Now they learn multiple skills needed in the maintenance of a complete household, because the husband can no longer carry forth his share of responsibilities. O'Bryant et al. learned of this process from widows of Alzheimer's patients who evaluated the past experience from their current perspective, once the burden of care was over.

Factors Affecting Caregiving Stress

The effects of extensive caregiving on the main caregiver depend on a number of factors, including the type of illness and its progress; the care needs throughout; the resources of the caregivers, personally and in terms of informal and formal aids; and role conflicts. The gender, age, and relationship to the patient of the caregiver also appear to influence the effects.

ILLNESS DIFFERENCES
IN CAREGIVING STRESS

One of the most difficult caring situations is connected to dementia, such as Alzheimer's disease. The patient exhibits a loss of memory and irrational, emotional, and often dangerous behavior. In a relatively modern society that idealizes self-control and mental competence, such illness is a source of embarrassment and shame for relatives, especially the spouse and children. America is still inadequately prepared for this type of illness. Long-term care facilities are financially devastating to families, and caregivers' needs for respite and assistance are not adequately met. Day care centers or in-house respite care services usually do not accept patients with behavior problems, and there is little that medical professionals can do besides sedating the person (see Straw, O'Bryant, & Meddaugh, 1991, p. 368). Usually, the caregiving wife is unwilling to reach out for help because of the nature of the problems. Friendships can wither in any long-term, serious-illness situation, let alone in one involving Alzheimer's disease. Thus, the whole burden falls on the family, mainly on the wife (Clipp & George, 1990). One of the few resources available to caregivers is support groups, frequently organized by hospitals or the national association. This situation, however, appears to be the hardest to face by any primary caregiver. One of the devastating aspects of Alzheimer's and related diseases is the total destruction of the marital relationship so that the conscious spouse becomes a personal widow even before becoming a full widow. The spouse lives on biologically but not emotionally or cognitively.

Another unique situation in caregiving surrounds patients with acquired immunodeficiency syndrome (AIDS) because of the epidemic nature of the illness and several characteristics of the population (Martin & Dean, 1993). In the early 1980s, little was known about AIDS and its transmission, and the gay male community was hard hit with it. The dying and the caregiving men in the community were in the prime of life but in societally stigmatized relationships. Research among AIDS caregivers found heightened psychological distress, including panic attacks about developing the illness, attempts to avoid thoughts and emotions about it, or suicidal thoughts and attempts as a preferred alternative. Caregivers constantly examined their own bodies for signs of AIDS. These and related symptoms combined with the usual problems of caring for visibly and painfully dying friends and lovers. The multiplicity and constancy of illness and dying made impossible the denial of its existence. Caregivers of nongay patients who acquired AIDS had similar problems in dealing with the outside world because of the immense fear of this illness, as evidenced in the cases of children who are not allowed to attend public schools or whose lives in school are made miserable.

GENDER DIFFERENCES
IN CAREGIVING STRESS

There is currently rapidly expanding research on gender differences in perceived strain from caregiving. Although the results are mixed, there are very interesting, and often confusedly interpreted, differences in the way women and men respond to heavy caregiving situations.

According to most studies, the most vulnerable to emotional and physical health problems are women, in order of strength of effects: wives, daughters, then daughters-in-law. Of lesser vulnerability are sons and, finally, husbands. Those who "occupy shared residence," and low-income providers are also highly vulnerable (see Wright et al., 1993, p. 183). The interesting thing is that the severity of impairment and duration of caregiving in general are not found to be significantly associated with depression on the part of caregivers. Certain aspects of the caregiver's personality, lack of control over the spouse's behavior, and the feeling that life had changed considerably due to the illness were associated with depression in the study by Wright and colleagues. This supports the previous conclusion that wives are more stressed in the caregiving of husbands than vice versa because women have less control over men due to the patriarchal nature of American society, especially among middle-aged and older members. The most likely to be involved in long-term, difficult caregiving is the wife, partly because husbands are more frequent patients, being older and of the gender that dies earlier. Straw et al. (1991) also attribute the preponderance of women in stressful caregiving situations to the whole ideology of female nurturance, which may even create guilt for not having protected their spouses from illness.

In one study, greater stress was reported by wives caring for cognitively impaired husbands than vice versa (see Miller & Kaufman, 1993, p. 19). The Alzheimer's diseased spouses of both genders had similar degrees of impairment requiring similar care activities by their spouses. The researchers had a different explanation for the differences of men and women's feelings of burden than was reported in other studies. They found that each gender held divergent belief systems. Women explained caregiving in personality and emotional terms, whereas men referred more to tasks of household and personal care and the need for physical strength. Women's socialization into sensitivity to emotional distress resulted in anxieties of competing obligations, confinement, and unpredictability of care needs. This was particularly true of women who had been full-time homemakers prior to providing heavy caregiving to husbands rather than of those who had been employed outside of the home. The homemakers reported role strain because they had to behave in ways they associated with "men's work." In other words, they held strong "gender belief systems and ideas about appropriate gender roles" (p. 21) that conflicted with what they had to do in relations with cognitively impaired husbands. The women had to learn more difficult skills, by their definition, than the men had to learn to manage the household and the care of their wives. Such perceived role strain was more typical of middle-class white women than of African American women of the same social class, who had already learned less gender specialized skills.

A study of caregivers, drawn through mass media and organizations serving the elderly who were likely to belong to support groups, reported greater strain by wives than by husbands, although the men took care of sicker persons and carried forth similar supports (Barusch & Spaid, 1989). The researchers had assumed incorrectly that the men patients would be more difficult to care for than women patients on the basis of degree of physical disability as well as cognitive and behavioral problems. Barusch and Spaid gave several explanations for the finding that wives were more burdened than the husbands. One was that the wives in the sample were younger, and younger caregivers report greater stress than do older ones, possibly because of role conflict. The main explanation, however, for the difference in experienced stress was that the men were more "active copers" in response to the needs, whereas women used more avoidance and a greater variety of different coping styles. These statements about coping strategies certainly reflect the influence of the traditional, patriarchal structure of the two-sphere world. They indicate that the wives had much less direct control over the husbands than the husbands over the wives. Therefore, they had to use a variety of coping styles to accomplish their caring aims. Lack of control over the situation has always been a source of strain.

Another study (Young & Kahana, 1989) concluded that caregiving daughters of a never-married, widowed, or divorced parent experienced greater strain from such care than even wives or husbands in marital units. This was explained in terms of younger age and role conflict. Wives took care of husbands in their own homes, and part of the caregiving involved regular homemaker supports, such as laundry and cooking. Work was not very different from what is carried forth when husbands were well. The daughters were younger and experienced more role conflict; half of them were employed, and most had their own nuclear families. Their roles of wife and mother were apt to suffer from the attention they paid their parent.

SUPPORT SYSTEMS AS FACTORS IN CAREGIVING RELIEF

Stroebe and Stroebe (1987) point out that forewarning of the coming death is one of the most important aids in easing strain for both the dying patient and the caregiving spouse. Such forewarning mainly comes from a supportive medical team:

> On the basis of psychoanalytic theory, one could argue that the fore-warned individual should be able to avoid guilt feelings by having the opportunity to make restitution. This should be particularly important for marital relationships characterized by ambivalence. (p. 204)

The importance of the caregiving wife's perception and her reality construction of the situation is evident in her evaluations of support networks as reducers of the strain of emotional caregiving. It is not so much the amount of actual support she receives as it is her feelings of unmet needs that lead to the depression of the caregiving wife. Thus, need does not necessarily result in sufficient or the right kind of support. A complex support network can actually contribute to stress—because each member of the social circle requires attention, even if only to provide training and instruction—at a time when the caregiver is absorbed by her spouse. The circle's members can also contribute their own emotional reactions, adding to stress. Smaller helping networks can be of greater assistance to wives of functionally impaired patients because they are more easily organized. Surprisingly, the studies found formal social supports, including counseling services, to be of little benefit during the height of caregiving. The wife may not be able to deal with even good counseling at that time.

A study by Thompson, Futterman, Gallagher-Thompson, Rose, and Lovett (1993) concluded that there are variations in the benefits provided to caregivers of frail and dementia-suffering elderly by different types of social supports. The most helpful were opportunities to "socialize and be engaged with friends and family" (p. 252). The feelings of burden experienced by the caregivers diminished with the opportunity to discuss problems and obtain supportive feedback from others but were even more diminished by pleasant activity with others that reduced negative feelings and distracted them from frustrations. Burdened caregivers may deprive themselves of recreation, feeling guilty over leaving the sufferer yet wishing for individuated freedom. A similar feeling is expressed by mothers of newborn children, who are cut off from the normal flow of social life by isolation in the home.

The authors even found interpersonal conflict with family and friends to be burden releasing, probably because it cannot be expressed in the caregiving situation. These findings suggest that support groups may not be sufficient substitutes for fun and recreation with friends and relatives.

Recommendations for Caregiving Relief

Many societal supports could ease the burden of caregiving. Tish Sommers and Laurie Shields (1987), cofounders of the Older Women's League, made a number of very practical suggestions as to legislative reforms, many of which have been in the public arena for years and that may actually be implemented through health reform. Their main suggestion is for a caregivers' movement to push for the following reforms:

1. Make respite care widely available and affordable through state and federal legislation.
2. Prevent the impoverishment of the caregiving spouse.
3. Cover long-term care for chronic illness—in nursing homes, in the community, and in the home—under Medicare.
4. Overhaul supplemental security income (SSI) and Medicaid.

5. Provide tax incentives for caregivers.
6. Increase the availability of comprehensive private health insurance for long-term care.

The Death of the Spouse and the Role of the Widow

Whether sudden or protracted, in an institution or at home, the death of the husband finally takes place. There are two major sets of consequences of this death for the wife: personal, in terms of her emotions and sentiments, and social, in that she takes on, at least temporarily, the role of a widow. We must remember that throughout these processes, the wife may not have been totally isolated, even if many of her roles had withered. The social circle of the dying husband contained, besides her, other people personally involved with him, such as the extended family and friends, as well as the professional teams caring for him as a patient. These may be hospital or nursing home professionals and assistants or all those involved in a hospice program. The wife of the dying patient had to relate to these members of the patient's social circle. She received rights from them, such as help with the care of the patient, information and advice about how to care for him herself and about his prognosis, and emotional and service supports. She, in turn, had duties toward them, even if just recognition of their presence and help but usually much more. She had to grant them the right to do their part in the process and to impinge on her relationship with the dying husband. She had to grant some of them the right to emotional reactions to what was happening, although she often felt that she was the only one with the right to such feelings.

The event of death may have been experienced directly by the wife, if she were present when it happened or if she found the dead husband, or indirectly, as when she learned about it from others. News of the death is often transmitted in less than an empathetic way, over the telephone or by someone who simply does not know how to cushion the shock (Charmaz, 1980). Hospital staff members or a chaplain connected with a health care facility often assume that a male member of the family, not the closest survivor, should be informed first and made responsible for communicating the news to others. Many cultures have a whole set of procedures by which the news of the death reaches more and more distant circles of people who are assumed to be influenced by it. Mass communication media, such as newspapers, carry obituaries that usually describe the person, the circumstances of the death, and close survivors. The person's brief history, place and date of birth, education, occupation, and membership in voluntary associations are often given. The list of survivors usually includes the spouse and children by name, parents, siblings by gender, and grandchildren by number. The obituary contains information as to time and location of a wake or visitation, religious ceremony and cemetery (if any), and family wishes concerning expressions of sympathy and donations. Generally, the wider the circle of interested people who would experience the loss of the person, the longer the announcement and the more places it appears. The death of a societally important person is usually eulogized in national magazines, with specification of their contributions to the society.

Naturally, the social significance assigned to the dead person by the community influences the role of widow during the whole mourning process. It is hard for a wife, and then a widow, if her husband were judged as a detriment to the wider society or if his death were connected with stigma, as in the case of a criminal, alcoholic, suicide, or, currently, in consequence of AIDS (see Hess & Markson, 1980, pp. 113-114). An example of the effects of the type of husband or the type of death was contained in Chapter 2 in which Israel's treatment of civilian widows was contrasted to that of war widows. Although the form of death and the honor accrued by the deceased are only indirectly influenced by the wife, the widow tends to bear the brunt of the judgment of the husband.

Interestingly enough, intimate but not legally recognized relationships are not acknowledged in the funeral preparations or rituals. Much fiction surrounds the problems of the heterosexual or homosexual lover who is cut out of the picture and cannot publicly express his or her sentiments. In some cultures, it is the parent, of even an adult child who has his or her own family of procreation, who is expected to be most bereaved. In others, the spouse is expected to be most bereaved. Children are often neglected in the rituals.

Whatever the lines of communication, the decisions regarding the treatment and the removal of the body, as well as of the location and style of rituals, are shared among the closest relatives and the widow in the case of a man's death. After all, the death is a family affair. Preparation for the funeral can be a source of family conflict, however, if its details have not been worked out by its members or specified by the deceased before his death (Rosenblatt, 1993). Rules of behavior, hierarchy of status, and responsibility for the procedures surrounding funeral events must be negotiated. Competition among the bereaved can make the situation very difficult. Some family members may come from out of town and must be "put up," or housing arrangements must be made. Modern families often contain members of various religious persuasions who cannot agree on what is to be done and said.

The importance of the person to wider circles in the society is reflected in the size of the setting for the wake or visitation, the religious ceremony, and the entourage of cars leading to the cemetery. It is also reflected in the media news coverage, as mentioned earlier. Some funerals, such as those of John or Robert Kennedy, are very public events, with televisions transmitting all the details to the nation and even the world.

Funeral and mourning rituals vary considerably by society the world over and by ethnic and racial communities in the United States (see *Ethnic Variations in Dying, Death and Grief: Diversity in Universality,* edited by Irish, Lundquist, & Nelson, 1993). One usual feature is the eulogy, often filled with stories and reminiscences, in which selected persons describe the positive characteristics of the deceased. Many religions and ethnic groups follow the burial (or cremation) ceremony, if there is one, with a social gathering featuring food and drink. This custom reinforces the ties of the living and indicates that life must go on, with sustenance assisting the process. One problem of modern life has been the pushing of death into formalized and depersonalized contexts, the stylized funeral home handling what used to be carried forth by the family and religious personnel (Gorer, 1967).

The functions of funerals have drawn considerable attention of social scientists (Kastenbaum, 1991; Lamm, 1969; Pine & Phillips, 1977). Backer et al. (1994) summarize these functions for the individual:

1. It increases the reality of death.
2. The funeral provides a "consensual validation" for the mourner, since the mourner is joined by others who are also feeling the loss.

3. . . . It provides the bereaved with something to do.
4. . . . [It] provides the bereaved with support . . . in grief.
5. . . . [It] helps people gain greater perspective on life and death.
6. The memory of the deceased gets rehabilitated.

The society benefits from funerals because they reaffirm the cohesiveness of the family, . . . act as a mirror of the values and expectations, . . . reinforce the social order, . . . reaffirm religious and ethnic identity, and . . . serve as rites of passage. (p. 291)

The funeral itself can be a cause of grief, not just because it formally establishes the fact of the death. As mentioned before, there is a great deal of decision making in its connection, with not all involved persons necessarily agreeing on its form. Funeral rites can be performed in a variety of places and followed by ceremonies in a variety of settings. The funeral can be extremely expensive, showing the family's importance or wealth, or it can involve minimal cost. Because there are usually several survivors involved besides the widow—children from this or other marriages, the parents of the deceased, his siblings, the widow's parents and siblings, and a variety of friends—advice and arguments can proliferate. As in all rituals, placement of survivors can be determined by protocol or negotiated. Closeness to the deceased can be indicated by the receiving line, the order of automobiles in the procession, the location of the wake or visitation, and the reception following the disposal of the body.

For ceremonies, the body can be in an open or closed casket or not present at all. It can be offered to science or cremated, although such procedures have not been frequent in America's past. According to DeSpelder and Strickland (1992, p. 126), only 14% of American deaths resulted in cremation in 1986, although the number is currently increasing. The ashes can be spread wherever the deceased had wished or can be contained and given to a special person. If buried, the location can be a source of competitive anger, as evident in the case of national heroes, especially if they die in "unnatural" locations as in wars.

The complexity of possible reactions to the death of a member of a community led Pine and Phillips (1977) to match figures on funeral expenditures to the status position of the family as measured by Warner's Index of Status Characteristics (ISC) that included occupation, source of income, education, and housing type. They found a direct association between the status group location and the funeral expenditures (see p. 424). In addition, they concluded that women spend more than men on funeral expenses within each status category (see p. 425). The "high cost of dying" has drawn much commentary since Jessica Mitford's (1963) *The American Way of Death* was published (see extensive commentary in DeSpelder & Strickland, 1992). The range of costs for the funeral, not including cemetery and associated expenses, is immense, and even average costs differ considerably by region and community (see DeSpelder & Strickland, 1992, pp. 212-231).

The effects of the death and rituals of commemoration do not end with the funeral. Many cultures have elaborate ceremonials for extended periods of mourning after the death or at anniversaries (Irish et al., 1993). Some cultures, such as Indian and orthodox Jewish, require severe changes in appearance of survivors for varying lengths of time.

American society as a whole does not demand dramatic expressions of grief during or following the death. The norms of appropriate behavior, however, are very specific among more traditional subcultures, and great stress is expressed by failures to observe them. The possibility of inappropriate action by persons attending funerals increased among the young, especially in the 1970s and 1980s. The appearance and demeanor of Jacqueline Kennedy after the death of her husband, President John Kennedy, is often used as an example of dignified behavior at a funeral. Although decreasing numbers of Americans are fully clothed in black as typical of European past and even current times, appearance and manner of funeral attenders are highly visible, much as in weddings.

Prior mention was made of the Jewish custom of "sitting shiva," whereby the closest bereaved in the family stay home, with various outward symbols of mourning, while relatives, friends, and associates of the deceased visit and allow for open grieving, reliving the life and the circumstances of death (Shuchter, 1986). This lasts a whole week and is reported by psychologists as beneficial to the bereaved. Periodic mourning rituals, such as at anniversaries of the death, officially remind the survivors of the deceased.

Involvement in the role of widow varies considerably in time, with appropriateness of leaving the role being strongly influenced by cultural norms. The length of time that the woman must carry the role of widow can depend not only on the status of the late husband but also on her expected future. Some widows are expected to carry forth the roles, albeit with changes, of the deceased, or at least his mantle, and to keep him socially alive. For the most part, Americans do not have such expectations of most women; a "proper" period of time for grieving is vague and not accompanied by continued physically identifying symbols. The end of the period of official mourning can often be formally established, or it may simply drift off. Although the bereaved may not feel any of the appropriate emotions, the formal mourning stance requires that they be expressed in behavior.

Summary

The processes by which a wife becomes a widow vary by time and place and by the circumstances of death of the husband. The circumstances, whether sudden or through prolonged illness; the extent to which the period prior to death involves a caregiving role on the part of the wife; the location of death; and the ages of the survivors and their alternative support systems all influence how these events affect the woman. There is a lack of agreement, however, in the cultural myths, and even in conclusions of social research, as to which form of death is harder on the survivor. Some believe that sudden death has the worst consequences for the widow; others believe that prolonged care of a slowly dying husband is worse.

Great variations exist in the content and duration of the processes by which a woman moves from the role of wife to that of widow and then out of that role into a partnerless person with a different role cluster. Throughout, the woman has the cooperation, sometimes the hindrance, of her main social circle of the temporary role of widow, as well as of the circles in her other roles. The transition out of the heavy consequences of the death tends to be very personal in American society, as support providers through caregiving, the death, and the funeral sequences move somewhat away, at least in terms of the woman's personal experiences of emotion and sentiment. Problematic can be the situation in which the associates and the widow have different expectations of her, or their, behavior.

Note

1. Schulz and Ewen (1993) also state that "young adults who lose a spouse to death appear to be at higher risk than older widows and widowers" (p. 405), again without evidence to support this statement.

5

Emotions, Sentiments, Resources, and Identities

Myth: Grief is a universal experience with definable stages and length of time (Lieberman, 1994).

Myth: Younger women suffer more in being widowed than do older women.

B efore going on with our discussion of the emotional effects on the widowed woman of the death of her husband, we need to define basic terms:

> *Bereavement* is the objective situation of having lost someone significant; *grief* is the emotional response to one's loss; and *mourning* denotes the actions and manner of expressing grief, which often reflects the mourning practices of one's culture. (Stroebe et al., 1993, p. 5)

I would also add that both grief and mourning reflect the culture of all involved and that this culture forms a foundation for the strength of emotional response to the death of others. In fact, Lofland (1985), in discussing "The Social Shaping of Emotion: The Case of Grief" points out that grief, or the emotional responses to the death of another, varies considerably in "shape, texture and length" (p. 181). The strength of the emotion is heightened by the degree of significance of that other to the self. She concludes that the modern Western world has decreased the number of people with whom an individual develops building blocks, or threads of connectedness of human attachment, that give meaning to the self (see p. 175). It has, however, increased the significance for the self of the few people with whom multiple blocks or threads are developed. It is Lofland's (1985) thesis that the individualization trends in modern society have increased the importance of a small number of highly significant others, which makes the death of such others more devastating than in societies in which the self has connecting threads with numerous others. "Intimacy (that is, the sharing of many facets of self, the multiple threaded connection, with only a few others) would appear to be a product of Western individualization, urbanization and industrialization" (p. 176).

Thus, in American marriages, individuals rather than larger social units, such as families or kin networks, form a basic bond for each person that is incorporated into the self-concept and modifies its prior content and dimensions. Modern individualization increases the importance of the marital bond, broken by the death of one of the partners. How much a woman's self-concept is disorganized by the death of her husband depends on similar factors that influence the degree of disorganization of her life: the degree of her dependence on him, on her married life, and on being a married woman for how she defined herself.

Another of the problems of grief in modern societies is the deinstitutionalization of much sentiment and ritual surrounding death (Gorer, 1967). In fact, death has become so distanced through medical technology, pushed off into later years and sterilized environments, that even attention to it is avoided. According to Gorer (1967) and Aries (1981), attitudes toward death in the past have incorporated it into the normal flow of life, not to be a source of fear unless, like in Scrooge's case, one's life had been "sinful and mean." The combination of having few intimates and of the changes in the meaning of death makes grief different and, possibly, more difficult in the modern world.

Grief

Sooner or later, the funeral and mourning rituals are over, and the role of widow fades as others return to their previous or modified relationships with the woman and to their own lives. The widow must go through the personal consequences of the death of her husband. As observers of the American scene indicate, and as we noted before, there is really no role of widow lasting beyond the mourning ritual, with its own social circle, rights, and duties. This was not true of traditional Hindu India, which allotted and forced a widow into such a role with visible symbols isolating her from the normal flow of life and lasting till her own death. There are, however, many vestiges of the role of wife and of the temporary role of widow that affect the immediate and later life of a woman. Above all, there are the sentiments and emotions in response to the death, the bereavement, and memories of the past. There is also a cutoff of the anticipated future that must be reconstructed. In this chapter, we will focus on the personal reactions, coping mechanisms, and self-introduced changes of the woman as an individual, from a symbolic interactionist perspective. In future chapters, we will examine how widowhood changes her relations with selected others. These two aspects of widowhood are obviously mutually interdependent.

Recent years have brought considerable attention to the subject of grief following spousal bereavement, a very complicated set of sentiments. Despite Lofland's (1985) clear analysis of the emotion of grief and the consequences of changes in world settings, there is little agreement among social scientists as to whether people who have experienced a loss or bereavement feel the same sentiments, let alone the same emotions. There are cultural variations in how people act when observers assume they are feeling grief, and even self-descriptions of what is felt vary by many factors. Currently, there are numerous popular models of timing and stages of grief, as we shall see later (Lopata, 1979).

One of the variations in the study of grief is disciplinary, and in all cases, the main problem is the difficulty in finding adequate methods of studying it. The discipline and theoretical framework influence the search techniques and interpretations of results. In the past, psychiatrists of a psychoanalytical background frequently treated grief as an illness or a form of depression and measured it in terms of physical distress (Shuchter & Zisook, 1993). Some have used the framework of stress theories, seeing death of a significant other as one of the important stressful life events, one that can even end in the death of the bereaved. The psychologist, Mort Lieberman (1994), is highly critical of psychiatrists who treat grief as a disease. Many psychologists of recent times have looked at it as a natural response to a loss and have analyzed it in terms of symptomatology and changes in cognitive and behavioral processes and interpersonal relationships (Stroebe et al., 1993, p. 5). As Lindeman (1944) and others have pointed out, grieving is necessary and requires many opportunities for its expression.

Increasingly, scientists interested in grief have pointed to its multidimensional nature. Comparative analyses of different kinds of loss are now likely to discover patterns of adaptation and successful responses to this life transition. Of course, successful resolution depends on what is defined as success and is usually based on psychological definition of normalcy in human beings. Sociologists are likely to focus on the social context within which the death and grief occur and the effect of death and dying on social roles and relationship in the family and the broader community. Social psychologists, especially symbolic interactionists, have focused on the meaning of death to all those involved and its effect on the self-concepts and construction of reality of the dying and of the survivors. Anthropologists have compared forms and expressions of grief cross-culturally.

There are also methodological problems with the study of grief. Most in-depth studies of grieving persons bring out the complexity of sentiments but are disadvantaged by obtaining them at only one point in time. Longitudinal, in-depth studies are ideal, but they are very expensive and usually use small, unrepresentative samples. Surveys of selected populations tend to generalize from simplistic scales with precoded questions concerning predefined physical and psychological symptoms. They cannot be used without prior in-depth understanding of the complexities and extensive pretests to determine the most appropriate language in the questions. On the positive side, surveys can, for example, provide comparisons between widows and widowers to help us understand the differences between men and women going through the same experiences. They can also indicate social class or racial variations in perceived sentiments. All studies that focus on the grieving person alone, however, lose the meaning of the configurations of the situation.

I have incorporated several frameworks in this analysis of grief, working around the symbolic interactionist perspective, which sees grief as a combination of sentiments and emotions. *Sentiments* are interactional feelings surrounding the self and the other that emerge over the period of a relationship as well as the self-images and feelings about the self and the other that emanate from contact with other people. We have learned through Adam Smith, Charles H. Cooley, and George Herbert Mead that we and society are twinborn. What is identified as an *emotion* and felt reflexively in any society at any time is combined into packages of appropriate and shared sentiments. Mourning rituals encourage certain feelings and their expression, defining others as inappropriate for that situation.

According to those symbolic interactionists who have been focusing on human emotions and sentiments, there is a strong connection between the social construction of reality and such feelings as grief (see the special issue of *Symbolic Interaction* on the "Sociology of Emotions," Franks, 1985). Human beings live in symbolic worlds and indicate to themselves how they feel and the reasons for feeling this way. The social environment into which a person is socialized and in which she or he negotiates social roles and individual relationships contains "structured accounts of emotions." These provide a script that defines situations within which human beings can feel in certain ways, defines these emotions, and indicates the appropriate ways such emotions can be expressed (Franks, 1985, p. 162). For example, a person may identify an experienced set of sentiments as anger, explain it in terms of the situation, and select what she or he considers to be an appropriate response to the anger in view of the situation. The situation includes the self, with its self-concept as a certain kind of person under these circumstances. The definition of the situation and what is being felt in it enables the person to act vis-à-vis it and other persons involved in it (see Franks, 1985, p. 163). Emotion is thus perceived and defined; internal as well as external bodily reactions and expressions are organized. Even the perceptions are influenced by what the person expected in anticipatory socialization. We know that we are supposed to feel grief over the death of someone to whom we feel attachment; others expect us to feel grief, so we define what we feel as grief, and the combination of perceptions influences and is influenced by our bodily reactions (Lofland, 1985). Of course, the depth and content of the grief depends on the significance of the person to us (see Lofland, 1985, p. 175). Part of the grief is for the self as the sufferer of grief. How this sentiment of grief is expressed depends on many factors, including the subculture and interactional situation or setting (see Lofland, 1985, p. 180).

NORMAL GRIEF

Psychologists are now focusing on the patterns of normal grief, pathological grief by their definition having different and longer-lasting characteristics that are best helped through intervention of counseling and therapy. The task of finding generalizable patterns of normal grief is difficult, because there are great variations in how people respond to bereavement, both in severity and duration, as well as in the final consequences. One of the most comprehensive analyses of its components has been developed by Shuchter (1986) from several studies of California widows and widowers (see also Shuchter & Zisook, 1993). The San Diego Widowhood Project concluded that grief has multiple dimensions, each with several components. The first dimension of "emotional and cognitive responses to the death of a spouse" includes shock, sudden high experiences of pain of grief in response to reminders, a sense of loss, guilt, regrets over the death and over missed opportunities to have made life better, anxiety and fearfulness, mental disorganization, feeling overwhelmed, loneliness, and even relief. This dimension can also include anger at the dead spouse and at everyone or everything connected with the death, such as the physician, God, and fate. The survivors may feel exploited by the whole process and by the representatives of formal agencies, such as insurance companies, the Social Security Administration, or the funeral parlor. In addition, intrusive images of the past and the deceased over which the widow has no control "appear spontaneously" (Shuchter, 1986, p. 33). These emotions do not necessarily occur at the same time or in the same combinations. They can be accompanied by positive feelings even at the most difficult times. "In the right circumstances, the bereaved can feel joy, peace, or happiness as oases amidst the sorrows" (Shuchter & Zisook, 1993, p. 30).

The second dimension involves coping with emotional pain and includes numbness and disbelief, suppression of strong emotion through self-control, altered perspectives, faith, both avoidance and exposure to stimuli that trigger grief, activity or "keeping busy," involvement with others, passive distraction, expression of inner feelings to others, and indulgence in pleasurable activity (see Shuchter & Zisook, 1993, pp. 30-33).

The third dimension focuses on "the continuing relationship with the dead spouse" and encompasses his or her imaginary placement in some setting, such as heaven; continuing contact through hallucinations and conversation; symbolic representation in the form of clothing, rings, and similar objects; use of living legacies that are extensions of the person borrowed and incorporated into the life of the survivor; rituals; memories; and dreams.

The fourth dimension involves changes in functioning, such as withdrawal from social settings and loss of work motivation and interest that can lead to mistakes. There can be a deterioration of health. A fifth dimension incorporates changes in relationships with family, friends who are brought either closer or distanced (see Chapters 5 and 6), and romantic engagements (see Chapter 8). The last dimension involves changes in identity. We will return later to the last two dimensions as methods of dealing with grief and introducing changes in relations and self-concept.

Original studies of what has been labeled grief in America developed a model of "stages of grief," following Kübler-Ross's (1969) stages of dying, with about 13 months' duration as the norm for the main part of the experience. Unfortunately, the stages and calendar of "normal" grieving became part of American culture, with detrimental effects (see Lopata, 1975b, p. 50). What made it problematic for the grieving person is that this society has very definite ideas as to normalcy and little tolerance for behavior and emotional responses it considers inappropriate. Close associates familiar with this theory and even those in secondary relationships tend to watch for the widowed woman's "normal" movement from stage to stage, commenting to her if she is entering or exiting too early or too late for each one. This can have devastating effects, especially if she takes this progression seriously, questioning even her sanity if she is defined as off time.

PATHOLOGICAL GRIEF

Prolonged and severe depression and excessive focus on the past or the circumstances of the death are often used as indicators of "bad" grieving. The descriptions of pathological grief come from psychoanalytic or attachment theories and focus on grief that is unresolved so that it becomes intensified rather than gone through or resolved. The subtypes include absent, delayed, inhibited, chronic, distorted, and unresolved grief. In many such cases, the typical expressions and sentiments of grief are absent, with people acting as though nothing had happened. In the long run, severe depression, low self-esteem, anxiety, and somatic and delayed stress disorders are experienced (Middleton, Raphael, Martinek, & Misso, 1993).

Grief Work

One of the most frequently used analyses of grief was developed by a psychologist, Eric Lindemann (1944), considered "the father" of such research. According to Lindemann, survivors of the death of a significant other must accomplish "grief work": "emancipation from the bondage of the deceased, readjustment to the environment in which the deceased is missing, and the formation of new relationships" (p. 43). Thus, grief work involves change, often unanticipated and almost inevitably forced on the widow at a time when she is still disorganized by the death. There are many complications contained in these processes of cutting ties, adjusting to the late husband's absence, and developing new relationships. Complete detachment is not possible because the deceased remains in her memory. Complete detachment cannot even begin, however, until the loss is defined, understood, and validated (see Rosenblatt, 1993, p. 102). The loss must be felt in relation to the self and to the world in which the self lives and is interacted with.

A major finding of my first study of Chicago-area widows (Lopata, 1973d), which was tested in the second, larger project (Lopata, 1979), is that the higher the education of the woman and the more middle-class the lifestyle she and her husband developed when he was well, the greater was the disorganization she experienced in self-concept, support systems, social roles, and lifestyle in widowhood. The main reason was the fact that, at least in modern American society, middle- and higher-class couples develop greater interdependence than is true of working- and lower-class couples or of couples in other countries and times. The level of significance of one marital partner to the other tends to be very high in these situations, with great interdependence and with what Lofland (1985) calls "multiple building blocks or threads of connectedness" (p. 175). They tend to communicate more (Komarovsky, 1967), share concerns over household and parental roles, and develop couple-companionate friendships. Many of the middle-aged and older wives were participants in two-person careers, in that they were the backup person to the employed husband. They were highly influenced financially in their use of time and space and in their whole lifestyle by the occupation of the husband.[1] The wife, who was so involved in her husband's roles and was so dependent on him, thus experienced greater disorganization than one whose marriage followed parallel tracks without much overlap. We have yet to see how the greater involvement of women in their own careers affects the lives of their husbands.

As to relationships with past associates, these must be changed, partly because others see the widow as a different person and change the way they relate to her. Relations with all the other members of all the social circles in which the husband and wife were involved must also be changed to reflect the man's withdrawal in death. Thus, the role of mother is changed by the absence of the father (see Chapter 6). Modifications in friendships are necessitated in the setting of a couple-companionate social world now that she is partnerless (see Chapter 7). She can remain as she always was only in those roles in which the husband was not a member of the social circle or in which widowhood does not enter as a pervasive identity.

Loneliness

One of the problems of identifying and studying grief is its close tie with loneliness. Loneliness can be defined as a sentiment felt when the level or form of interaction or relationship is considered inadequate (Lopata, 1969). This can result from the construction of a particular situation in terms of relative deprivation, compared to other situations or compared to what it is assumed others are experiencing. Just being alone does not produce the feeling of loneliness. One can be lonely for a particular person or event, or one can just feel lonely in general. Weiss (1973) categorized loneliness into two kinds, emotional and social. Loneliness of emotional isolation "appears in the absence of a close emotional attachment" whereas loneliness of social isolation is "associated with the absence of an engaging social network" (p. 19). "Such feelings are likely to arise when the habitual or expected depth of relations with other people is judged as temporarily or permanently unavailable, broken or underdeveloped" (Lopata, 1969, p. 249).

The widowed women our research team studied in the Chicago area experienced both emotional and social loneliness as a result of all the events surrounding the death of their husbands. Interestingly enough, however, the expression of loneliness in widowhood did not appear in interviews on support systems conducted in non-Western, nonmodern communities with extended families and public life among neighbors (see Lopata, 1987a, 1987b, 1987c, 1987d, 1987e). In fact, as many psychologists and sociologists have pointed out, the very concept of privacy and individuality so prominent in America is a relatively new phenomenon and absent in many developing countries (see, for example, Aries, 1965, for an early analysis of the development of the concept of privacy in Europe). In many such societies, the husband was not as important a "close attachment" on whom the wife depended for most emotional supports as is true of American middle-class intact marriages.

We found loneliness to be one of the major problems facing American women who had been married and living with her husband before he died. Initial examination of what women meant when they reported being lonely led me to the realization that this sentiment has many forms and components. Widows (and this can be true of anyone whose significant other dies or otherwise vanishes) can be lonely for that particular man, for being a love object or for having a love object, for a sexual and loving partner, and for someone who treated them as an important person. This last form of loneliness was brought out by one of the respondents I happened to interview. She explained that she and her husband argued all the time. Now there is no one who thinks what she says is worth arguing about. Her children just say with irritation, "Oh, ma!"

Loneliness can be for an escort to public places or social events, a companion with whom to share even comments regarding a television show, or a partner in couple-companionate interaction. Wives often become involved in social events, such as conventions, banquets, or other forms of social activity, through the husband. A drop in income can make impossible even activities the widow could enter alone. Although "modern" women may have trouble believing this, many older widows miss working and scheduling life around a husband. Also difficult is being alone in the household, usually for the first time in an older woman's life. All in all, loneliness for the whole lifestyle and the companionship of the husband can become quite depressing.

Not all widows experienced all these forms of loneliness. In fact, there were strong social class differences in the forms. For example, a working-class woman who simply saw her husband as someone around whom she had to organize work and time, still missed having that source of filling in a schedule. Some lower- and even middle-class wives were relieved by the death of their husbands, who had been unpleasant, even frightening elements in their lives. Yet with the help of some polishing in memory, they could report feeling lonely in the empty house and for the excitement of interaction. Conflict is of itself a source of stimulation, as indicated earlier in the example of the woman with whom no one now will argue. For many middle- and upper-class women, however, life at present lacks both social and emotional supports made possible by the late husband. The past looks better than the present or the future, and it can never be reproduced.

Risk Factors in Bereavement

Although people vary considerably in their experiences following bereavement, depending on numerous factors, certain patterns are often evident. These do not occur in the same sequence, combinations, or strength. As noted in Chapter 4, there is some debate among social scientists and psychologists as to the contributions of "anticipatory grief" that takes place before the actual loss to the grief process following the death (Hill, Thompson, & Gallagher, 1988; O'Bryant, 1991a). Those who assume that grief can be worked out before the loss see it as a specific, measurable thing and believe that anticipatory grief cuts off part of the grieving so that less of it is left after the event. Thus, the longer survivors know of the impending death, the more time they allegedly have to anticipate grief and experience at least partial withdrawal. Glick et al. (1974, p. 14), however, concluded from a longitudinal study of the bereaved that anticipatory grief and grief following the death are different experiences. In addition, as O'Bryant (1991a, p. 229) points out, it is not the length of forewarning that eases grief. Rather, the death itself can ease grief if it followed prolonged suffering on the part of the husband and difficult caregiving on the part of the wife. We must remember that unless he is completely comatose, the husband is still around until the death so that the shock of his absence does not hit until later.

In any case, sudden death appears more devastating, as indicated in Chapter 4, leading to shock and disbelief at the highest level. Unfinished business lingers, and the feeling of powerlessness can be overwhelming (see Sanders, 1993, p. 263).

Age as a factor that can affect grief has produced mixed results in research. The assumption that younger people suffer more from bereavement than do the elderly has been found to be more complex than the statement implies. Typically, myths oversimplify reality in this way. Wortman, Silver, and Kessler's (1993) extensive study of Americans' changing lives found that "younger respondents are initially more affected by the loss of their spouse, but (that) they recover more quickly than older respondents" (p. 360). Widowhood at an older age may be experienced as "on time," so it is less disturbing than when it occurs off time (Hill et al., 1988). Of course, many other factors can affect the extent of disorganization in widowhood by age. It may be less disorganizing for older people because fewer roles and responsibilities are involved. On the other hand, the older widow may be more dependent on the husband than is a younger one with competing roles.

Recently, researchers have concluded that men have a harder time than women when widowed and that younger men suffer most after the unanticipated death of the wife (see Stroebe & Stroebe, 1993a, p. 195). The idea that widowers have a hard time because they are not accustomed to taking care of themselves and to developing or retaining social supports comes from a study by Berardo (1970) of aged widowers in the state of Washington. Several other researchers found widowers experiencing greater stress than widows, although women express a higher level of death anxiety (see Kastenbaum, 1991, p. 19). There are, however, several explanations for the differences:

> It appears that women's primary source of vulnerability following widowhood arises from an increase in financial strain. In contrast, men's greater vulnerability stems in part from their more limited social relationships and from the difficulty in assuming tasks previously handled by their wives. (Wortman et al., 1993, p. 359)

In fact, Wortman and associates (1993) found that widowers had strained relationships with their children, whereas widows did not. The authors suggest that such strain may arise from an earlier distance between father and children, "combined with male difficulty in expressing the need for support" (p. 359).

In general, bereavement can have strong physical effects on main survivors. DeSpelder and Strickland (1992, pp. 245-247) report numerous studies of the high mortality rates associated with bereavement. Some of the research found death rates of survivors to be "nearly seven times that of the general population." Other scientists found chronic disease rates and diminished immune responses resulting from grief to be very common. Evidence of the vulnerability of men comes from their high mortality figures in the United States, higher than those of widows, factors such as age being held constant. The causes of death are also different for the genders. Longitudinal studies find that many men die within the first 6 months of bereavement of causes such as suicide, accidents, cirrhosis of the liver, infectious diseases, and heart problems. These causes are often defined as indicative of a wish for death combined with improper and even dangerous lifestyles. The fact that men are expected to hold back their expressions of grief, whereas women are socialized and culturally allowed to express their feelings may also contribute to earlier death of widowers. Women are more likely to die later in widowhood and of more chronic problems.

The most likely to die after bereavement are people who move into a chronic care facility, live alone, report having no one to whom they can telephone, and in general lack support systems (Stroebe & Stroebe, 1993a, p. 185). Shuchter and Zisook (1993, p. 43) reported from their San Diego study that 13 months after bereavement women more often than men felt helpless (22% vs. 5%, respectively) and lonely (41% vs. 33%) but able to express their feelings (66% vs. 47%). There were other interesting gender differences. More women than men reported feeling that the late spouse was watching over them (52% vs. 33%) and that the spouse was with them at times (66% vs. 55%). Men fought acceptance of the death, were much faster in developing new romantic relationships, and were more likely to turn to alcohol for relief (Schuchter & Zisook, 1993).

Widowers who remarry decrease the probability of early death, but remarriage does not help widows very much.

> Gove argued that marriage benefits women less because they do not receive so much gratification from their one major role, that of being a housewife, whereas men obtain gratification from being the head of the household and breadwinner. (Stroebe & Stroebe, 1993a, p. 192)

This is really an outmoded view of the roles of women and men, probably applicable to older couples, although less so to the more "modernized" woman.

There is some evidence of racial differences in response to bereavement. Wortman and associates (1993) reported that "whites are hit harder initially, and take longer to recover, than do black respondents" (p. 360). Social role complexity, in the form of multidimensional life space, cushions the effect of spousal bereavement (see DeSpelder & Strickland, 1992, p. 326). The authors attribute this to the purpose in life provided by such involvements. I would add that such complexities decrease the dependence of the survivor on the deceased, possibly even before widowhood.

Other risk factors, resulting in especially hard or prolonged reactions to bereavement include loss of economic resources, loss of social status, or both; personality problems, such as inflexibility; inadequate use of existing resources; and an accumulation of negative events following the loss (see Sanders, 1993, p. 258). According to Stroebe and Stroebe (1993b, pp. 217-218), widowed persons with previous emotional stability who are feeling in control of life fare best. Psychologists note that it is not necessarily the woman who reports a very satisfactory marriage who suffers intense, overwhelming grief but the woman who had an ambivalent relationship with the husband (Raphael, 1978). Poor health prior to the husband's death usually carries over to the following years, making any kind of adjustment difficult. As mentioned before, stigmatized death, such as in suicide or AIDS, contributes to problems, as do multiple surrounding deaths, as exemplified in disasters or wars.

Other Problems Experienced Early in Widowhood

Of course, the path of widowhood is not isolated from the paths of social roles and other aspects of life. Although one of the myths surrounding mourning posits the sufferer as at least temporarily cushioned from events occurring around her and able to suffer in peace, this simply does not happen. Other small and large troubles and problems emerge.

PERSONAL RELATIONS

Problems in the relations with children appear to be not as difficult for widows as for widowers, as documented earlier. Still, the death of the father creates tensions and emotional responses. The children can react by revolting or with passive resistance instead of understanding and supporting the mother in her heavy grief. Many widows are simply unable to deal with the grief and the resulting behavioral outbreaks of their children. Our respondents explained that the children were either too young or too old to be affected by the death of the father. Yet when asked about how the children's lives were changed, the widows reported problems at school, negative consequences to having plans cut because of a lack of money in the family, refusal to cooperate with increased work in the household, even deviant behavior. It is probable that the mother simply could not admit that the death created problems for anyone but herself.

Life brings forth constant irritations and more serious problems. Lawns and gardens can become problematic if no one cares for them and neighbors are critical of the appearance of the household; dogs bite children, the car refuses to run, other people get sick, and the widowed woman herself suffers symptoms both frightening and irritating. Insomnia and depression leave her wishing to be left alone, but the family must be fed and clothed. Where is the supportive network that is supposed to be there? Why did the husband desert her when she needs help so much? Autobiographies by widows report terrible sentiments of anger and frustration (e.g., Caine, 1974; Lerner, 1978; van den Hoonaard, 1993).

Sentiments of loneliness are exasperated by interaction with friends, especially married friends who simply drop the widow or those who try to see her in situations completely different from in the past. This usually means situations without the husbands. Many friends simply avoid the woman entirely, originally stating that she needs to grieve in peace and later never returning to the intimacy of interaction. Younger widows are particularly likely to report jealousy on the part of married friends in the presence of the husbands of those friends. Dinner parties do not include a "fifth wheel," as some women call themselves.

Other problems face widows as they are trying to forge a new life. Many older ones never learned to drive a car or feel uncomfortable driving under certain circumstances, such as at night. The car has traditionally been a male object, and the whole culture of the car salesroom, repair garage, or even service station can be overwhelming.

Widows often fear being taken advantage of because of their ignorance. A recent trend of women entering car sales and even automobile service may ease these concerns; Lawson (1990) reports greater trust by women of women than of men in this generally distrusted occupation. The very lack of confidence in dealing with that whole world makes many widows unwilling to retain the family car (Lopata, 1979), which makes them dependent on other people or mass transportation. The latter, however, is organized around the needs and abilities of employed workers and healthy riders in general. Also, women who are unfamiliar with legal and financial matters either must have the economic means to hire trustworthy advisers or must depend on informal "experts," many of whom often offer useless and even bad advice.

In view of frequently heard complaints by widows about bad advice, we asked in the support systems study (Lopata 1973d) what advice our respondents would give new widows. One strong recommendation was not to listen to self-proclaimed experts concerning important decisions for the first year of widowhood. The worst mistakes the widows themselves reported were those regarding finances and housing. Almost always, these mistakes were made on the suggestion of one of the members of the widow's primary group rather than advice from a professional counselor. Frequently, the adviser is speaking from her or his vantage point rather than completely taking the role of the other—seeing the situation through the eyes of the widowed woman. Adequate role taking is hard in the best of circumstances and especially so when the adviser does not really want to put herself or himself in the shoes of the widow. That is why programs such as Widow-to-Widow are reportedly of great help (Bankoff, 1990; Silverman, 1986, 1987).

Another problem faced by widows is that other people either do not want to hear about the death at all or get tired of hearing about it. The widow tends to see herself as the only sufferer in her environment; her associates have problems of their own and want to get on with their lives. They certainly do not want to hear about the death over and over. American culture is youth and life oriented and ignores death as a personal event and depersonalizes it on television, whether fictional death or that involving many people far away. The achieving society wants to hear of achievements, not personal tragedies.

FINANCES

> **Myth:** The reason widowed women are often poor is that they are inexperienced in money management during marriage and do not discuss survivor plans with the husband.

American women whose marriages have ended through divorce or widowhood have a higher probability of being in poverty than do never-married or still-married women (Morgan, 1989, 1991a, 1991b). In fact, women who are widowed in midlife are more apt to have been at the margin of poverty in marriage because all the factors that contribute to poverty also contribute to a shorter life span of the husband.

A longitudinal Panel Study of Income Dynamics showed that 64% of all widowed women "experienced some interval of poverty over a 10-year period" (Morgan, 1989, p. 88). This is particularly true if their family income was on the edge of poverty while the husband was alive, but it is also true of many previously more comfortable women. Poor older women are in general more likely to lack personality resources, such as skill in living alone in complex urban environments, that are needed to pull themselves above poverty. National longitudinal surveys (Morgan, 1989) in which women's postmarital income was obtained for three periods of time—1 to 2 years, 3 to 4 years, and approximately 5 years after widowhood—indicate that many slid into poverty or near-poverty levels more than once. Widows were more likely than divorced women to experience a drop from the prewidowhood level immediately after the end of their marriages. For example, 15% of the women were poor, and 18% nearly poor while married, but 26% were poor, and 31% nearly poor within 1 to 2 years after the death of the husband. As far as frequency goes, 54% of the women never reached poverty or near poverty, 26% went below the line once, 14% were there twice, and 4.5% went below the line three times (see Morgan, 1989, p. 94). This means that, although 40% of widows went through poverty at least once, this was frequently a temporary condition.

The fact that so many women end up below or near the poverty line is sometimes explained in terms of their lack of experience in management of their financial resources, resulting in the loss of these resources through bad advice or plain victimization, as indicated in the myth just mentioned. Morgan (1986) found that only about 20% of a large sample in the Longitudinal Retirement History Study entered widowhood with "no daily money management experience during marriage nor a discussion with their husbands regarding financial plans for the survivor" (Morgan, 1986, p. 665).

Almost 46% of the widowed women in that sample had managed the family finances during marriage, and an additional 20% shared financial management. In addition, almost 40% of the wives had discussed such matters with the husband. Nearly a third had been employed at the time of the death, and another 12% returned to the labor force after becoming widowed. Despite these indications of financial knowledge, half were below the poverty line in their income at the time of the study, and a fourth reported a decline in their standard of living since widowhood. This means that many had been poor even when their husbands were alive. In fact, Morgan (1986) says this:

> These findings suggest that it is not lack of experiences with finances or poor advice regarding money matters, either before or after loss of spouse, which can be blamed for the poverty found among older widows. . . . While the economic problems associated with widowhood may not, to the extent previously thought, include inexperience with managing money, the very real problems of poverty and limited economic alternatives remain. (p. 668)

These figures indicate, however, that many widowed American women are able to maintain an above-poverty standard of living without having to continually earn money or be dependent on their relatives. In the historical past, nonrural widowed women often had to take in boarders, lodgers, sewing, or laundry or to run businesses or make objects for sale (Abbott, 1913). Many were dependent on charity or the earnings of children, some of whom were quite young (Kleinberg, 1973). The 1935 Social Security Act and its 1939 amendments, however, provided economic support for retired workers and the widows of entitled workers who cared for his minor children or who were themselves aged 65 or over (see Lopata & Brehm, 1986, pp. 71-75). The shift of emphasis of all the amendments since 1935 from protection of the individual wage earner to family protection has also enabled many a widow to stay in her own dwelling rather than moving in with relatives or having them move in with her.

The support systems study of widowed women who were or had been beneficiaries of Social Security in metropolitan Chicago in 1979 showed that two thirds lost income with the death of the husband and one third were living on an income that fell below the poverty line (see Lopata & Brehm, 1986, p. 215). The women receiving benefits in 1978 were in five beneficiary categories: mothers of dependent children, old-age beneficiaries, recipients of only a lump sum payment to help defray funeral costs, former beneficiaries whose children were grown, and former beneficiaries who remarried. The most economically advantaged were mothers of dependent children, who were younger than the others and who often combined several sources of income. The remarrieds were the next best off economically, especially if they could combine the husband's income with the children's benefits from their late father. The poorest women were those who received only old-age benefits and the lump sum recipients who did not have dependent children and were too young for old-age benefits. The sum that the latter widows received did not even cover funeral expenses, and many could not find jobs that paid well, having been out of the labor force for many years while working full-time as homemakers.

The two main sources of income for women in American society, employment or remarriage, were not available to the majority of these Chicago-area widows (see Lopata & Brehm, 1986, p. 215). In fact, 40% of the women had never been employed, and 48% had worked outside of the home only since widowhood; only 28% were holding a job at the time of the interview (see Lopata, 1979, pp. 59, 305). The most likely to be working at that time were mothers of adult children (73%) and the women who received only lump sum benefits (54%). Over half of the mothers of dependent children had to supplement their benefits through employment. The fact that so few respondents were employed is partly due to their age: 60% were age 65 or over, a consequence of the Social Security subtypes drawn for the study. In addition, 58% had less than a high school education, making it difficult for them to find and maintain a job. The most likely to be employed were widowed women aged 45 to 54 who had more than a high school education. Steinhart (1977, pp. 21-22) computed the widow's income adequacy, meaning the total family income minus the woman's wages in terms of the U.S. "Labor Department's income adequacy index for that size family," (p. 41) and concluded that mothers with three children had to hold a job because the maximum Social Security benefit covered only two children. On the other hand, women with four children were most destitute because most were unable to get a job. In all, the poorest widowed women had several children and only a grade school education. An important point is that a lack of adequacy of income from other sources among widowed women does not ensure that a job will be an economic resource for them.

Some of these financial patterns are undoubtedly different in the 1990s because the life course of American women has changed (Lopata, 1994a). Only within the past two decades or so have women remained in the labor force long enough to gain good salaries or wages and to receive benefits on their own records. Many a past generation of American women has been economically dependent on husbands, living in the two-sphere world that discouraged women from taking seriously a need to support themselves financially. Those women in the Chicago area who never married earned more than either their married or formerly married counterparts (see Lopata & Brehm, 1986, p. 215). The cohort of married respondents aged 25 to 53 in the late 1970s was contributing on average only one third of the family income (Lopata, Barnewolt, & Miller, 1985). Members of this cohort are now considerably older and are not likely to have earned enough through their employment careers to decrease dependence on their husbands' Social Security benefits. Thus, marriage has been a serious deterrent to a woman's own income sufficiency, despite the growing number of women who do not retain an income-producing husband for all their years.

The Chicago women who were employed since widowhood found many positive features of their jobs. We will return to the contributions of occupational roles to various supports of women in a later chapter.

As indicated earlier, two thirds of the Chicago-area widowed women were living above the poverty line for a family of their size in the late 1970s. This proportion is higher than generally presented for American widows as a whole, the latter figure being closer to half (see Morgan, 1986, p. 668). Morgan (1991a, 1991b) concludes from an overall analysis of statistics concerning the economic security of older women that the future looks better than the present due to a combination of many factors. Among these is increased and more continuous labor force participation, especially in non-sex-segregated and inferior-pay jobs, in organizations that provide private pensions and Social Security. Factors interfering with upward economic movement include (a) continued sex segregation of occupations, (b) poor pension plans without guarantees, (c) changes in the labor market with the growth of smaller and nonunionized companies with lower likelihood of pension coverage and with few male workers choosing survivor options, and (d) impractical retirement decisions on the part of the women. Also problematic are women's continued main responsibility for family life and the frequency of divorce, which deprives women of a major source of income.

Personal Resources in Response to Widowhood

Although the more educated and middle-class widowed women in the Chicago-area study suffered more disorganization of life and self-concept than did their lower-class counterparts, they had more personal resources with which to create new lifestyle and modified self-concepts (Lopata, 1979). These included economic, health, knowledge, and self-confidence resources. This conclusion is supported by many other studies (Atchley, 1975; Morgan, 1991a, 1991b). Poorer women have a harder time in marriage and in widowhood than do their more fortunate sisters in the long run, although poorer women may go through less conscious reconstruction of the world and themselves. Poorer, less educated women also experience widowhood earlier in life (Hyman, 1983).

HUSBAND SANCTIFICATION

One of the main tasks of grief work, according to Lindemann (1944), is cutting ties with the deceased. This is hard to do, because the present time for human beings rests on memories of the past, and the widowed woman's past contained the dead husband. In addition, most cultures, at least the American one, contain an obligation not to forget the dead. The question then is, How can the widow cut ties with the deceased and yet preserve his memory? The Chicago-area widows whom I studied provided me with the answer to this question in the form of reconstructed memory. I had tried to find out about their support systems prior to the late husband's fatal illness or accident and often heard of his constant contributions to all supports, even when other parts of the interview indicated that he was not so available or so positively contributive (Lopata, 1981). Memory of the past is a complex matter, because it is constantly reconstructed from the vantage point of the present. There is a tendency among most Americans, begun in the eulogy, to reconstruct the deceased in one-sided ways. The interviews indicated that many women had developed an extremely idealized image of their husbands and their lives with them.

I finally constructed a "sanctification scale" composed of two segments. One segment contained a semantic differential method (the respondent circled one of seven positions between two extremes), measuring the extent to which the husband became identified as extremely good, useful, honest, superior, kind, friendly, and warm. The second segment obtained the extent to which a wife judged their marriage, life together, agreement on issues, happiness of the home, and the husband's parenting as "above average." The bottom line stated "My husband had no irritating habits." Over a quarter of the women agreed strongly, and another quarter simply agreed with this extreme statement. More women were willing to give their husbands extremely high marks as individuals (the first segment) than placed their life together (second segment) at that level. Interestingly enough, memory of the husband as superior was not frequently associated with warmth or friendliness. Those two characteristics were more connected with kindness.

The relations segment of the sanctification scale also showed some very interesting patterns. Men who were identified as very good fathers were not seen as having shared leisure activity or feelings with the wife, nor were they absolved of irritating habits. Extremely good fathers were apt to have been in gender-segregated, traditional marriages. A happy home contained marital sharing with an honest husband but not necessarily a superior one. The respondents who least often remembered the late husband in sanctifying extremes were nonwhites with low education and low incomes during marriage. In fact, the least educated women often expressed hostility against the husband. Although length of time since the death of the husband proved insignificant in the degree of sanctification, younger women were less likely to sanctify their husbands than were older ones, possibly because they were left with much unfinished business with the deceased (see Lopata, 1981, p. 449). The widows who were most likely to sanctify their husbands were older, white, and had a strong ethnic identification, or middle-class lifestyle. Age had less influence on whites than on nonwhites in the extent to which life with the husband was seen as very good. The most educated women refused to go so far as claiming no irritating habits, but there was a positive association between education and the tendency among nonwhites to see the husband and the marriage in a positive light. The more education, capped with a degree, that a widowed nonwhite woman had, the more positive was her memory of the husband and marriage. In general, however, nonwhites, most of whom were African American, were least likely to consider their late husbands as having been superior, good, or honest. The life together segment of the sanctification scale did not bring out as many differences between whites and nonwhites as did the semantic differential segment of the husband's qualities. Education and degree had less direct association with sanctification among white women.

In addition to being culturally approved, sanctification, or at least idealization, of the late husband can perform some important functions for the widow. In the first place, if such a saintly man had married her, she must be a pretty worthwhile person, which she often questions in the depression of grief. In the second place, the process converts the late husband into a benevolent spirit, lacking mortal tendencies of jealousies and criticism. He remains in the memory as a positive adviser, not a critic of how she is managing money or raising the children. Finally, life in the past can be defined in positive terms, removing unpleasant scenes. There are, however, disadvantages to this process in that it discourages friends and potential mates. Friends who knew him as a mortal with very real irritating habits become impatient by the new, repeatedly drawn, image. What other man, interested date, or potential husband can compete against this ideal? Hunt (1966) claims in *The World of the Formerly Married* that divorced men do not like to date widows, because each has a completely different attitude and set of sentiments toward the prior partner.

The sanctification scale has been used in other studies since its creation. Gay Kitson (Kitson, Lopata, Holmes, & Meyering, 1980) used it to compare the attitudes of divorcées and widows toward the ex-husband and found, not surprisingly, a reverse pattern.[2]

THE HOME

One of the resources women considered important in widowhood was their home. Heaton and Hoppe (1987) have traced historically the demographic changes in living arrangements of both widowed and married Americans from 1900 to 1980, finding that, although few households were three generational even in the early years (because few people lived to old age), the frequency of both men and women living alone in widowhood has increased dramatically. Unless a widowed woman has extreme economic needs, poor health, little education, and little knowledge of American city life, she prefers and is able to reside by herself (see also Lopata, 1971a). Men are less likely to live alone, mainly because their wives are still alive or because they remarry soon after widowhood. "Of the noninstitutionalized widowed population in 1900, approximately 16% of women and 24% of men aged 65 and over resided alone; by 1980 the proportions had risen to 67% and 64% respectively" (Heaton & Hoppe, 1987, p. 264). Dissatisfaction with housing arrangements is one of the factors contributing to negative feelings about life among widowed women. Most widowed women studied in Columbus, Ohio, felt deeply attached to their homes and wished to remain in them, even if occupying so much space was economically impractical. Having their own rights over the property, and over the rhythm of routine within it, provided one of the major satisfactions to these women (O'Bryant, 1987).

OTHER RESOURCES

Other personal resources or methods of adjustment to the death of the husband and to the whole situation of being a widowed woman include developing feelings of competence through learning new skills and decision making in many new situations. Such decisions have to do with finances, such as selling or buying homes and other belongings; traveling; dropping or starting new relationships and group affiliations; and even occupational training and job searches (Lund, Caserta, & Diamond, 1993). Professional help is sought by relatively few widows, most Americans not being accustomed to expressing their feelings to strangers, but the prolification of self-help groups, such as the Widow-to-Widow program, indicates the popularity of this movement. Widows learn to accept the ups and downs of their emotions, avoiding situations in which the downside creates problems in social relationships and life complications and using confidants whenever possible. One characteristic of the identity of some widows that appeared to protect them from many problems was their religious beliefs and involvements. Belief in an afterlife in which one will be reunited with the deceased changes the nature of death, making it more of a natural event in the life course.

THE SELF-CONCEPT

Lindemann (1944) presented grief work as having three major tasks: cutting ties with the deceased, adjusting to the world without him, and the formation of new relationships. To this, I would add the job of reconstructing the self-concept. A major element of change following widowhood can, and usually does, occur in the woman herself. This is not only a matter of identity but also of the content of the self-concept. The self-concept, according to Rosenberg (1979), is "the totality of the individual's thoughts and feelings having reference to himself [sic] as an object" (p. 7). It contains packages of pervasive identities, such as woman, black, old, widow (in societies in which it really is a pervasive identity); of social role identities with their idiosyncratic variations, such as wife and friend in couple-companionate relations; and of what I call the "generalized self," or images of the self as a certain type of person that transcend role and situational contexts (Lopata, 1986a). The various parts of the self-concept are organized in dimensions with boundaries and reconstructed with transitions and important events.

Marriage brings forth a reconstruction of reality, including the reality of the self and of the spouse. The reconstruction of the self is allegedly undertaken more extensively by women than by men in America and by middle- and upper-class women more than by lower-class ones (Berger & Kellner, 1970). Until recently, American women have taken the husband's name, being identified simply as Mrs. John Doe. In addition, the person with whom a wife lives and interacts daily provides a potent source of self-concept, self-feeling, and symbolic world construction. The interaction itself gives meaning to the situation, including the self and the other, as well as to all those with whom they relate. The setting of life includes the home and household, each given meaning in relation to the self and the other (Lopata, 1971a; Rosenblatt, 1993).

People develop what Lund, Caserta, Diamond, and Gray (1986, p. 237) define as social anchorages of the self, measured by the Twenty Statement Test. In this test, respondents are given a piece of paper and asked to list 20 answers to the question, "Who am I?" Lund and colleagues administered the questionnaire six times for 2 years after the death of the spouse to trace changes in the complexity of the sources of social anchorage. They found that the death of a spouse in a long-lasting marriage created a great deal of dislocation in the survivor's social relationships that form her or his social anchorage and that the effects are evident in changes of the self-concept even after 2 years.

Several aspects to the changes can be experienced by a woman as she leaves the role of wife and enters temporarily the role of widow. In that role, she can see herself, and be treated by others, as the suffering heroine, the center of attention. Once the role of widow is over and the circle drawn to it recedes, she is left in a limbo situation as far as marital status is concerned: She cannot remain in the identity of wife or reenter the identity of a single woman, and the identity of divorcée is so much worse that even divorced women define themselves as widows once the former husband dies (Lopata, 1986a). The obvious way out of the limbo location is to drop any marital status identity—that is, to be in roles and relationships in which this identity is not pervasive. Older women often did not have alternative identities to bring forth into central position in the role cluster. The most frequently chosen role identity among traditional women could be that of mother, yet by the time most women become widowed, the children are grown and focused on their own lives. Unless forced by feelings of obligation to care for a frail mother, a widow cannot even fill the emptiness left by the death of her husband with the role of daughter. Besides, no other role can replace the set of relations, emotions, and sentiments of the role of wife. Even remarriage brings a different set of feelings and relationships. The failure to reconstruct identity and the worldview can lead to the kind of disengagement studied by Cumming and Henry (1961).

Long-term marriages involve some form of interdependent partnership, usually with gendered specialization in skills and knowledge, so part of the change brought by widowhood is in learning to do what the husband did before or learning to do without that resource. The widowed woman can thus add or subtract part of the generalized self from the self-concept as she observes what she is now doing. She can see herself as increasingly competent—or incompetent—in skills or activities previously mastered by the husband. Other forms of situated action bring other self-images. She must construct the self with the emotions of the past left in the memory of the past and develop new attachments and sentiments. This is hard to do and takes time. In addition, the conscious reconstruction of the self-concept is a very cognitive and reflexive process, and people vary in their desire, ability, and opportunity to do so.

When asked how they had changed since the death, many of the new Chicago-area widows responded with negative self-perceptions. They felt incompetent in facing situations and problems previously handled by the husband. Responsibilities for the automobile and finances were the most bothersome. Older widows especially had not solved any of these problems; some had not even learned to drive (O'Bryant, 1991b). Automobile care and repair personnel are almost inevitably male; men are accustomed to dealing with men in garages and car salesrooms, sharing a male culture. Women are usually uncomfortable in such surroundings. Even self-help gasoline stations can be forbidding to someone who has been accustomed to relying on her husband and showing ignorance in such matters.

Widows may also have to deal with experts with whom they are not familiar, such as health and life insurance agents, lawyers, realtors, or bankers. Their financial situation may require major life changes that threaten the self-concept, such as movement to a less desirable area or dropping prestigious social activities. One of the ego-diminishing experiences frequently reported by widows is being dropped by former associates. One woman, the widow of a prominent businessman, reported to me in great anger that her husband's associates had obviously been nice to her not because they liked her and because she contributed to their social life but only because of the importance of her husband (Lopata, 1979). Such situations did little to boost the self-esteem of the widow.

Women interviewed later in their widowhood, on the other hand, were much more likely to report changes to the self in a positive direction. They learned new skills and felt more competent and well-rounded than in the past. Many started new ventures and experienced new ways of being and relating to others. The degree and direction of change varied considerably, depending on the original self-concept and the self-confidence to initiate such new experiences.

The higher a woman's education, initially or in later life, the more she was likely to engage in self-concept reconstruction. Widows with little education often reported no change in the self, perceiving change negatively, as threatening whatever security they had (Lopata, 1973a, 1973b). It is interesting that there appears to be a connection between social isolation, education, and perceptions of change in the self (see Lopata, 1973a, p. 416). Women with more education are more socially integrated and perceive change in themselves in widowhood more than do less educated and more isolated women. Generally, education makes people more self-conscious in objectifying reality. It is also possible that other people help the socially involved widow identify changes in herself. In addition new relationships bring forth new actions reflexively perceived by the woman herself. On the other hand, there were women who reported no major change in their lives with the death of the husband because the couple led parallel lives that infrequently intersected anyway.

Widows use various means of solving temporary bouts of loneliness. These fall into three major types: keeping busy, developing new roles and relations, and focusing life on one social role (see Lopata, 1969, p. 257). The most frequently given advice to new widows is "keep busy." Women reorganize their schedules to fill in the hours when loneliness is most likely, usually hours when the husband was home. One widow, for example, made a point of not having her mail delivered so that she would have to go out every day. Baking for others continues to serve as both busy work and an excuse for contact with others. Some make dinner, movie, or card-playing dates in the evening with other partnerless women. New widows often learn to develop closer relationships with other widows, seeking out those they knew in the past or joining, at least temporarily, groups such as Widow to Widow (Silverman, 1986). New roles and relationships can be formed through special-interest groups, in churches, or in the occupational setting. In each such situation, those who are active in internalized constructions of the self can recognize new images from these new relationships and from watching the self in them.

Some women move geographically closer to one of their children, usually a daughter, in widowhood; others concentrate on occupational, organizational, neighboring, or friendship roles or any combination of these. There are many ways human beings can handle stressful life events, with the help of internal or external supports. The initial numbness is undoubtedly useful as a means of going through all the processes and rituals of mourning. The initial disbelief must vanish, and funeral directors claim that having the corpse on view, and its internment in the earth are helpful devices in convincing people of the reality of death. Other coping means include intellectualization or rationalization of the whole event, especially practiced by the more educated survivors. Finally, some of the many means of coping with the emotional problems of grief work included church involvement and religious faith; humor; avoidance; keeping busy; passive distraction; involvement with others, through supporting their own investment in others' welfare; compensation with such things as pets; expression of painful sentiments to others; and indulgence in external sources of gratification, such as food, alcohol, tobacco, other drugs, or sex.

Summary

Death is followed in most situations with community rituals acknowledging this event and establishing a continued social existence for the deceased. The wife temporarily enters the role of widow, but then the circle disbands, and she must go through the emotional, relational, lifestyle, and self-concept changes basically alone. Grief as an emotion is experienced in many ways throughout an indefinite period of time. Grief work involves breaking ties with the deceased, sometimes assisted by a sanctification process that removes him from daily life. It means learning to live without the deceased and the future they had constructed for themselves as a couple and that the woman had constructed for herself individually. Social relationships and the more complex social roles must be modified to various degrees depending on the involvement in them of the late husband or her changes in life circumstances and of social identity. Changes in the self-concept are a consequence not only of change in marital status but also of modifications in past roles and relations and the addition of new ones.

The process of change involved in grief work is not lineal and does not follow a specific schedule or set of stages. It is accompanied by many additional problem situations as well as many varied resources with which to deal with each problem or combinations of them.[3] The problems can be internal, such as loneliness with accompanying immobilization, or external, as in the behavior of children or friends.

Various means are used by the women to deal with these problems, more or less successfully at first but often with increasing competence. Except in cases of sudden death, which is relatively unusual in nonwar times, the wife is very likely to have taken care of her husband during his illness, even if he finally died in an institution. Age is an important factor in grief work and the resources for solving problematic situations. This means that it is experienced differently by younger than by older widows, but there is no agreement in the grief literature as to which type of woman suffers more. Similar complications contribute to the myth that sudden death is or is not harder on the younger widow.

One of the major findings of most studies of widowed women is their resilience (Lieberman, 1994; Matthews, 1979). However hard they are hit by the death of the husband and related or subsequent problems and however limited their resources, most widows reach a relatively acceptable level of life satisfaction. They work through memories of the past and tie in the present to a reconstructed future. In addition, with a few exceptions in which life was not strongly disorganized by the death (usually because the couple was not living together and not interdependent in lifestyle), great changes have occurred in the process of becoming and being widowed. These changes can be dramatic, in self-concept, sentiments, and emotions; in relationships with everyone from the past; in entrance into new social roles and individual relationships; in lifestyle; and in life space.

Some widowed women learn to enjoy being alone a lot of time, responding to their own needs rather than constantly worrying about the needs of others (Silverman, 1987). They enjoy their freedom, especially if they have health and financial resources. They learn new areas of competence and self-identification. Past restrictions no longer constrain them, although past resources may be withered or absent. The widows most likely to express happiness after the period of heavy grief, loneliness, and immediate problems is over have usually been initiating, self-confident, and autonomous even within interdependent relations. They create and define new needs and modify self-defined old ones. All this is not done in isolation but in symbolic interaction with many others in many social circles. Of course, there are socially isolated and lonely widowed women and those with very limited social life space. Despite the tendency of observers to assume great unhappiness in such situations, in actuality, few widows express such feelings. People adjust to great variety of life circumstances, and there is a great variation among widows, as there is among women in other marital statuses. Let us now examine how the relations and interaction with others change with widowhood.

Notes

1. Readers interested in the concept of the two-person career and the influence of the husband and his job on the life of the wife can turn to Janet Finch's (1983) *Married to the Job*. Hanna Papanek (1973, see also 1979) coined the concept of the two-person career. The husband has the position in an organization (or in self-employed professional work) but can perform the job only in cooperation with a backup person who solves all problems on the home front, performs officially unrecognized work, and adjusts to all the demands of the occupation. Coser (1974; see also Coser & Coser, 1974) called the jobs that demanded such cooperative work "greedy institutions."

2. The sanctification scale was included in the *Handbook of Family Measurement Techniques,* edited by John Touliatos, Barry Perlmutter, and George Holden (Sage Publications). The first edition appeared in 1990 and was so popular that a second edition is forthcoming.

3. I have been avoiding the concepts of adjustment, coping, and so forth, so frequently used in discussions of widowhood, because of their passive tenor. As a symbolic interactionist, I see human beings interacting with the various elements of their environment—other people, roles, and life circumstances—constructing and creating this world. Of course, people vary in the degree to which they are active and creating in such constructions, but they do not merely adjust to what others or the setting provide. There is a strong tendency to see widows through the prism of such passivity stances. This may be a consequence of many factors: their pervasive identity as women, the response of observers of death over which they had no control, ageism, or any combination of these.

6

Kin Roles in Widowhood

Myth: Widowed mothers are heavily dependent on their children for financial, service, social, and emotional supports.

Myth: In widowhood, women are likely to turn to their siblings for major supports.

Widowed women can continue, with modifications depending on the prior involvement of the late husband, in many kinship roles. Relationships with different direct relatives or the extended kinship group vary by many factors. Of greatest significance and salience to most widows are the roles of daughter, sister, mother, and grandmother. I will first discuss the role of mother, then the other roles, because these are usually, although not always, of secondary importance to a widowed woman who has children.

The Role of Mother

Some widowed mothers in America are heavily dependent on their children for all their supports, but there are not many of them, and those who are have distinctive characteristics: They are usually quite old, feeble, and poor with limited sources of income. They are poorly educated, and in general, they do not have the skills to take advantage of the variety of resources available in American society. Frequently, the husband was the main connecting link to the broader community once the children left home, and his death resulted in even greater social disengagement. The children, usually a daughter, gain in importance as providers of remaining supports. The higher the education and socioeconomic lifestyle of the widow and the less limiting her health, the broader is her support network and the less she is dependent on any one person (Lopata, 1979).

THE ROLE OF MOTHER IN HISTORICAL PERSPECTIVE

The processes of modernization, especially since the 18th century in Europe and America, have increased the significance of the mother in the lives of her children. Several interdependent changes have contributed to the idealization of the role of mother and the heavy burden of responsibility placed on a mother. In traditional societies, the care and responsibility for children were undertaken by the extended family and the community. Mothers gave birth to children or adopted children born to other women and nursed them; then the young ones melded into the larger unit. Mothers had numerous pregnancies, and many children did not survive. The death of newborns and even older children was taken as inevitable.

According to Aries (1965), the family of the middle ages in Europe was not a private and isolated social unit. Rather, it was part of an extended manor house or a village. In addition to the owner, his wife (joint ownership is a modern arrangement), and their children, the manor house could contain hundreds of servants, apprentices, workers, and visitors who stayed for considerable time due to the distances covered by slow-moving transportation. Giving birth, dying, working, eating, and sleeping took place in large, common rooms. Village life was also very public. People interacted across age, gender, and even social class lines.

In countries such as England, the first phase of industrialization involved the whole family—men, women, and children—in cottage industries. Textile work was farmed out to them by middlemen. The second phase pulled the women and children into factories and mines while the men remained in farming. Hard work was considered good for children, teaching them discipline and keeping them out of trouble. Gradually, however, reform movements in Europe, and later in America, opposed the labor of children. In addition, as agriculture decreased in importance as a source of subsistence, men turned to the new forms of employment, which encouraged the removal of the children and also of women from the workplace (Oakley, 1974a, 1974b). Childhood became redefined as a separate stage of life, not simply as small adulthood but as a stage that required special care and treatment. Removed from the factories, however, children tended to roam the streets in gangs, as Charles Dickens so dramatically portrayed in his novels. The reformers encouraged the supervision of children by their families, which began to be limited to their mothers. The idea of mass education spread as nation-states solidified and industrialization required formally educated workers.

All these changes accompanied the rise of a two-sphere ideology, the public sphere of jobs and politics separated from the now privatized sphere of the family. This could be done only through the reconstruction of the reality of the home and motherhood. The home became idealized as a haven and motherhood as the source of emotional support and nurturing of the children and of the husband when he came home from the harsh and competitive public sphere. The mother, biological or adoptive, became imbued with virtue, "culture" (meaning music, religion, and art), and "doing good" in the community. This was, of course, a middle-class portrayal, but it became an ideal aspired to by upwardly mobile lower-class people, especially in American society with relatively open boundaries between these two classes. The ideal for the ever-expanding male population was to be such a "good provider" as to enable his wife to stay home and to have both her and the children out of the labor force (Bernard, 1983). "The Century of the Child," so labeled because of the idealized and protected image of the child, emerged in America by the mid-18th century (Ehrenreich & English, 1979).

The result of all this is a variation of the role of mother unlike that of the past or of most other places on earth. The mother is the one person totally responsible not only for the physical health of the children but also for all their behavior in youth and "how they turn out" in adulthood. She is allegedly helped by a whole social circle made up of the father, relatives on both sides, pediatricians, school personnel, protective police, and a variety of social groups to which the child can belong, be they gangs or scouts. The trouble is that the privatized image of the family in a society that idealizes individualism makes many of the members of this social circle of little help to her. A recent movement in America is to punish the parent for the misbehavior of the child, even though the mother often has little control over this child once he or she leaves the home. The complexity of the society, the anonymity of many neighborhoods, and the unwillingness of the community to provide services to "other people's children" all make the mother's role very difficult (Grubb & Lazerson, 1983). Gone are the servants and the extended family within easy reach. Grandmothers are apt to be employed or financially independent and unwilling to take on the care of grandchildren. New ideas as to the care and socialization of children appear constantly, and the mother is often confused or anxious about doing the right things. This anxiety was the main problem facing Chicago-area homemakers whom I interviewed in the 1950s and 1960s (Lopata, 1971a). No other role worried them as much as that of mother, deinstitutionalized as it had become with no single set of guidelines. This burden of worry was particularly true of middle-class suburbanites, who felt that everything they did would have an effect on the physical, and especially the psychological, development of their children. Gone was the comfortable assurance that personality was inborn and nothing could be done about it. Of course, the all but recent ideology of "true motherhood" assumed the presence of a father in the social circle who would provide the family with economic support and be an active participant, although generally not an equal coparent.

The Death of the Father

The effects of the death of the father on the role of the mother are complicated and depend on many factors, especially ages of the children. These effects are influenced by the contributions and problems involving the rest of the social circle of the mother and the social circles of her other roles. In cases in which the father was also the husband of the mother and an active participant in those other roles, the effects of his death are multiple. I will first discuss the general effects and then specify differences by the age of the children.

The death of the father affects the children directly through the same set of circumstances that affect the wife in the death of her husband. That is, sudden death has different consequences than does prolonged illness followed by death. The grief of sudden death can leave the mother unable to deal with the children's problems with understanding what happened. On the other hand, the father's illness can deflect the mother's time, energy, and attention from her children, leaving them deprived of both parents.

What affects the children has repercussive effects on the role of mother. She has to deal with their reactions, often at a time when she herself is still cocooned in numbness or in heavy grief. Their distress can be acted out in demanding and even destructive behavior with which she may not be able to deal. The children can also be responding to the mother's grief over the loss of her husband as well as to the loss of their father. Her manner of coping with her grief thus affects the children (Silverman & Worden, 1993). At the same time, the children's demands on the mother to help with their grief and to replace the supports previously supplied by the father can create role conflict for the woman. In fact, this is a frequent occurrence reported by young widows (Lopata, 1979). Children can also be of little help, coming and going at their own rhythms. Guilt can hit the whole family if prior problems led to avoidance or anger at the husband and father. On the other hand, the children, or at least some of them, might feel that the mother or siblings did not do enough to support the father in his illness. All in all, the times before and immediately after the death can be fraught with emotions that are hard to control.

The death of the man may also change the social circle of the mother in other ways. We found in the Chicago-area studies that in-laws, to whom the husband was the connecting link, may lose contact with the survivors. Being relatives of the deceased, in-laws are expected to assist with the funeral, other mourning arrangements, or both. Most of the widows reported receiving help at that time (see Lopata, 1973d, p. 57). When asked, however, whether the in-laws had been helping with the children or giving children gifts or money, about half of the widows stated "never," and about a third found the question inappropriate because they had no in-laws who could help. In fact, only 12% of the respondents reported that in-laws visited or invited the children over, and 43% responded that there were never such visits. Unfortunately, we do not know if the man's relatives were active in the mother's social circle while the father was still alive. Certainly, in traditional patriarchal family systems, the male line is expected to—and barring geographical mobility or family problems, does—contribute to the rearing of the children and even to their inheritance. Absence of grandparents and aunts or uncles from the circle of the mother can be advantageous in that they do not interfere with her relationships with her children.

The woman can be affected in widowhood in the resources she has available to carry forth her duties and receive the rights of the mother role. An important right is continued economic support if the deceased had been a major contributor to family income. Some husbands ensure survivor benefits, and American society covers some of their obligations to the family through Social Security. The husband's death also removes a member of the woman's other social circles. The more he was involved in her various social roles, the more each removal affects her role of mother, even if indirectly. The same holds true for the children. The more the father was involved in their various roles and the stronger or more ambivalent the emotional ties they had with him, the more his removal affects their lives. The mother then has the double burden of "grief work," to work through her own emotions and supports as well as to help the children work through theirs.

Becoming Widowed and
Being a Widow in Midlife

BECOMING WIDOWED
WITH YOUNG CHILDREN

The most disorganizing to the role of mother, at least in this society, is the father's death while the children are small, especially if he has been a full member of the family. If the father was in the household, his very presence influenced what the mother could and could not do in relations with her children. A division of responsibility along traditional lines usually left the disciplining and socialization of the boys to the father. In fact, he could be the disciplinarian for all of the offspring, as the famous statement "wait till your father comes home" shows. The presence of the father can also relieve, at least temporarily, the need for full-time attention toward young children. In traditional terms, the father can "play with the children" while the mother turns to other roles, such as homemaker. Fathers can help with decision making concerning large and small issues of child rearing. They can share the emotional drain when problems arise or the joy when something good happens. As many a mother has found out, it is impossible for her to be a mother and a father at the same time. The widow must, however, take over some of the father's duties and provide the children with much of what they gained from their father while he was alive and well, or she must find substitutes. Widows report turning to male members of the family or friends to "take the boys to the ball game," in the gender-specific style of parenting. Some of the father's contributions to the children simply get dropped. The children themselves may try to take over some of the husband's duties toward their mother, increasing the rights element of that role.

There may be some positive consequences for the role of mother arising out of the death of the father. The Chicago-area study of homemakers indicated that in many households the father contributed more to the complexity of life for the mother than to easing strain and conflicts (Lopata, Barnewolt, & Harrison, 1987; Lopata et al., 1985). Fathers can create problems in child rearing if they interfere with mothering by contradicting the mother or depriving her of necessary resources. The children may have had serious problems in dealing with the father while he was alive and well and even worse ones while he was sick and dying, so his death may actually have calmed and simplified life. Fathers can create even greater problems by abusing the children, sexually and through physical and psychological violence (see Davidson & Moore, 1992, pp. 384-389). Unsteady income from the father may have made the provision of child rearing necessities very difficult. The death of the father can thus remove problems and may stabilize family life.

BECOMING WIDOWED
WITH ADULT CHILDREN

There is a great deal of difference in the effects on the role of the mother in consequence of the father's death when the children have already reached adulthood than when they are young. The forms and content of relations between a widowed mother and her adult children vary by gender, birth order, and personal preference. One important factor affecting their relationship, especially in the historical past, was the method of receiving and the size of the inheritance that the widowed mother and the children gained with the death of the husband and father.

A 20th-century trend in American society has been for the wife to inherit the goods and wealth from the marriage and to pass it down to the children only after her death (Sussman, Cates, & Smith, 1970). However, the American legal history contains several separate inheritance practices. The plantation system of the southern colonies favored primogeniture so that the land was concentrated in the hands of a single offspring. In the New England colonies, sons tended to inherit equally. The widow was limited to only a part of the inheritance, or dower, whereas the children inherited what was considered their shares (Clignet, 1992).

A study by Sussman et al. (1970) in Ohio during the 1960s found the following:

> If the testator [the deceased who made a will] was survived by a spouse and lineal kin, the overwhelming majority named the spouse the sole heir. By doing so, the testator provided the widow or widower with assets in order to make it possible for the spouse to continue an independent existence and to have a legacy to use in bargaining for services from children and other relatives later on. (pp. 289-290)

The older the man, the more likely he was to leave a will, which determined the distribution of the inheritance. If the deceased had no will or died intestate in Ohio or other noncommunity property states, the estate was usually divided between the spouse and the "issue." According to records, the children often transferred over their shares "to the surviving parent, because of filial responsibility, a realistic appraisal of their parent's financial condition, and a sense of justice that the surviving parent had earned the legacy" (p. 290).

The researchers also found that exceptions to the spouse-gets-all pattern occurred if there were a large estate or in cases of remarriage. As we shall see in Chapter 7, one of the problems of widow or widower remarriage is the objection by children, not only because of their attachment to the deceased parent but also because of their fear that in community property states, which represent the majority of states in the 1990s, the new spouse could deprive them of their inheritance. This would happen if their surviving parent died and the new spouse inherited everything.

The shift over to the spouse as the main inheritor for as long as she lives, with rights of property disposal, is one of the strongest indicators of change in the family institution over the past two or so centuries. It puts the marriage bond ahead of the lineal succession bond. This is a dramatic transformation from prior times, when the widow could not inherit because she was considered peripheral to the male line and inheritance was used to ensure family continuity. Then, she either shared with or became dependent on the inheritor. Now, she is considered a major contributor to the family estate and is no longer a legal minor unable to conduct business. She no longer needs a male guardian, be it a son or a bank representative. She is seen as the rightful possessor of goods inherited or acquired during the marriage and is trusted not to invest unwisely or to squander the children's inheritance. In fact, the widow in modern times has the right to do what she wishes with the inheritance unless the testator made other arrangements in the will. The society assumes that the parents had provided the children with sufficient background ability to be able to support themselves.

Another indicator of change in the American family institution is the fact that all of the children are now likely to share the inheritance when it finally comes to them. The tradition of male primogeniture and of buying off the daughter with a dowry because she could not inherit from the father is basically gone. Clignet (1992, pp. 174-186) found that the inequalities in wills according to bequest or controls among the children based on gender or in favor of one child decreased considerably between 1920 and 1944.

The subject of inheritance, formally and informally passed on, is a very emotional one, frequently causing rifts in families. Family held objects can become so symbolic that their inheritance indicates the importance of the receiver to the testator (Rossi & Rossi, 1990). Of course, goods are transferred within families at times other than death, often to prevent taxes or the items ending up "in the wrong hands." Rossi and Rossi (1990) found few gender differences in the type of material goods or the number of types of goods inherited except that never-married women reported "a much higher average number of things they received from someone than never-married men do" (p. 464). The same advantage on the part of never-married children is evident in the inheritance of parents' insurance policies, and here, sons have the same benefits as daughters. The marital status difference in inheritance may be a result of variations in support systems. Unmarried children are leaned on more than the married.

BEING A WIDOWED MOTHER IN MIDLIFE

Most sociologists of the family have found a steady flow of supports from parents, especially from mothers, to their adult children as these enter new family roles (Sussman, 1965). Increasing longevity of Americans, especially of American women, has prolonged the time they and their children can relate to each other, including the time of adult life when neither is highly dependent upon the other (Wood, Traupmann, & Hay, 1984, p. 227; see also Baruch & Barnett, 1983; Fischer, 1981, 1986; Lopata, 1994a). Once children grow up, leave home, and establish their own households, the relationship between parents and offspring changes considerably. The modern mother has little power over her adult children, who are able to marry and create their own families of procreation even without the mother's approval, let alone mate selection rights. They are free to settle their households at any distance from the mother, enter any combination of roles, and raise their own children in a style quite different from that of the mother.

The large and consistent amount of support and contact between these two generations of adults in American society, mother and adult children, is therefore significant, because it is voluntary rather than legally or culturally enforced. We asked widowed women in the support systems study (Lopata, 1979) for the inflow and outflow of economic, service, social, and emotional supports and found an interesting pattern. Women did not list themselves as providing transportation, housekeeping, or shopping supports to children living in the home, only to children living apart. They also did not report an inflow of service supports from household residents unless they were made by special arrangement. In other words, such actions are part of the normal flow of life in a household. Anderson and McCulloch (1993) also found that instrumental supports within a marital dyad appear to be so "embedded in everyday life" (p. S141) that they are taken for granted, especially when part of the gender division of labor.[1]

During the adulthood of children, gender differences in relationships with the mother take a new turn or at least become more visible. Mothers in American society, as discussed in Chapter 3, are strongly encouraged to allow their sons to grow away, breaking the early emotional tie to join the world of men (Chodorow, 1978). Adult sons are expected to become focused toward their occupations and families of procreation rather than being tied to their families of orientation. This is certainly different from the situation in traditional India and similarly patriarchal societies, as discussed in Chapter 2, in which the mother-son tie was considered the closest in the family and the care of the elderly widowed mother was the responsibility of the son. There are several reasons for such an arrangement in these settings. Men carried down family continuity, often in the name; inherited and managed the property; contributed productive labor to the family; and ensured a proper afterlife of deceased ancestors where such religious rituals were practiced. The daughter-mother tie was not considered as important, because the young woman had to leave home and become attached to the husband's family. Her obligations were to the mother-in-law, not to the mother.

The American relationship between mother and daughter, often stormy in earlier years due to the revolt of the young against parental authority, becomes much closer after the young woman matures and enters the roles of wife and mother (Fischer, 1986). This is especially true if she reproduces the same life pattern as the mother, combining social roles in the same way. It is less close if the mother, for example, stayed home to care for her children, whereas the daughter tries to balance a career, wifehood, and motherhood in a manner disapproved of by the mother. Fischer's (1983, 1986) research indicates, however, that this was not a serious problem in the early 1980s, and few studies have focused on this relationship under such circumstances. All evidence points to a mother's closer relationship with one of the children, a daughter, even if there are others in the family.

Exchange theory provides some explanation of the asymmetry of a mother's relations with her children. According to this theory, support exchanges in present relationships are dependent on past or anticipated future exchanges. We do not know enough about favoritism in new families, however, nor do we have sufficient knowledge as to the selection process in support exchanges between a mother and her children. This process becomes extremely apparent and important when the mother becomes frail and dependent, as we shall see later in this chapter. In the meantime, the exchanges between a widowed mother and each of her children are known and mentally recorded by the siblings. Jealousy on the part of children over perceived inequities is often reported by mothers.

Although social scientific research documents extensive exchanges of supports between widowed midlife mothers and their daughters, it also notes some problems on both sides. Daughters may find request for help from the mothers quite burdensome, especially if they create role conflicts. Focus group studies of widowed women found numerous negative comments about demands from relatives, both parents and children (see Morgan, 1989).

The modern woman in midlife tends to be quite competent, feeling mastery over her life (Baruch & Barnett, 1983; Baruch & Brooks-Gunn, 1984). The widowed woman past the strong experiences of grief and moving out into a more autonomous life is especially likely to have a multidimensional life space. Such a woman may resent requests for help from the daughter, especially if they impinge on her new freedom. One frequently mentioned source of tension is baby-sitting. Adult children often assume that a widowed mother has nothing else to do and would love to be with the grandchildren. The catch is in the term *baby-sitting*. It contains the very feature of the situation that upsets the older woman. She often wants to be an active grandmother, whereas her children do not want her to do so if it means that she countermands their policies or tries to socialize the young in a way they do not approve. What they want is someone to literally sit (and play with, of course) and watch the children. In addition, the concept of baby-sitter implies a servant, hired to sit while the parents are out having a good time. Often, the mother would rather be taken out for a good time herself. Taking care of the children can be a pleasure under certain circumstances when it has a limited and agreed-on time span, if there are not too many or too young children and if the grandmother has the resources for keeping everyone happy.

Widowhood on the part of the mother does not necessitate the children's return to the mother's house, which is anyway not likely to be an ancestral home or even the home in which the younger generation was raised. Despite the withdrawal of husband and children from the household, most of the widowed mothers who are economically relatively independent continue living in their own dwelling so that the economic, service, social, and emotional support systems flow across households. If the widow shares the household with an adult child, it is likely to be a daughter who never moved away or one whose personal or marital problems have led her to return to the mother's home (Brody, Litvin, Hoffman, & Kleban, 1995). In other words, coresidence is retained or reformed for the benefit of the adult child. Only when the mother becomes quite frail is sharing of a residence accomplished for her benefit.

The Chicago-area women we studied and those studied by others in other locations were very specific about not wishing to live in the same household as their children, especially one run by a daughter-in-law. They preferred to live alone and were able to do so unless they were uneducated and unfamiliar with American culture and urban life (Chevan & Korson, 1972, 1975). In fact, according to survey researchers, "About 8 out of 10 of the 5.9 million [older persons] who live alone are widowed," and "in 1985 approximately 41% of older women age 65+ maintained separate residences" (O'Bryant, 1988a, p. 93). The days in which sons or daughters remained in the family home in which the older woman was the head and matriarch, able to control the behavior of coresidents, are gone. If the widow lives with anyone, it is likely to be an unmarried child (Lopata, 1971a). There is a greater probability of an African American woman living with married children than there is of a white woman doing so, simply because of economic need. Even here, however, such arrangements tend to be transitory (Lopata, 1973d).

Widows explain their unwillingness to live with married children in the latter's dwelling in several ways: They like to manage their own homes, organized their way and with their belongings. They also like their own rhythm of working, eating, sleeping, and using the bathroom. The women do not want to be periphery members of another household. As one mother explained to me, "I never took orders from my husband, and I sure as hell couldn't take orders from the children" (Lopata, 1973d, p. 122). Sharing the role of housewife can also present problems, with the widow's either having to fit into the system developed by another person or to take over. The widows with whom I talked felt that they had already kept house and cared for children at one stage in their lives and did not want all that work again.

Widowed mothers have visited or stayed for extended times with their children and know how frequent are the possibilities for conflict with the offspring, the in-law, or the grandchildren. Mothers tend to find their offspring unfairly treated by the spouse or vice versa, and many cannot help advising the younger generation on raising the grandchildren. Widows even use folklore phrases to justify their feelings: "Two women in the same kitchen are no good." If it is actually believed, such commonsense knowledge can prevent feelings of guilt or rejection on both sides. One woman explained the situation to me in such a way:

> Well, I went down to New Orleans to visit my daughter after Sam died. My son-in-law is a doctor and they have a very nice home. My daughter said: "Ma, you could move here with us, but, ma, you are going to have to keep your mouth shut." Now you tell me, what's the fun of living if you have to keep your mouth shut? (Lopata, 1973d, p. 120)

An additional problem arises in cases of social mobility of the younger generation. The son or daughter's family moves into the suburb or a posh neighborhood and develops new friends and a new lifestyle that makes the mother very uncomfortable. A problem also can emerge if the mother is too busy to provide supports for the new family unit. Yet it appears that many mothers are able to provide needed services and emotional supports. Marriage and motherhood by a daughter bring her closer to the mother as they share life experiences (Fischer, 1981). As soon as the children are less confining, the midlife mother and her daughter, and to a lesser extent the son, are able to enter a relationship that involves "continuous negotiation" (Wood et al., 1984, p. 230). The content of the negotiation varies over time and circumstances, but it tends to even out. Bengtson and Robertson (1985) point out that this dyadic relationship must be able to change with changing roles and expectations, balancing dependency and autonomy, the giving and receiving of supports, and the handling of events that could become divisive.

The Older Widowed Mother

Of great interest to social gerontologists has been the growing need for caregiving to a rapidly expanding proportion of older, frail American women. Medical advances have decreased the death rate of women at younger years and prolonged the number of years of life. Although most of those years are spent in increasing independence in relatively modernized societies, the last years tend to be characterized by health problems. These are usually met by the spouse of the frail person, with the help of outside support givers. The increasing divorce rate, however, leaves many an older person without a spouse to care for her or him. In addition, one of the two marital partners almost invariably dies first, and the survivor often needs outside supports.

Discussions of the supports of an older widowed parent occur more often in families of widows than of widowers simply because of the demographic distributions. Only 21% of women aged 75 and over were living in 1979 with a husband, whereas 67% of all men of that age were living with a wife (see Hagestad, 1985, p. 35). Widowed fathers may require greater support if they lack daily life skills. The remarriage rate and the shortage of time of widowhood by men make them less frequent targets of concern. Previously independent mothers can become frail and dependent on new social, emotional, and even service supports to replace the supports provided by the husband or by a multidimensional support network.

Which Child?

As we have noted throughout this chapter, modern American families have somehow placed the responsibility for the care of older widowed women on the daughter rather than on the son or the community. This reflects what appears to be lifelong closer relationships of mothers with daughters than with sons (Fischer, 1983, 1986; Lopata, 1991b). One widowed mother in the Chicago-area study explained rather bashfully that she gets much more help from her daughter than from her sons because the "boys" live far away (Lopata et al., 1985). The question arises as to why there is such a divergence in distance from the mother. In this case, the respondent justified the sons' moving away in terms of their job demands.

Innumerable studies indicate that the first line of support for widows is the daughter, if there is one, whereas other children provide care of various forms and degrees. The situation of parental caregiving, however, is rather complicated. One study of parent care by a research team at the Philadelphia Geriatric Center found daughters to be in their middle years of life, married, and with children of their own so that extensive care for the frail mother often became a burden and caused serious role conflict (Brody, 1990; Moss, Lawton, Kleban, & Duhamel, 1993). Employed daughters provided less personal care and less cooking help than did full-time homemakers, but they substituted with purchased services. The two types of daughters, however, employed and not, "provided equal amounts of help with shopping, transportation, household maintenance, emotional support and service management" (Brody, Kleban, Johnson, Hoffman, & Schoonover, 1987, p. 201). Daughters who reduced working hours and experienced the most disruption in their lives to provide care for the mother felt the greatest amount of stress, more than the homemakers or the employed women. That is not a surprising finding, but it points up the problems of such situations. The authors note in this study, and Brody (1990) in her other work, that America is one of the few industrial societies that does not provide at least some assistance to people caring for frail parents in the form of respite and day care services. It does not even provide an attendant's allowance.

> Some countries provide benefits such as Social Security credits for the years that caregivers remain at home, pensions for those who have taken care of an elderly or disabled person, and shorter working hours for caregiving wage earners. (Brody et al., 1987, p. 208)

Horowitz (1985, p. 613) studied a sample of primary caregivers of frail elderly people known to a day care center, a homemaker agency, a local meal program, and a visiting nurse service in New York City. The research focused on the differences in the care given to a frail parent, usually the mother, by sons and daughters and supported the general finding of gender concentration and segregation. Three fourths of the children who were primary care providers were daughters, and many more of the daughters than of the sons agreed to the interview.[2] The sons who undertook primary responsibility were either only children, had only brothers, or were the only geographically available child (p. 614). Only about one fourth of the parents were living with the adult child. The differences in caregiving were gender based, with the daughters doing more hands-on care, whereas the sons took care of financial management or assistance and dealing with bureaucracies. There was no difference between the gender of the children and the use of formal services. This means that formal services did not "fill the gap of care when a son was the primary caregiver" (p. 615).

One of the important findings that gives credence to the theme of continuity in the patriarchal family systems was the contribution of the spouse of the adult child to the care of the mother. The sons, most of whom did not offer much personal care and who were less frequently involved than the daughters, were able to depend on their wives for the psychological support of their efforts and for actual care. Daughters reported a "neutral response" from their husbands toward their obligations and little if any actual care. Thus, it is the woman who is involved directly in caregiving or through the obligations of the husband or son. As in other studies, the daughters experienced much more stress as a result of their caregiving than did the sons. Horowitz (1985, p. 616) explains the difference in terms of the emotional distance of the sons and recency of their involvement with the mother, the distance in the forms of the care, and lack of role conflict due to the cooperation of the spouse. The daughters were more emotionally involved with the mother, performed more personal care, and faced role conflict with their family of procreation. The question Horowitz asks is, Will changes in the socialization and family experiences of sons in "modern" times increase their personal caregiving to the mother and, thus, the strain experienced by such involvement?

Both of my studies of widowhood in the Chicago metropolitan area focused on role changes and support systems of the women. I became aware of a differentiation of the types of supports provided by sons and daughters during the pretests. As a result, our interviewers in the second study asked who supplied 65 different supports, organized into four systems: economic, service, social, and emotional, as mentioned earlier. The economic and service systems included an inflow and outflow of supports. The respondents could list up to three persons for each support. Few of these noninstitutionalized widows obtained any economic supports in the form of gifts or help in payment of rent, food, bills, travel, or anything else from their children. At least they did not report any such support. Few of the widows provided economic supports, except in the form of gifts to children or grandchildren. A few of the sons provided care of a car. The daughters helped much more often than did the sons with transportation, shopping, housecleaning, and care in illness. These services were given on a regular basis and were important to the mother. Household repairs and care of the yard were provided to the mother mainly by the sons, and both gender offspring contributed financial and housing advice, but all these supports were reported quite infrequently (Lopata, 1991b).

The children living outside of the mother's home appeared less often in the social supports as companions in public places or for special meals, games, travel, and so forth than did friends or neighbors. Children were most often mentioned as the primary persons with whom holidays were spent. Daughters appeared in this support system much more often than sons, probably because it is the women rather than the men who are family "social secretaries." For example, daughters were mentioned twice as often as sons as visitors or companions in restaurants or travel. In actuality, about half of the widowed women reported never going out to public places except to church.

I finally separated the daughters from the sons as they appeared in the mother's emotional support system. The children were by far the most important contributors to this system. The only place that they appeared infrequently was as persons who most often made the mother angry. Children were most likely to appear as contributors to the woman's feelings of closeness and enjoyment, those to whom she would turn to in times of crises, and those who made her feel important and respected. A surprising finding was that only a third of the references to confidants of problems were to the offspring.

Daughters dominated the emotional support system. Sons appeared as sources of anger more often than daughters, possibly because they did not meet expectations. At the same time, sons (maybe, but not necessarily, different ones from those who caused anger) also contributed more frequently to feelings of security, but the gender differences here were not great. Daughters were listed much more frequently as persons to whom the mother felt closest and told problems, whom she most enjoyed, and who most often comforted her. Despite earlier hypotheses, we found the women more likely to turn to daughters than sons in times of crisis. The surplus of daughters was low in the self-feeling segment of the emotional system, but then few women listed an offspring in several of these areas. The fact that the mothers obtained a feeling of being respected and useful from others (mainly from the children) while they credited themselves with the feelings of independence and self-sufficiency supports the theoretical framework of symbolic interactionism. The first two self-feelings depend on relationships, the second set on self-evaluations.

Of course, who supplies the supports depends on who is available to do so. The gender composition of the offspring is an important factor. O'Bryant (1988a) did such an analysis for the sample of widowed mothers she studied in Columbus, Ohio. The widows were divided into four groups—those with at least one son and no daughters, those with at least one daughter and no sons, those with both gender offspring, and those who were childless.

> Childless widows and those with daughters only received help with significantly fewer traditional male types of support than widows with sons. . . . Although there is evidence of some substitution for missing sons from sons-in-law, brothers, other kin, and friends/neighbors, in general these groups probably do not feel as obligated as sons to provide help. (p. 101)

On the other hand, mothers without daughters could draw "from other available females" (p. 103).

In sum, then, all research, including some very carefully controlled analyses, indicates that daughters are *much* more likely than sons (3.22 times vs. 2.56 times) to provide help to impaired parents with activities of daily living and other forms of social and emotional support (see Dwyer & Coward, 1991). In addition, Brody (1986) concludes that "the evidence indicates that adult children now provide more care and more difficult care to more elderly parents over much longer periods of time than ever before in history" (p. 177).

Most mothers do not become so dependent on their daughters as to create serious problems in their relationships, or the period of their heavy dependence is rather short. In fact, widowhood can free even an older woman from the restrictions of marriage and decrease role conflict between the roles of wife and mother.

Stepmother

Widowed women can acquire stepchildren if they remarry and the new husband has children from his prior marriage. There are several possible variations of this situation. In the first place, the method by which those children lost full involvement with their mother has important consequences for their relationship with the new mother. Their ages at that event and at the remarriage of their father are also important factors. There is a growing literature on *fused, mixed,* or *stepfamilies,* whichever term is used for this configuration. The death of the stepchildren's mother leaves scars but also a vacuum that the new mother can fill, especially if the children are small. Frequently, mother-orphaned older children take over the running of the home and care of the father. In such cases, they may resent the woman brought in by the father as their stepmother. Several of the remarried widows whom I interviewed pointed out their advantage over other circumstances of remarriage because the new husband had been a widower rather than a divorced man and either had no children or had adult offspring who had left home and built their own families some distance away. The main problem the stepmother had with adult stepchildren was the latter's resentment over the use of family property and the fear that if the father died first, much of it would be lost to them (Lopata, 1973d). Ambivalence in the children's feelings about the stepmother is introduced by the kind of sentiments they hold about the biological mother, especially if they spent many years with her. The stepmother-in-law appears to have few rights unless she is the one who raised the children that the in-laws married. Grown children, however, often express relief that the father is happy and that someone is there to take care of him.

More complicating for the stepmother is the situation of divorce and child sharing between the divorced parents. In most cases, their mother has custodial care of the children, the father having visitation rights only. Increasingly, however, there is a joint custody arrangement, and in a few cases, the father gains custody. All these possibilities influence how the widowed woman can build relationships with the children. Of great importance is the housing situation: If the children share with the father and stepmother, tension can emerge over who has what dwelling rights, and how the integration takes place. The experiences of the children of divorce are varied. The degree of disorganization in their lives is reflected in how they view the new marriage and household. The most difficult for the children is conflict between their parents before, during, and after the divorce, especially if each parent tries to build loyalty to the self by downgrading the other. The children may be very torn by all this, either turning to the stepmother or rejecting her initially and even over time. The original mother is an ever-felt presence. If the children see the stepmother only during visits, she has greater rights over the setting than the children do, and she must try to make them feel at home. The part played by the husband (and children's father) is, of course, of primary importance. As Cherlin (1978) has noted, remarriage is an incomplete institution, meaning that there are no easy-to-follow procedures for integrating the new family in view of the constant reminders of the old family—even of two old families.

The widowed mother who remarries has some of the same and some different problems, again dependent on whether the new husband has children of his own and the characteristics of her own children. Symmetry in cost and benefits for all involved is seldom achieved, especially if the stepchildren still have an active mother. Blended families are those that may have "his children," "her children," and even "our" children. It is easy for the mother to be very thin-skinned concerning her own children, fearful of having them hurt by the stepfather or stepsiblings and yet not wanting to antagonize those people.

Widowed Daughter

The main way widowhood can affect a daughter is to free her into a closer relationship with the mother as competition from the role of wife is dramatically decreased.[3] The increased closeness or at least increased contact can benefit either the daughter or the mother. Brody and her associates (1995) found widowed daughters more likely to share households with their mothers than do married daughters. One reason was that the widows were considerably older than were the daughters in other marital situations. They also had less family income than the married or remarried daughters, increasing the advantages of shared housing. Widowed daughters were also most likely to have the mother or both parents move in with them if the elderly needed caregiving. The effect on the younger daughter was more often depression if she were widowed, divorced, or separated than if she were married, due to the supports provided to the married women by the husband. Often, the widow had a long history of caregiving, having provided it to the husband before providing it to their parents.

Younger widows with children often benefit from the willingness of the parents, especially the mother, to care for the offspring so that the daughter can take a job or be involved in a wider social life space than is possible in the absence of caregivers in the home.

Widowed Sister

There is a great deal of debate as to the contributions made by siblings to each other in older age. One of the assumptions is that the decrease of competition from the roles of wife and mother increases the need for new support providers and that siblings are able to substitute for prior ones (Shanas, 1973). Martin Matthews (1987, 1991) found strong emotional bonds between widowed women and their "families of orientation, including especially sisters" (Martin Matthews, 1991, p. 42). Her studies in Guelph, Canada, found siblings in contact several times a month, and 54% of the widows were involved in social supports with a sister and listed one as the person to whom they felt closest.

On the other hand, I (Lopata, 1979) found Chicago-area widows very unlikely to list a brother, even a sister, within the four support system. Twenty percent of the weighted sample of more than 85,000 widows who were at that time or had been beneficiaries of Social Security had no living brothers or sisters. As noted before, the widows were asked about contributors to the economic (both inflow and outflow), service (both inflow and outflow), social, and emotional systems for a total of 65 supports. They were encouraged to list up to three persons for each support. This means that a brother or sister had a total of 195 chances to appear in the woman's support systems (Lopata, 1979). The findings were disappointing to our assumption of sibling involvement in the network: The vast majority of women claimed not to receive or give economic support. Only 4,380 widows helped anyone with rent or mortgage payments, and 10% of the recipients were siblings. Only 4,380 gave help with food, and 14% of the recipients were siblings. Ten or less of the service supports were provide by or to siblings. Twenty percent of the people whom the widow helped with yardwork were brothers, but only 4% of the women provided that kind of support. Most of the widows listed companions in holiday celebrations, and 10% of those companions were siblings. The siblings made only rare appearances in the emotional support system. Although most widows acknowledged such supports, only 10% listed a sibling as the person to whom they would turn in times of crises (Lopata, 1978a, pp. 359-361). All in all, siblings appeared in only 26% of the sentiment segment of the emotional support system (closest, enjoy being with, tell problems to, is comforted by, etc.) and 13% of the feeling status (makes me feel respected, useful, independent, accepted, self-sufficient, and secure). The respondents saw their sisters or brothers on an average of only 3.37 times a year (Lopata, 1979, p. 69). These findings certainly are not an indication of the importance of siblings in widowhood.

Anne Martin Matthews and I have discussed on several occasions the possible reasons for differences in the involvement of siblings in the support systems of widowed women in Chicago and in Canada (see Lopata, 1987d; Martin Matthews, 1991). Chicago is a metropolis with a highly mobile population, both geographically and socially. Many of the widows in my studies are first- or second-generation migrants from other countries or from other parts of the United States. This mobility has led to a socioeconomic and geographic dispersal of many siblings and made them unavailable to serve in the active support network. This is not true of most of the Guelph-area widows studied by Martin Matthews. Hers is a relatively stable population that grew up in the local area with greater kin availability (see Martin Matthews,

1991, p. 45). On the other hand, the widows in metropolitan Chicago had more children still living, some even in the home, than did the Guelph women. One reason for this is that my sample consisted of widows of all ages, whereas hers was of only older ones. Women of younger ages, according to the literature and our own studies, are likely to be involved in more multidimensional life spaces than are the older ones, partly because of difference in education and familiarity with social resources. Martin Matthews (1991, p. 45) reports that according to Connidis's 1989 study, London, Ontario, women have more active ties with siblings in widowhood than in prior marriage. He stressed the importance of marital status similarity.

O'Bryant (1988b) reported,

> The likelihood of receiving help [from siblings] may depend not only upon the sociodemographic characteristics of the widow (e.g., age, health, and income) but also upon the existence and proximity of children, and the sex, marital status, and proximity of the siblings themselves. (p. 175)

The relatively small size of the community and the relative immobility of families may also account for the fact that Adams (1968) found that over two thirds of young siblings living in the same city saw each other at least once a week. They were involved, however, in few support exchanges. Cicirelli (1982) reported very few siblings are turned to for help among the elderly.

> Some 7% of all elderly interviewed reported turning to a sibling as a major source of psychological support; a smaller number of elderly regarded a sibling as a primary source of reading materials, help with business dealings, source of social and recreational activities, protection, and help with homecoming. (p. 279)

Cicirelli goes on to say that siblings "stand ready to help one another in time of need, although most people do not call upon this resource frequently" (p. 279). Any way one looks at the figures, the siblings in his study were certainly not involved in active supports.

O'Bryant (1988b) concluded that "siblings of different marital statuses have different potential benefits for the recent widow" (p. 174). Brothers-in-law do not appear frequently in the support systems of widows in most studies. Sisters-in-law appear only somewhat more frequently. It is possible that siblings-in-law are resistant to active involvement by their spouses in the sister's supports. The reports of support by siblings are influenced by the time frame under analysis. The Chicago sample consisted of women at varying stages of widowhood but usually quite some time after the death of the husband. Siblings may enter the support systems early in widowhood to then return to their normal lifestyle afterward. That may explain why so few appear in any of the numerous supports we studied. The same is true of the O'Bryant (1988b) findings. It is important to note that the healthy (by self-report), Ohio widowed women who had a married sister nearby and saw her frequently reported positive feelings or affection. O'Bryant (1988b) speculates that her feeling of well-being may be due to "having a married sister who is willing to share her husband" and who "challenges her away from self-pity" (p. 181). All in all, although those women who report active sister relationships appear to benefit from them, few widows are able to be so involved.

Widowed Grandmother

Again, we can assume that the role of grandmother can increase in importance with widowhood. On the other hand, the death of the husband and grandfather may decrease the opportunity for contact if he had been the driver and transportation becomes a problem for the widow. Adult children often move away from the parental neighborhood. Their suburban or other community residence may be not only far from the mother's household but also in a territory foreign in lifestyle to the older woman. She may be uncomfortable in these surroundings when she visits, either for short or extended periods of time. All research indicates the importance of frequent contact for the development and maintenance of close relationships between a grandmother and her grandchildren (Bengtson & Robertson, 1985; Cherlin & Furstenberg, 1986).

The most likely to be in frequent contact, of course, are people who live in the same household. In some of these shared facilities, the grandmother takes over many of the child care duties and rights of mothering, the most intensive form of grandparenting. Burton and Bengtson (1985) found, in a study of several-generation African American female lineages in Los Angeles, that the women on whom the role of grandmother was thrust off time by their teenage daughters experienced tension and conflict because of their own age and role conflict. Grandmothers who acquired this role later in life were able to adjust to it with greater ease. Thus, "both timing of entry and generational structure affect grandparental role behavior in different ways" (p. 76). According to Ludwig (1977), Puerto Rican grandmothers living on the mainland have the community-approved right to take over the mothering of their grandchildren if they do not approve of the way the parents take care of the young.

Little is known about the variations in grandparenting styles between widowed grandmothers and those in other marital situations (Cherlin & Furstenberg, 1986). Cherlin and Furstenberg studied the differences in grandparenting activities between grandmothers and grandfathers and concluded that the gender of the grandchild also influenced the relationships. Grandfathers were most involved with their grandsons, and grandmothers tried to bridge the generation gap with both genders of grandchildren but succeeded best with granddaughters.

The Widow and Kin Networks

Kin relations are almost invariably modified by the death of a member, depending on the centrality of that person, the structure of the network, and his or her relation to the others. The death of an adult male affects the relationships between his widow and other members of the more or less integrated network in various ways. One of the findings of my (Lopata, 1993a) role modification study of Chicago-area widows was the almost total withering of interaction with her in-laws—that is, with the late husband's relatives. Closeness of contact was facilitated only by proximity and ties that went beyond that marriage. The presence of children also increased the possibility of closeness, especially in upper-class cases or in ethnic communities. The possibility of inheritance of sufficient size or importance generally ensured continued interaction. Modern American kin groups, however, have become quite voluntary in their relationships, and although a son may insist on maintaining contact with his family of origin, his widow may not feel that kind of obligation. In-law jokes abound and indicate that such ties are not some of the favorites of those available to adults (Lopata, 1991a).

Summary

The traditional family of myth or reality surrounded a woman throughout her life. The family of orientation, consisting of parents and siblings, was a relatively insignificant part of her support system in highly patriarchal, especially patrilineal, systems because she left it to join the husband's family of orientation. Modernization, with the decrease of importance of the male line on the new nuclear unit meant that a woman could remain close to her birth relatives during her life. The changes in relationships especially increased the bond between mother and daughter, with emotional, service, social, and economic supports flowing down in early years and flowing up as the mother got older and in more need. Most American women, however, are not extremely needy most of their lives, so the myth of total dependence on the daughter is simply that—a myth that exaggerates the problems of some mother-daughter dyads throughout the relationship.

The effects of the death of a father on the social role of the mother depend on a number of factors, the most significant one being the importance of the father to the children and his contributions to the role of the mother. The ages of the children are also of significance, both in how they are affected and in how the children can help the mother deal with the problems produced by the death. Once children have reached adulthood, both the effects of the death and the relationships with the widowed mother become more stable. The difference in such relationships by the gender of the offspring become apparent in support exchanges in adulthood when neither generation is heavily dependent on the other and again much later when the mother becomes frail and needs increased support. The shift of the responsibility for the care of the mother from the son, as typical of heavily patriarchal family systems, to the daughter, apparent in modern America, reflects changes in the whole configuration of the family. Daughters, and daughters-in-law when the son has the main responsibility, tend to take on the personal care of the elderly widowed mother, the instrumental and more distanced support coming from the son. Sons-in-law are not reported as providers of supports as frequently as daughters-in-law.

Whenever she can, a widowed mother generally prefers to live in her own home than to move in with a daughter and especially a son and their families. Two sets of factors appear to influence this situation: the wish for, and ability to maintain, independence on the part of the mother and the worry over possible conflict and undesired work. Of course, studies of widowed mothers usually present only her perception or definition of the situation. It is possible that the children do not want the mother living with them and indicate this in a variety of more or less subtle ways, picked up by the parent. Whatever relationship develops between the mother and each of her children, the fact of widowhood is constantly present if the father had been active in the family unit.

Despite the prevalent myth as to the return of siblings to their alleged closeness in childhood, very few American widows develop extensive support networks with a sister, let alone a brother. Many factors contribute to the failure to use siblings, especially in cases in which children are available for support. One may be the lack of closeness in childhood, another the emotional, lifestyle, and geographical dispersal of the family of orientation in adulthood. More stable communities, in terms of mobility, provide evidence of viability of some sibling networks, but this is not a frequent situation. Involvement in other kinship roles is often a matter of choice and availability on all sides.

Notes

1. Here, an interesting insight comes from the actual language used by respondents. Traditional wives or mothers often speak of the *help* they get from others. That very word designates the woman as the main person responsible for the task, with some form of negotiation with others resulting in offered, willing, or passively resisting help. This is a source of intergenerational and marital conflict when it comes to instrumental tasks such as housekeeping or care of children. An excellent analysis of how all this takes place is contained in Hochschild's (1989) *The Second Shift*.

2. The unwillingness of male family members to be interviewed was also recorded by Cherlin and Furstenberg (1986). They concluded that one reason for the difficulties they had in getting a grandfather sample reflected "the greater reluctance of grandfathers to talk about their family lives" (p. 127).

3. One of the obligations of a wife carried into widowhood is to preserve, sometimes even sanctify, the deceased husband. This can continue a problem in the widow's relations with the mother, if the latter did not, and still does not, like or approve of the late husband.

7

Friendship in Widowhood

> Myth: "With respect to the elderly, the popular view is that widow-hood limits people's involvement with their friends" (Allan & Adams, 1989, p. 54).
> Myth: Courtship among the elderly moves at a slower pace than among the young.

American society has developed a romanticized image of friendship that appears to be almost impossible to achieve for most people in most situations. The perfect friend, portrayed in song and story, film, and television, is available when needed, pushing other relations into the background; willing to make sacrifices (the shirt off the back, blood for transfusion); supportive of tender egos; a confidant who respects privacy (Lopata, 1990). Fascinated by this image, a number of us sociologists decided at one time to focus on friendships in different contexts, in the military, in the clergy, on a kibbutz, and so forth (see Lopata & Maines, 1990). Interestingly enough, each chapter in our *Friendship in Context* began with this statement: "One would think that this situation (or setting) would be perfect for the formation and maintenance of friendship, but . . .". We then described all the constraints preventing the ideal friendship from developing. When it really comes down to everyday life, Americans consider other roles—wife or husband, mother or father, occupation, or even volunteer—to be more important than that of friend (Daniels, 1988). Young people are allegedly free to put friendship in the center in their role cluster—

but in many cases, only if it does not interfere with success in the role of student.

Friendship must be handled with care and constraint in situations in which undertones of sexuality, heterosexual or homosexual, could lead to inappropriate behavior. Friendship is not supposed to create conflict in a marriage or impinge on relations with one's children. Adults busy with multiple roles often believe that retirement or old age in general can open possibilities for completely supportive friendships. In such a portrayal, widowhood, especially in older age, would be an ideal ground for the development or vitalization of such relationships. The marital partner is dead, children have created their own families and lifestyles, and occupational commitment, if ever strong, peaked a long time ago. On the other side of friendship expectations is the disengagement theory that posits that, as people age, they and society (other people and groups) gradually withdraw from each other until the final break with death. The actual situation, however, is not as simple as either extreme holds.

One of the problems of studying the complications of friendship is that it means different things to different people. David Maines and I (Lopata & Maines, 1990) decided not to define this relationship for our respondents or authors, and most other social scientists who have studied friendship also allow the respondents or subjects to provide their own meanings (Adams & Blieszner, 1989). People have no trouble doing this, although their responses vary considerably by gender; ethnic, racial, and religious identities; age; and involvement in other social roles. There appear to be strong cultural differences not only in the definition of friendship and its components but also in the importance assigned to it in people's lives. For example, Latin American men seem to attach great importance to friendships (De Hoyos & De Hoyos, 1966; Sanchez-Ayendez, 1988), whereas North American men allegedly do not develop or even desire the emotionally involving confidant type of friendship (Adams, 1989; Bell, 1981; Nardi, 1992; Rubin, 1985; Wright, 1989; see also Kimmel & Messner, 1995).

Analysts of this social role point to friendship's many emotional, sentimental, and behavioral components. The components are both expressive and instrumental, forming emotional, social, service, and even economic support systems within dyadic or even network friendships. Such networks vary in their size and duration as well as in their individual relationships. Friendships do not exist in a vacuum but are lodged in specific contexts and settings. They are limited by these boundaries, although they can be transferred from one locale to another. For example, friendships on the job can be limited to such a setting or carried into leisure time activities. Individual friendships can remain independent of marital roles or be converted into couple-based friendships. These must then be transformed if the people involved are no longer coupled. Most of this chapter deals with the friendships that people bring to marriage, the development of couple-involving friendships in marriage, what happens to them after the death of the spouse, and the creation of new friendships in widowhood. The latter section of the chapter deals with cross-gender friendship, romantic relationships, and remarriage. I will limit the discussion of couple-companionate friendship to the middle class, because working- and lower-class Americans seem to confine themselves to relations with kin rather than with nonfamily "outsiders" (Bell, 1981; Komarovsky, 1967; Lopata, 1979; Rubin, 1985). There is less of a geographical scatter among such families, making members available for supports (Aulette, 1994; see also Bott, 1957, for the initial statement of this pattern). In addition, there is less companionship between men and women in lower-class families (Komarovsky, 1967).

An interesting aspect of the American scene commented on in cross-cultural studies of friendship is the very high rate of mobility, both social and geographic, of much of the population (Allan, 1979). Such mobility makes difficult the maintenance of contact with family and of lifelong friends. Middle- and upper-class women and men have developed norms of companionate relations that can be transferred from one location to another. Such members of societies are also likely to associate with different kinds of friends (Gouldner & Strong, 1987).

> They need long-term friends to oversee those activities associated with roles that tend to be stable over a lifetime, such as ethnic and religious ones, as well as those activities based on their early years that they seek to preserve. They need intermediate-term friends to manage activities associated with slowly changing roles, such as occupational changes, marital shifts, residential moves, and alterations in parental roles. Finally, they need short-term friends to deal with immediate and rapid changes in roles, such as those associated with being a newcomer in a retirement community, activities during a vacation trip, or peer interactions in a nursing home. (Litwak, 1989, p. 66)

Recognition of the geographical and social mobility of Americans by entrepreneurs and voluntary groups has resulted in the creation of multiple resources for the development of friendships at any level, especially of the intermediate and short-term kind (Allan & Adams, 1989; Litwak, 1989; Lopata, 1990). Whole books on etiquette, Dale Carnegie's (1936) much reprinted *How to Win Friends and Influence People,* and many kinds of courses teach people the "social graces" and accompanying skills of companionate eating, conversation, dressing for different occasions, entertaining and being a guest, and engagement in different sports and games. The increase in leisure time for many people and the shift from the Protestant work ethic, which approved of "recreation" only to re-create energies for the next day's work, to a positive evaluation of nonwork activities have contributed to an emphasis on friendship in the past century or so (Dulles, 1965). An additional factor is the democratic ideology of human choice. For Americans influenced by all these factors, achieved friendships are above relationships that have a flavor of obligation, such as family (Adams, 1968; Aulette, 1994). It is interesting that Americans often make a clear distinction between kinship and friendship, sometimes simply by stating that a relative (e.g., sister) is also one's best friend (Bell, 1981). Part of the reason friends are favored among the middle class is their symmetrical nature. Kin relationships tend to have a past or future history of asymmetry as they go through the life course of dependencies. Finally, social mobility of an uneven rate among family members or old school friends and neighbors increases diversification of lifestyles, values, and attitudes. One of the main conclusions concerning friendship is the similarity of basic orientations, made more likely in modern societies to occur among occupational, social class, and interest group members than within families of adults. The diminishing of significance of kinship relations appears less frequent among the two extremes of upper and lower classes (see Chapter 5; Adams, 1989; Gouldner & Strong, 1987; Lopata, 1990; see also various chapters in Lopata & Maines, 1990).

There are great variations in the development, forms, and depth of friendships. For a variety of reasons, cross-gender friendships appear to be more prevalent among the young than among older people unless they are part of couple-companionate relations (Litwak, 1989; Wright, 1989, p. 203). Working- and lower-class people have fewer and more setting-limited friendships than do middle-class people whose relationships "flower out" from their original meeting locale, so defined by Allan (1979, pp. 58, 70). As we shall also see, when analyzing problems with married friends in widowhood, there is a great deal of difference between what Kurth (1970) calls "friendly" relationships and friendships.

Friendships of Married Americans

Entrance into the role of wife requires a reconstruction of reality, as discussed in Chapter 3. Such reconstruction is more typical of middle-class couples than of their lower-class counterparts, and I believe that wives undertake it more extensively than do husbands, even in modern times when women have other major involvements and multidimensional life spaces (Lopata, 1993b, 1994a). In addition, entrance into the role of wife or husband modifies relationships within all other social roles that are affected by this change in marital status, including in friendships. Of course, some relationships, such as those formed through one's occupational role, may require little change after marriage. As Rubin (1985) so perceptively notes, "The friendships we form separate from the couple, then, remind us of our own identity, enabling us to retain the 'I' without getting lost in the 'we' " (p. 134).

When asked to name their best friends, most American couples will list couples with whom they share leisure hours. This form of companionate interaction, so typical of modern, middle- and upper-class relationships, I have labeled *couple-companionate friendship*. Znaniecki (1965) defined relationships of polite companionship "as culturally patterned relations between individuals who carry on social intercourse regularly for the purpose of common enjoyment" (p. 172). Rules of conduct and propriety establish the boundaries of behavior and sentiments appropriate to different kinds of social relationships (Denzin, 1970), including those that transform casual relationships into friendships (Suttles, 1970).

Limiting ourselves now to the discussion of friendships of partners in marriage, we can find great variations in the sources of such relationships and how they involve each partner. A husband and a wife can have separate friends. Either one of them can convert prior or independently developed friendships into couple-companionate ones with more or less symmetry of emotional, sentimental, and behavioral involvements. Of course, this requires the cooperation of the spouse and of the friends. Kin network members, school friends, or those made in any role interactions of either husband or wife can thus be converted into couple friends. A couple can also decrease the significance of prior connections and form only new ones as a couple. It is usually necessary, however, to move away geographically from locales affiliated with such associates to distance them socially and emotionally.

There are usually some problems with converting into a symmetrical arrangement relationships to which one marital partner was previously close, but many couples really try to do so. As stated earlier, most studies of marital couples point to the social class differences in the combinations of sources and closeness of friendships of a couple and to the fact that family-based primary relationships are harder to make symmetrical than are friendship ones. Yet transitional, and certainly the modern, married couples try to develop companionship in the marriage, which leads to a desire for couple-companionate friendship (Aulette, 1994; Lopata, 1975a).

Problems With Old Friends in Widowhood

Many problems may begin to occur in previously formed friendships following widowhood. The death of the husband can certainly be counted as one of the "disruptive external events" (Rook, 1989, p. 179) that affect all relationships, even ones that were not deeply involving. Many people avoid all connection with death and thus with people involved directly in it (Caine, 1974; Glick et al., 1974). Others handle interaction with the bereaved so awkwardly as to cause a decrease in future contact. Widowhood changes many aspects of life, decreasing similarity with persons who are not in that marital situation (Blau, 1961). Loss of income makes much socializing difficult, if not impossible. Clubs and hobbies may be dropped, residence changed, or a time-consuming job taken on. Face-to-face contact, so necessary in more casual friendly relations, may be made difficult. In addition, the widow's emotions may be so altered by widowhood as to make former close associates uncomfortable (see Rook, 1989, p. 170). Norms of symmetry and sharing that were developed and successful in the past may no longer work. Friends of recently widowed women are put off by the repetitious life review and husband sanctification. They have their own problems and resent the widow's constant imposition of hers. The relationship no longer remains symmetrical in give-and-take manner.

The original lines of connection between each marital partner and other people, including couple friends, that were developed after marriage become apparent in widowhood. One of the major problems of widows is the clarity with which the death of their husbands brings out loyalties and commitments in friendship. Autobiographical accounts and in-depth research of women as they enter widowhood abound with stories of strain, conflict, and even complete disintegration of prior friendships (Caine, 1974; Lopata, 1973d, 1979; van den Hoonaard, 1993, 1994).

Many of the widows I interviewed in the Chicago metropolitan area were appalled over being dropped by the late husband's former associates, let alone by couples they considered to be in symmetrical relations. One told of finding out after the event about a dinner party to which she would have been invited with her husband. Another arrived at a "gala" of an organization in which she and her husband had been active members, often sitting at the head table, to find herself placed not with friends but at a table with other widows. The realization that she was no longer important to the social circle because her husband was dead had two components: (a) that she was only peripheral to the relationships in the past and (b) that she no longer counted as a person.

Van den Hoonaard (1993, p. 14) quotes many women authors of autobiographical accounts of becoming widowed and problems in relations with couples they had considered their friends. Caine (1974) details at length such situations for a widow:

> There comes a time when she discovers that she is ostracized by our couple-oriented society. When she is yearning for comfort, for companionship, to be included in the world of families where she used to belong so naturally, then she finds that she has been excluded from most of the intimacies of her old friends, the social life she used to take for granted. (p. 141)

Both the depth of disappointment in relations with married friends and the fact that new constraints appear in these may be partially explained by the confusion to which Kurth (1970) drew our attention between friendly relations and friendships. As stated before, American society has developed, or borrowed from countries of origin, the norms of polite companionship that make possible pleasurable interaction (Suttles, 1970; Znaniecki, 1965). These are woven into social exchanges typical of couple-companionate relations. Many people appear to identify these as the same as friendships rather than just "friendly" relations. The depth of involvement is actually confused, in that friendly relations lack "the sense of uniqueness," level of intimacy, affection and related sentiments, and feeling of obligation characteristic of real friendship (see Kurth, 1970, pp. 138-142). Thus, widows may expect all the feelings of friendship, including that of obligation, to have existed in their couple-companionate relationships when they in fact did not reach that depth of commitment. The widows then become disillusioned when the relationship does not result in highly supportive behavior from these friends while they themselves go through the role of widow and emerge as a partnerless person. If, however, the couple-companionate relationship had been only that, a friendly one, then it lacks the complicated foundation and depth of friendship to carry it through one partner's hard times. Once the base of pleasurable activity is made difficult or even awkward, the relationship is dropped, more or less subtly.

Many situations can create awkwardness. For example, married friends of recent widow explained to me that it was hard to include her in a dinner party because everything is organized in pairs. This is especially true if the hostess cannot match her friend with another person, either because of the recency of the widowhood or because of refusal on the part of the widow to be matched. Then there is the problem of transportation if the widow cannot, or will not, drive. Someone coming to the party has to pick her up, or the host must leave to get her instead of helping in the preparations for the party. Returning the friend back to her home, if at a distance, can create new problems.

Going out with a widowed woman friend presents other problems to couples. Men in this society, especially but not exclusively those of older cohorts, are accustomed to paying the bills for any social event, including restaurant meals. Husbands often resent having to pay for someone other than a member of their family, yet they are embarrassed if the single woman insists on giving them money for her part or asks for a separate check. Even the separate check solution is sometimes impossible if the restaurant does not have such a policy.

Friendships that were not based on couple-companionate relationships can also be strained by widowhood. Caine (1974) and other women who have written of their experiences in becoming widowed often comment on the negative images of themselves emanating from friends. The term *widow* when used by still-married others can somehow appear to imply incompetence.

Wiseman (1986) notes that strains can develop in friendships with "the violation of taken-for-granted personality and/or character traits" (p. 197). Such personal relationships depend on the acceptance of the other as known, with traits important to oneself accepted and traits annoying to the other ignored. Women change in widowhood, and they may modify friendship-based, taken-for-granted behavior, even replacing it with objectionable actions. The widowed friend may not wish to engage in certain activities shared in the past. Her grief and husband sanctification may antagonize the former friend. The two women no longer have a common base of interest or meet in the same set of circumstances as before. They move apart as the widowed friend moves into a new cultural milieu. Another problem may arise if the widowed friend demands more support than the other can offer or does not reciprocate when the partner is in need. Friendship culture, according to Wiseman (1986, p. 203), involves an unwritten contract that is broken when the symmetry of benefits and costs becomes skewed.

On the other hand, same-gender friendships that were reconstructed and readjusted after the marriage of one friend may be able to again adjust to changes brought about by widowhood without too much strain. This is particularly true if marital status was external to bonds of common interest.

The Development of New Friendships

There are still many Americans—especially widowed women of the older cohorts—not socialized into the modern, urbanized, industrial life who consider only family or childhood friends as resources for personal relationships. Most people in more modernized societies, however, know that there are procedures for the development of friendships (Allan, 1979; Gouldner & Strong, 1987; Lopata, 1990).

As stated at the beginning of this chapter, the willingness to make friends and the knowledge of the procedures and rules of relevance have expanded in modern, mobile, urban, and non-kinship-restricted people. Converting acquaintances into friends varies considerably by social class. Working-class women whom I (Lopata, 1971a) initially studied in Chicago and its suburbs, as well as those studied by Berger (1960) in a working-class suburb in California, were very limited in their friendships. The same pattern emerged in my different studies of widowhood. One woman, a widow of a minister, explained to me all the steps she took when she moved from the home of one of her seven children to that of another. Other widows simply agreed with the statement that "your relatives are your only true friends" (Lopata, 1973d). Allan (1979) concluded that middle-class women in England were also able to "make friends," the relationship "flowering out" (p. 58) from one setting to another. Working-class people tended to restrict friendly relations to one setting, usually considering their homes as off-limits to nonrelatives. Working-class Chicago-area widows, similar to people of the same stratum in England, did not "entertain," the very concept of invitational exchanges being foreign to them (p. 75). Such organized events were typical of more educated women (see Lopata, 1979, p. 84).

The process of conversion of strangers into friends depends first of all on people becoming acquainted in some sort of setting (Jacobs & Vinick, 1979). There are settings especially formed for such purposes, such as clubs, bars, sports or other centers, the homes or other locales of friends, and so forth. Friendships are reportedly now being formed through the Internet. All sorts of settings in which people meet for a variety of reasons also can provide opportunities for making friends. Joining clubs or going to places in which there is a possibility of meeting potential friends, especially in a new community, is typical of middle-class women (Booth & Hess, 1974; Hess, 1972). Their working-class counterparts are usually limited to the church as a source of contact. Such interaction then remains within that setting for working-class women, whereas middle-class women tend to expand it into social events in restaurants or homes.

In fact, being thrown together can create a fusion between a social role and friendship relations, either complementary to the performance of that role or in competition to it (Hess, 1972). That is, the friendship can help each, or at least one, friend in carrying forth role rights and duties, or it can compete with such obligations. Most studies find that people who identify each other as friends tend to be similar in that they share similar feelings and behavior. Physical proximity with people of the same race, ethnicity, or age makes possible testing "at a distance" without intensive decision making in early stages of the relationship (Hochschild, 1973). Initial positive reactions to meeting others can be of dislike, disregard, or liking. My original study of older widows in the Chicago metropolitan area found greater religious and nationality heterogeneity than expected (see Lopata, 1973d, p. 186). Only about one fifth of the respondents claimed that *all* their friends were of the same religion, and only a few more said that all were of the same nationality. At the same time, two fifths stated that *most* of their friends were of the same religion, and one fifth said that most were of the same nationality (see Lopata, 1973d, pp. 185-186). This, however, left over two fifths of the friends being of a different religion and three fifths being of a different nationality. This is in Chicago, a city with numerous almost self-contained ethnic communities in which many of the older widows were brought up.

Given an initial possibility for friendly relations among people in contact, any potential friend can initiate or accept initiation by others of greater opportunities for interaction in the future. This is not apt to happen in cross-gender contact unless there is a sexual or at least a romantic element involved (Booth & Hess, 1974; Wright, 1989). In fact, initial contact between a widow and a married woman is not apt to develop into sociable interaction with that woman and her husband, but if expanded past the initial locale, the relationship tends to remain gender segregated. Increased face-to-face contact can increase awareness of similarities (see Adams & Blieszner, 1989; Bell, 1981). According to Jackson and Crane (1986), however, contact is not enough to offset prejudice of any segment of the population. I do not know of studies of same- or cross-gender friendship among widows in America that cross racial lines. Of course, that may be because the high rate of racial segregation offers few opportunities for repeated contact in pleasant circumstances. Research in integrated senior centers or nursing homes may bring forth new data on cross-racial friendship.

Friendships vary in the time they take to develop and in the complexity of emotions they combine, partly in response to starting and developing skills on both sides (Gouldner & Strong, 1987). They also vary by the setting in which they are located. Friendships differ socially in how they are embedded in other relationships and personally in how deeply they involve the individual personalities and life spaces. Compartmentalization of modern life through the separation of institutional spheres may constrain friendship to a particular role or pervasive identity, in that the total personality is not shared. At any rate, friendships must be maintained through continued efforts at symmetry.

The same factors that make relations problematic between a married woman and her widowed friend can restrict or reverse the formation of new dyads or networks. According to exchange theory, the costs of maintaining such relationships cannot outweigh by far the benefits. "Studies of late-life friendship dissolution reveal that older persons rarely report actively ending friendships. Instead, they attribute their loss to external causes . . . diverging life-styles and pathways" (Blieszner, 1989, p. 121). Of course, friendships developed in widowhood among either very young or much older women may simply lack extensive side bets of commitment, which are present in long-term relationships sustained by many emotions and surrounding relations (Litwak, 1989; Lopata, 1994a).[1] Even the norms of polite social interaction can create barriers that are difficult to cross for the development of more meaningful relationships (Johnson & Troll, 1994; Kurth, 1970). Often, it is difficult to determine if the other person is simply being polite or is sincere in the attempt to deepen the interaction. Norms of propriety can discourage personal disclosure or expressions of even positive sentiments. Violation of such rules of conduct can repel others.

Jerrome (1981) found older respondents joining clubs and recreational associations and converting neighbors or ex-colleagues into resources for friendship foundation. Those who scored high on the role-of-friend scale tend to have been widowed a relatively short time (1 to 4 years), to have had some college education, to have a Protestant rather than a Catholic background, to have comfortable finances, and to have adequate health. They were likely to have been married to managers, salesmen, or service workers (several of whom were African American with higher education). An isolation scale, built from a number of aspects of social relationships, was statistically associated with a lack of friendship. In other words, there were no substitutes for friends in the support systems of such women (Lopata, 1975a).

The support systems study of Chicago-area widows found some women who claimed not to have had any friendships before the husband took ill and not to have any at the time of the interview (see Lopata, 1979, p. 211). One type of such a woman was family oriented and did not trust "strangers." A second type simply lacked the skills necessary for the development of close relationships. She considered herself surrounded by constraints (Blau, 1961). A third kind of widow held idealized images of friendship and experienced disappointments in the past, so she had ceased trying to develop intimate interaction. Although forming only 16% of the sample, all three types of widowed women were apt to be at the bottom of the socioeconomic ladder, based on education and total family income when the husband was well and at the time of the interview. The women themselves had been in lower-paying and low-prestige occupations, had been full-time housewives, or both.

Friends as Providers of Support in Widowhood

Elizabeth Bankoff (1990) studied the contributions of three subsets of a widow's friendship network—married friends, widowed or single friends, and neighborhood friends—on the well-being of women in the early and later phases of widowhood. Early widowhood was named the *crisis loss phase,* and the sample consisted of women widowed 18 months or less who reported themselves as still in intense grief (p. 116). Women in the *transition phase* had been widowed for more than 2 years, and although still feeling grief, they reported it at a lower level than in the past. The two groups were similar on basic background characteristics.

> Our data suggest that whether or not friendship support helps, hurts, or is inconsequential for the well-being of widows during their long process of adjustment depends on at least three factors: the problems and adjustment tasks currently faced by the widow, the specific type of support provided, and the source of that support. (p. 134)

During the crisis loss phase, the widow needed "social companionship and assurance of emergency assistance" (p. 120) from the total friendship network, but she needed intimacy support only from married friends. She needed to unburden her problems to such friends, whereas talking with her single or neighborhood friends made little difference. Bankoff speculated that only a widow's long-term friends, who know her well and who are likely to be her married friends, can provide emotional support when the pain of losing the husband is still fresh.

On the other hand, nonmarried and neighborhood friends contributed most to the woman's well-being by comforting her and providing guidance about how to handle specific problems of widowhood.

A change in the friendship needs of Bankoff's (1990) respondents occurred later in widowhood. The support supplied by married friends became dysfunctional in the transition phase when the woman was trying to build a new life for herself. It was then that the guidance of widowed friends contributed most to a widow's welfare. She needed new ways of organizing her life, and unmarried friends could help guide her in this direction, whereas married friends held her back to the past. The study found that widows who continued to confide in their married friends were worse off than those who turned their attention to nonmarried ones. As the new widow changed in life situation and interests, the bond she previously had with married friends decreased in importance and even hindered her development.

The importance of neighborhood friends also varied in time. They were much more important during the transitional phase than in the prior phase because they contributed emergency assistance and the security of knowing of its availability. Although the researcher did not have an explanation for this, neighborhood friends also provided guidance in the solution of problems and even emotional support as the widow moved out of heavy grief and into attempts at a new life. The main reason given for the importance of neighborhood friends is the decrease of attention from other friends quite early in widowhood. Neighbors remained as an emergency resource while the widow, less burdened by grief, moved to solve day-to-day problems (see Bankoff, 1990, p. 133). Those neighbors who were also widowed may have simultaneously been the main suppliers of emotional support, whereas married friends faded into the background.

The interviewers of the study of the Chicago-area women who had been widowed for varying lengths of time asked for specific areas in which friends appeared in the support systems. Few of the widows obtained economic supports from personal associates, and people who were identified as friends simply did not enter such supports as givers or receivers. The friends who exchanged service supports were most apt to provide or receive help in transportation and shopping (see Lopata, 1979, pp. 80-81). In fact, many more widows claimed to help their friends in these supports than receive such supports (18% vs. 39% of listings in transportation; 12% vs. 34% in shopping). The respondents were also much more likely to consider themselves as givers than as receivers of advice and "legal aid" to friends. Friends appeared most often in the social support system. In fact, one can easily conclude that the main contribution of friendship in widowhood is social in nature rather than service oriented or even emotional. If women undertake such activities at all, they are apt to go to public places, visit and entertain, eat lunch, or play games with friends. The respondents listed at least one friend as a companion in such socializing. On the other hand, few widows traveled out of town or celebrated holidays with friends, children being the main participants in such activities. The more education, middle-class lifestyle, and good health a woman had, the more likely she was to share social supports with friends and the more likely to have a multidimensional support network in general.

The contributions of friends to a widowed woman's emotional support system varied considerably but increased dramatically from the reported time "before your husband's last illness or accident." The husband was remembered through the prism of the idealized past as the main contributor to most sentimental and self-feeling supports, although much of the sociological and sociopsychological literature concludes that women's emotional support comes from other women. The husband is more apt to list the wife as the main supporter, usually because he lacks intimate male friends, but the wife of a living husband usually lists another woman (Bell, 1981; Rubin, 1985; Wright, 1989). A dead husband, however, was remembered by the Chicago-area widows as the person to whom she felt closest, enjoyed the most, turned to in times of crisis, and told her problems and from whom she obtained comfort. He was practically the only person who made her feel important, respected, useful, secure, accepted, and much less frequently, independent and self-sufficient. Even in these parts of the emotional support system, 40% of the references were to the late husband. The children were surprisingly infrequently listed as main contributors. Only 23% of the women listed the late husband first as the person who made them angry. Here, again, we must assume that the sanctification process is operating, in that assumably more wives of a living husband would claim that he made them angry most often.

The situation was quite different at the time of the interview. The late husband was replaced mainly by the children as primary providers of emotional supports. Friends did appear but not as often as we assumed on the basis of literature on friendship. That is, friends appeared as one of the first three persons to whom the widow felt closest in only 10% of the listings. Only 16% of the widows listed a friend as the person with whom they most enjoyed being, 12% as the confidant, and 11% as the comforter. The highest frequency with which friends appeared in the emotional support system was as the person who most often made the respondent feel accepted (19%). Thus, enjoyment of being with a person and feeling accepted by the other did not lead to deeper sentiments or self-feelings. Of course, as I noted elsewhere (see Lopata, 1979, p. 223), it is possible that the respondents felt obligated to list their children as the main contributors, thus pushing friends and other relations out of the picture.

Cross-Gender Friendships

As mentioned before, studies of friendship have concluded that such relationships are most likely to develop among people who have many things in common and who are in contact often enough to discover these commonalities (Lopata, 1990). This also applies to cross-gender friendships. The contact can be direct, face-to-face, or indirect (as through correspondence, evidenced by numerous exchanges of letters between famous friends). Human history is replete with cross-gender friendships and friendly relations. The American ideology of the two-sphere world, however, assumes that men and women have little in common except sex, procreation, and family maintenance. Such an ideology ignores the realities of modern societies in which men and women share schooling, occupational involvement, recreation, religion, political activity—participation in all the institutions of life. Of course, there are many pockets of two-sphere gender segregation (in many jobs, organizations, and political activity) in America as well as in other allegedly developed societies. Internal variations abound. For example, the lower the social class in America and England, the more isolated are the social worlds of men and women, even if they are in physical contact in the family (Bell, 1981; Booth & Hess, 1974; Bott, 1957). One can hypothesize that the greater the ideological, psychological, and behavioral isolation of the genders from each other, the greater will be the emphasis on sex, with its various ramifications, as the main bond between them. In such situations, cross-gender friendship is very difficult because each encounter is dominated by sexual concerns. The greater the emphasis on sex, the greater the societal barriers against barrier-free, extensive contact between men and women judged as inappropriate partners for sexual involvement. Although this has certainly varied by time and place, this would include members of families covered by the incest taboo, people judged already monogamously involved, members of different racial or religious groups, and so forth. Visible symbols, such as a nun's habit, priest's clerical garb, or a wedding ring, can alert others that a person is allegedly unavailable for sexual encounters.

Usually, organizations discourage romance among members if other goals are paramount, because primary relations are considered destructive, or at least distracting, to the main functions. Whole sets of norms and policies are designed to make irrelevant the sexual characteristics of people in frequent contact in roles having something other than sexuality as their main function. Pervasive gender identity has many aspects, and its sexual component can be pushed into the background. Colleagues, bosses and employees, leaders and followers, and many other role partners in modernizing or modern societies are expected to leave out romantic or other sexual components. The fact that the sexual aspect of human interaction can still create problems in such settings is documented by the numerous attempts to control what is now defined as "sexual harassment."

Whether a woman or a man is married or not is supposedly irrelevant in the formation and maintenance of cross-gender friendships. Vestiges of the two-sphere world again appear, however, when there is some hesitation concerning such close relationships for married people unless both are part of a couple-companionate foursome or a larger social network.

> Studies to date have indicated that cross-gender friendships occur more frequently among single adults than any other group. . . . Marriage in and of itself seems to have the effect of reducing the number of cross-gender friendships of both women and men. . . . Cross-gender friendships among the elderly are rare. (Wright, 1989, pp. 209-210, 215)

The relationship between age and the scarcity of cross-gender friendships—older people having fewer—is particularly true of women, according to Booth and Hess (1974). Of course, there are also fewer men with whom friendships can be developed. Despite the prevalence of the stereotype, supported by some research, concerning the impossibility of cross-gender friendships, several studies show that it is the lack of opportunities for meeting members of the other gender rather than other factors that contribute to their infrequency. Bell's (1981, p. 99) respondents felt that cross-gender friendships had a different quality than did same-gender ones, especially along the self-disclosure dimension. Men reported many more opportunities for meeting women who became friends than did women, especially full-time homemakers who did not participate in mixed-gender organizations. O'Connor (1993) studied both same-gender and cross-gender friendships among the elderly aged 70 and over who were Social Service Department clients in England and found that the majority of cross-gender dyads involved two elderly people rather than age-divergent couples. Some of these lasted for years and could be traced to prior couple-companionate relationship; to current sharing of lodging, as in a retirement hotel; or to being old neighbors. He identified these as "pseudospousal, typically lacking a sexual component and not being the main source of practical care" (p. 27). They involved a wide range of helping behaviors and provided feelings of security, closeness, being cared for, and pleasure. Platonic interaction sometimes included quite personal services.

Romantic Relationships

Many myths and even social science studies send contradictory messages concerning a widow's sexuality. Of course, these vary considerably by the age of the woman. Younger widows who had developed sexual intimacy in marriage are assumed to become sexually frustrated with the serious illness and death of the husband. The sexuality of older widows draws even more convoluted assumptions: that their cohort was never really sexually oriented; that elderly people, especially elderly women, lose interest in sexual relationships; and, finally, that elderly (even maybe younger) widows are likely to feel relieved of the necessity to submit to their husbands' demands. On the other hand, there remains the image of the "merry widow" going to great lengths to attract men and the frequently expressed worry by married women concerning the possibility of sexual interaction between their husbands and widowed friends (see a complex analysis of this attitude in Lopata, 1973d).

Loss of affectional and sexual interaction is often mentioned by women following widowhood, and that was one of the main forms of loneliness expressed by the Chicago-area respondents (Lopata, 1969, 1979). Malatesta, Chambless, Pollack, and Cantor (1988) studied 100 relatively healthy, community-dwelling widows between the ages of 40 and 89 and concluded that "younger widows, when compared with their older counterparts, viewed changes in body image, the dearth of unattached men, and financial resources for social activities as representing significant sexual barriers" (p. 49).

One of the complications regarding the sexuality of widows, and of anyone for that matter, involves the definition of this emotional and biological involvement. The frequent assumption of Americans is that sexuality refers only to sexual intercourse. Malatesta et al. (1988), however, found that the widows were less unhappy over the loss of sexual intercourse than expected:

> For the sample as a whole, greater unhappiness was expressed with the loss of nonsexual, heterosexual activity (e.g., conversation with a man, going places with a man). Results also indicated that, regardless of her age, activities pertaining to her children and grandchildren, wearing attractive clothing, and expressing her spirituality are all effective in meeting affectional and sexual needs aspects of single life for not-so-young widowed women. (p. 49)

The desire and opportunity for the development of different forms of interaction with men depend on many factors. Even casual romantic or sexual relationships may be awkward after years of marriage and aging (McKaine, 1969; Nye & Berardo, 1973; Peterson & Payne, 1975). Whereas younger widows with small children often do not have the time to search for male companionship, older ones frequently find the "single's scene" difficult and feel either "horrified" or at least uncomfortable about the new norms of casual sex (Hite, 1987). They worry about the inadequacies of their bodies or sexual habits when compared with women in modern magazines or in dating situations. Finally, there is the problem of reputation (Chandler, 1991). Adams (1985) appropriately titled her article about cross-gender interaction "People Would Talk: Normative Barriers to Cross-Sex Friendships for Elderly Women."

The strong disapproval of sexuality, or even of romance, among the elderly defines it as strange, if not indecent, in this youth-oriented society. For example, studies of love in nursing homes point to the numerous barriers against the development of such feelings and behavior, especially the lack of privacy.[2]

Older widows were also apt to be unhappy over the absence of someone with whom to share responsibilities, in addition to sharing conversation and going to public places with a man. Younger women reported going out on a nonromantic date, going on a romantic date, and dancing as the activities that were most helpful in "satisfying a widow's affectional and sexual needs," whereas older widows enjoyed most being with children or grandchildren and doing crafts (see Malatesta et al., 1988, p. 58). Of course, part of the reason for such an age divergence and claimed disinterest in sexual intercourse may be the tendency to give age-appropriate responses by the elderly woman, but another part may be simply a lack of interest in more sexual activity. These researchers report that age, not length of widowhood, was the distinguishing factor in expressions of desire for heterosexual intimacy when income, education, heterosocial involvement, and family contact were controlled (p. 49). A lack of interest in sexual activity tends to accompany health problems, illness, and disability (see Rice, 1989a).

As Malatesta and associates (1988) point out, assumptions about the asexuality of the elderly, including elderly women, have been questioned in recent decades as a result of a number of studies. They quote Masters and Johnson that " 'significant sexual capacity and effective sexual performance are not confined to the human females premenopausal years' " (p. 50). Social gerontologists have increasingly become aware of sexual needs among the elderly so that there is more literature on the subject available for people to read, allegedly taking the subject "out of the closet." American society in general has recently "discovered" the cross-gender socializing needs of the single elderly, as evidenced in the proliferation of clubs, organizations, and programs directed toward them. Bulcroft and Bulcroft (1985) studied some of the couples who participated in a singles club in the Twin Cities in Minnesota and found that they depended on such groups or general-membership organizations rather than on informal resources of family and friends for introduction to prospective dating partners. Any social events that brought together people with similar backgrounds for a variety of companionate activities provided opportunities for repeated contact. The club they researched admitted people aged 40 and over. The couples' dating behavior reflected their cohort norms. Men were expected to pick up the women and pay the expenses, although long-term relationships varied the monetary arrangements.

The dating relationship, however, sometimes moved into cohabitation without marriage, for many practical and, possibly, psychological, reasons. It is still economically beneficial for people not to marry if each is receiving social security. Family wealth, even if minimal, does not have to be jeopardized without marriage. Variations on the cohabitation pattern included maintenance of two residences, "with the dating couple typically spending two to four nights per week together at one of the residences" (Bulcroft & Bulcroft, 1985, p. 121). Such an arrangement made each partner feel independent and able to maintain the appearance of singleness before family and friends. These relationships definitely had a sexual component, with the authors finding that intercourse was expected to take place by the fourth or fifth date. According to the authors, and in contrast to mythology, older dating relationships are developed at a more accelerated pace than is typical of younger couples (see Bulcroft & Bulcroft, 1985, p. 122). This is explained in terms of a sense of constricted life space —the partners are too worried about the amount of time they have for such relationships to be willing to play the usual courtship games, especially those they played when they were younger and the norms of dating were slower. Although the researchers expected one of the major motives for dating among the young, mate selection, not to be as important among older people, their study found it to be primary. Even the respondents who desired a new marital partner did not necessarily want to marry the person whom they were dating at the time of the study. They appeared to be waiting for a more perfect husband or wife. Of course, there were older people who had no desire for remarriage because they did not want to give up their independence and privacy. Nevertheless, they wished to continue having intimate relationships and active social lives. Women also felt that having a man interested in them was a source of prestige.

Cohabitation without marriage among the elderly appears in many communities. Chandler (1991), however, recommends in *Women Without Husbands* that partners draw up cohabitation contracts to protect their own assets, similar to remarriage prenuptial contracts. Peterson and Payne (1975) reported in *Love in the Later Years* that single elderly often actively seek love relationships or drift into them through a process of increased intimacy. They are not likely to enter "swinging" relationships or to find partners in cocktail lounges or single's bars; instead, they usually meet each other in community centers, clubs, or churches. Some social scientists, cognizant of the great disparity in the numbers of widows and widowers, have advised that they practice some form of polygamy. However, most American elderly are not prone to enter such relationships, having been socialized to, and having lived in, monogamy (see Peterson & Payne, 1975, p. 94).

Elderly singles appear to be much more tolerant of sexual involvements of their peers than the myths lead us to predict. Liberation seems to have trickled up in age cohorts. Sexual behavior among the elderly includes greater emphasis on touch and cuddling than is typical of the young. Of course, according to many magazine surveys of the American scene, even younger women prefer greater touching and tenderness to intercourse in their sexual activity. Advice books for widows often recommend less traditional means of satisfying emotional and sexual needs than remarriage. These include heterosexual cohabitation, including group sharing; stable adulterous and homosexual relations; casual encounters with members of both genders; and masturbation (Malatesta et al., 1988).

One problem with a widowed woman's development of new relationships with men is the attitude of her children. Younger children may resent outsider men to whom they are expected to relate coming to the home. Children of all ages may resent someone's taking the place of their father. On the other hand, the children can be happy not to have to worry about loneliness on the part of the widowed parent and to have that parent enjoying life (see Jacobs & Vinick, 1979, p. 186). Even friends who came on the scene when the woman was widowed may resent her movement back into the dating circles. All associates worry that the match may be disadvantageous to their own member of the family or friend.

> Some of the Chicago area widows report that their offspring resent any man who enters the house as a companion or potential marital partner of the mother. Respondents carefully explain that they would not subject their children to a stepfather or even to the presence of a male lover, others that their children made things so difficult when men came for dates that they ceased such activities. (Lopata, 1973d, p. 100)

There are great variations in widowed women's attitudes toward romantic and sexual relations. For example, 41% of the Chicago-area blacks and only 6% of the whites agree that "it is [all right] for a widow to have sexual relations with a man without planning on marriage." On the other hand, only 26% of the blacks and 20% of the whites agree that "I wish I had more male companionship" (p. 330).

Remarriage

As indicated at the beginning of this chapter, the assumption that the elderly take a long time in courtship is only a myth. Recent research indicates that courtship, movement into sexual interaction, and even marriage among the widowed take place at a much faster pace than among the young. "Most couples wasted little time getting married" (Jacobs & Vinick, 1979, p. 191). This is especially true of people who had already known each other, but even the newly met marry fast once they decide that the advantages outweigh any actual or potential problems. Many of the couples studied by Jacobs and Vinick had festive weddings, with parties for friends and relatives. A major decision faced by the remarrieds was the place of residence, made complicated in cases in which one or both lived in housing for the single or in quarters that were inadequate for two people.

The situation concerning the remarriage of widowed women in America is complicated not only in terms of the attitudes of others but also by demographic factors. Attitudes toward the remarriage of widows have varied considerably in time and place. Chandler (1991) found such a change in marital status by women in preindustrial Europe to be stigmatized by the church and communities. Basing her conclusions on the work of Aries (1981), she states that "remarriage was a denial of her chastity and constancy, qualities valued and extended to beyond her husband's death" (p. 154). The needs of families, especially those with children, however, often necessitated remarriage, which was much more common than culturally defined.

Although there are no strong sanctions against remarriage of widows in America, there appear to be some negative feelings about it in certain circles, often among primary associates. This society does not favor a levirate system, by which a male agnate of the deceased takes over some of the functions of the late husband, or automatic widow remarriage (see Chapter 1). The main problem for those American women who wish, or would not object to, remarriage lies in demographic facts.

> Even as late as the 1920s, brides and grooms who were remarrying were more likely to have been widowed than divorced. . . . By 1987, 91 percent of all brides and groups who were remarrying were previously divorced, and 9 percent were widowed. (Cherlin, 1992, p. 27)

Women outlive men so that the older the woman, the lower the statistical probability of finding an unmarried man. Widowers, rare as they are, tend to remarry very quickly. They are "on the market" for a very short time, but they also marry much younger women this time around. DiGiulio (1989, p. 130) reports that although 49% of widowed women remarry, the percentage decreases with age so that fewer than 5% of those who are older than 55 do so. DiGiulio found in his sample that only 40% of widowed women respondents "stated that they wanted to remarry, while 31 percent clearly said they did not" (p. 132). Those declaring unwillingness to remarry dropped from 80% of those under age 35 to 47% of those older than 55. His figures are high compared with those of other studies.

The advantages of remarriage offered to DiGiulio (1989) by the widows include counteraction to loneliness, security of a fulfilling relationship, love, financial and emotional support for women with young children, and even a new identity to offset the identity of widow. Younger widows frequently mention the importance of having a father, even if it is a stepfather, for the children (Lopata, 1979). Remarrieds of both genders, although especially the men, have longer and healthier life spans and higher morale (DiGiulio, 1989, p. 132). Most are also more apt to be above the poverty line and were less dependent on their children and other family members.

Widowed women in various studies, however, have explained many disadvantages to remarriage, some strong enough to prevent even its contemplation. Widowed mothers worry about subjecting their children to a stepfather who may not treat them well or who would go against the mother's method of raising children. Disapproval of remarriage by the children of all but the youngest age or of the potential husband and conflict with them over this may be a strong deterrent. Interestingly enough, such offspring are often reported as pleased if their father remarries, unless there is property involved, but they are usually against the remarriage of their mother. It is possible that they see a new wife as someone who will save them care of the father as he gets frail, whereas a new husband is perceived as someone who will require care by the mother, distracting her attention from them. In either case, children are often worried that the new community property laws will deprive them of their inheritance (see Chapter 4). Despite the negative, and even demeaning, attitudes toward romantic interaction and remarriage by the younger generation and the society in general, increasing attachment can lead to refusal to accept antiremarriage advice from children. There can also be a problem with stepchildren, not only in how the stepmother relates to them but also in how the reconstituted family works together.

Older women with either financial resources or home- and family-maintaining skills often worry about being taken advantage of (see Lopata, 1979, p. 148). Whole subcultures, such as that of the Polish Americans, contain warnings against remarriage (Lopata, 1977). Many widows also assume that any man not already involved in a romantic relationship or marriage may have habits that they would eventually find repulsive. This is particularly true of women who have sanctified their late husband and marriage. Taking care of another man, even in health, requires a great deal of work. Women widowed for several years may enjoy their independence and consider remarriage equivalent to losing it.

We asked the Chicago-area remarried women in the support systems study (Lopata, 1979) what advice they "would give to a widow about remarriage," including the steps to be taken to prevent problems. Some of the advice included the following:

- Be careful; there's a lot of jerks in the world; don't jump from the frying pan into the fire. There may be problems with families, if he was married before.
- Be sure their husband-to-be has a will made out; it would save a lot of problems if he has children. And, make sure he is in good health.
- Do not marry for children or family. Place high value on yourself. I don't think widows should try to be nuns because of widowhood as far as physical needs. (pp. 172-173)

Financial and legal advisers have recently stressed the importance of settling appropriate matters between a future bride and groom in a nonfirst marriage (Johnston, 1992; Savage, 1992). The anticipated problems that can be avoided through a prior agreement include not just major rights but also day-by-day details of life. Many responsibilities need to be specified, according to the experts, including child care, bill paying, ownership of major assets, and "prospective support agreements and division of assets if the marriage should fail" (Savage, 1992, p. 62). Each partner of an older-age remarriage comes into the relationship with assets and liabilities, such as debts, that need to be specified. Remarriage can affect tax filing, Social Security, and other pension rights. Where the couple lives is a major decision and must be considered with financial consequences in mind. For example,

> For older people who remarry, an important consideration may be the once-in-a-lifetime exclusion of $125,000 in capital gains tax on the sale of a personal residence. But the exclusion can be used only once by a married couple. So if each party to a marriage owns a residence, each should sell before the remarriage so the exclusion is not lost. (Savage, 1992, p. 62)

Remarriage can create inheritance problems for the children of each partner, who can make life miserable for the new couple if they fear loss of what they consider to be rightfully theirs. New health and life insurance policies may have to be planned to the best advantage of the couple. In fact, the advice for getting a formal prenuptial agreement is given in the mass media for all couples considering remarriage, not only for those with a great deal of wealth to settle.

There is reportedly a rather consistent explanation of remarriage given by women who have entered such a relationship or seriously considered it, and that is a wish for companionship. DiGiulio's (1989) respondents listed mutual love even more frequently, but the Chicago-area women, for example, stressed companionship above all else.

Bernard (1956) found five basic "sets of forces that help select those who remarry:

1. the desire to enter into such a relationship,
2. the absence of inhibiting influences,
3. the opportunity for meeting prospective intimates,
4. community and family pressures inhibiting or pushing a no longer married woman in that direction, and
5. all the personal qualities and nonpersonal factors that make one attractive to prospective mates." (p. 116)

Smith, Zick, and Duncan (1991) used a nationally representative sample of widows and widowers from the Panel Study of Income Dynamics and concluded that the main factor influencing the timing of remarriage, besides age and gender, was the duration of widowhood. Younger people remarried sooner, and men remarried sooner than women. Remarriage rates increased right after the "appropriate period of mourning" and decreased with time. They hypothesized that the decrease in the rate may be due to a decrease of interest as people learn to live satisfactorily as unmarrieds. Of course, it is also true that health and financial problems facing people as they grow older decrease interest in, and efforts at, remarriage.

Tucker and her associates (Tucker, Taylor, & Mitchell-Kerman, 1993, p. 125) obtained data on remarriage and romantic involvement of older African Americans who formed part of the National Survey of Black Americans conducted in 1979-1980. They found that most males were either married or in romantic relationships. Women wishing cross-gender intimacy, on the other hand, were faced with the lack of eligible marital partners throughout their lives. Furthermore, the black women were often reluctant to "become partnered with someone who would be a drain on their finances" (p. 128) or who would have to be taken care of through a major illness. The older the woman, the more likely it is that she will have to care for a new partner. It is interesting to note that higher-income black women were more apt to be involved in romantic relationships than to be remarried. The 10% or so of men not involved with a woman in older age were deemed by the women to be completely undesirable in that they lacked any material or personal resources or they were isolates. The authors predicted an even lower proportion of married older African American women of future cohorts because of the death rates of younger men and the recent decrease of marriage throughout the life course.

> Although most Black women will marry at some point in their lives, the overall proportion who ever marry could range as low as 70 percent or 80 percent. . . . Since Blacks in general now marry later, have higher rates of separation and divorce, and spend more time in separated and divorced statuses, it would appear that Black females as a whole will spend a greater part of their lives in an unmarried state. (Tucker et al., 1993, p. 130)

In addition, a larger proportion of black women will spend a greater proportion of their lives in widowhood. Both white and, to a lesser degree, black women tend to live alone by choice, and increasing numbers of them have the resources to do so. Cherlin (1992) concluded that "the growth of households that do not contain a married couple has far outstripped the growth of husband-wife households" (p. 69).

Gentry, Rosenman, and Shulman (1987) studied three groups of widows in the St. Louis area: those who stated that they had not considered remarriage, those who considered it but had not done so when interviewed, and those who had remarried. The first group was the oldest, being on average 59 years of age. Both those who considered remarriage and the ones who took the step averaged about 49 years of age. The remarrieds had the youngest children. Reasons given for at least considering remarriage included, primarily, love and companionship. Those who actually remarried also had considered this move to solve other problems, such as financial and child-rearing ones. In the long run, such people did not develop as satisfactory marriages as did people who gave love and companionship as main reasons. Over half of the remarrieds reported that they had experienced conflicts with children or other family members over the remarriage. Those who did not even consider remarriage enjoyed their independence and did not expect to find a good husband the second time around.

Based on an earlier pilot study of 90 widows, Gentry et al. (1987) developed a list of 23 need areas and administered the list to their three samples. The remarried widows reported the fewest areas of need, those who had not considered remarriage reported more, and those who considered it but had not gone through with it reported the most. Thus, remarriage appears to decrease the areas of need experienced by widows. The specific areas in which the remarrieds differed from the other two groups were loneliness, housing, home maintenance, and finances—they did not identify these as major needs (p. 165). This set of differences is not surprising, in view of the traditional supports of marriage. Those who had not remarried identified loneliness as the biggest problem. The remarrieds were significantly more concerned with problems with children, partially in consequence of their ages but also possibly because of stepparent relationships. The women who were not considering remarriage were also most apt to be worried about future plans and medical issues. All three groups, however, claimed the same amount of stress in their lives.

McKaine's (1969) *Retirement Marriage* involved in-depth interviews with 100 Connecticut couples in which the bride was at least 60 years of age and the groom at least 65. Both the man and the woman had been married before, and this marriage had lasted 5 years. One reason this study is interesting has to do with the traditional, conservative attitudes and feelings of the wife and the husband concerning all circumstances preceding and during the remarriage. The interviews took place in 1966, so they involved a cohort of the elderly that is less and less representative of the elderly of the 1990s. "Almost one half of the husbands and wives were born in a foreign country" (p. 15), many on farms or in peasant villages of Eastern Europe. In such villages, there existed a familistic culture and rigid norms of behavior that allowed men even violent behavior toward women (Thomas & Znaniecki, 1918-1920/1958). Both marital partners in Connecticut had very little formal education and had worked in low-status jobs, if employed, so they had low incomes in retirement. Nevertheless, "nearly three-fourths of the couples owned the house in which they lived" (McKaine, 1969, p. 18), and most were in relatively good health. Within the sample, educational level, health, and income influenced how active they were in the community and in contact with children. Three fourths attended church. McKaine (1969) was interested in the processes by which they ended up married, the quality of the marriage by the respondents' standards, and factors contributing to success measured by five sets of indexes observed by interviewers:

1. Signs of affection and respect during the interview
2. Obvious enjoyment of each other's company
3. The absence of serious complaints about each other
4. Signs of being proud of each other
5. Signs of consideration of each other

Unlike the couples studied by Peterson and Payne (1975), the Connecticut remarrieds did not mention prior cohabitation and rarely volunteered information about their sexual relationships. The problems they experienced with remarriage included feeling disloyal to the deceased spouse, negative pressure from family, and the perception that the remarriage was not generally approved. This is apparent from the fact that although they varied considerably as to courtship activities, most either kept the wedding plans a secret or had a very simple ceremony. Their traditional upbringing is also evident from the fact that they wanted a church ceremony or one at the home of a clergyman rather than going to a justice of the peace. Reasons for marriage were above all for companionship, but they also mentioned sex and the desire for security, to feel useful, and to be needed. Entrance into such a relationship decreased, for the most part, dependence on the children, and for some, it even provided a home. Some of the men appeared to marry to get a housekeeper and cook, whereas the women gained someone who could do the heavy work around the house. The respondents tended to marry people very much like themselves in social characteristics and used knowledge from what worked in the prior marriage to both evaluate prospective mates and work out living arrangements. Many of them had known each other for years; some were even related by marriage (see McKaine, 1969, p. 23). Many of the remarried women studied by Jacobs and Vinick (1979, p. 177) also knew the new husband in the past. Both belonged to the same friendship network while married and turned to each other in widowhood.

Successful remarriages among the Connecticut 1960s couples were most likely if they had known each other in the past, if the husband had more education than the wife, if the man were widowed less than 3 years, and if the woman were widowed either less than 3 years or 10 or more years (see McKaine, 1969, p. 53). Success was made easier if the remarriage involved housing other than that lived in by either spouse in his or her previous marriage, because of memories associated with such a dwelling and the tendency to compare home management patterns. Sufficient income to carry forth desired activities was also an important factor contributing to success in remarriage. In addition, couples who were involved in and shared a variety of activities had more successful marriages than those who were limited to one or two activities. Couples with traditional Eastern European backgrounds, especially on the part of the husband, fared much worse than did American-born couples, living as they did in a more egalitarian society that disapproves of some of the ways men treated women in the "old world."

Widowers in the McKaine (1969) study, and according to all American census data, remarried much faster than widows and married women even younger than the first time around. Part of the explanation for such differences lies in the demographic characteristics of the population (almost five widows for each widower). It is also possible that Jessie Bernard (1973) was right in contending that men gain much more from marriage than do women. Berardo (1970) found older rural widowers incapable of taking care of themselves and so lacking in social skills that they needed a wife. The need for the contributions of a wife to daily living also appears to be important for the Connecticut men. Younger generations of men have been socialized into, and are more involved in, activities of daily living than prior cohorts, so the reasons for men's remarriage may change over time. The increasing independence and economic resources of women may decrease their need for instrumental supports. In both cases, desire for companionship may remain as the main reason for remarriage. It may also lead to cohabitation or any other form of social contact without remarriage, especially in a society with much freer sexual and other relational norms.

One assumption frequently expressed about the remarriage of widows is the relation between happiness in the late marriage and the willingness to remarry. In actuality, the connection between satisfaction with a prior marriage and the desire to remarry is complicated. Only one fourth of the Chicago-area women who idealized their late husband and marriage wished to enter another marriage (Lopata, 1973d). In addition, many of the widows believed that remarriage does not bring happiness. Seventy-two percent of the blacks and 49% of the whites agreed with the statement that "many widows who remarry are very unhappy." The others were pleased with their independent state and so did not wish to reenter marriage. There was an interesting connection between a woman's defining her marriage to the late husband as above average and her unwillingness to consider remarriage. Widows who tended to idealize the late marriage felt that no other man could match the late husband: "You can't trust the men available for remarriage." "Remarriage is no good." "I don't want to care for another ill man." The respondents who agreed with the statement that "my sexual relations with my husband were very good until his last illness," however, were much more likely to wish remarriage than those who disagreed with that statement. They tended to be much younger than those rejecting a new relationship. Those who had been widowed a long time stated that they did not wish to remarry, mainly because "no one would want me now."

Remarriage often decreases interaction by either spouse with children, other relatives, and friends due to a mutual, although often unexpressed, desire or to a decreased need for support. The new spouse takes over many of the supports, and other intimates are relieved of doing so. Sometimes, this creates strain or awkwardness, if the supporter had been dependent on the new husband or wife. The difficulties increase if friends, relatives, or both feel that the newlywed is unhappy in that relationship. Thus, the conclusion reached by Altergott (1985), after a review of the literature concerning primary relations in later life, that "marriage reduces the duration of non-household interaction" (p. 70) applies to remarriage. In American society, at least, marriage tends to be exclusionary; it encourages privacy. The courtship and a new marriage create their own barriers of interaction. There appear to be the same processes that took place in the first marriages as to the conversion of old friends into couple companionate relations, a decrease in interaction with those who cannot be converted, and the need to develop new couple friends. There may be an additional complication if the older husband and his younger wife had traveled in different circles before they met.

Summary

Friendships go through various life courses, depending on other life course events of participants and the mutuality of their involvement. Whether same gender or cross gender, they grow from a symmetrical wish for such a relationship, in settings conducive to the discovery of commonalities and frequent contact, through the usually gradual development of all the components of intimacy and mutuality. In highly mobile societies such as the American one, people are frequently dislodged by choice or decision of others from the primary groups within which they grew up. Because of this, complex rituals and procedures have been developed to help people convert strangers into associates of greater closeness. Many "friendly" relationships, aided by social events and work- or leisure-based groups, stand somewhere between acquaintance and friendship. Same-gender friendships abound in youth, and cross-gender or group interaction can foster closer feelings among all or some members. Marriage in couple-oriented America tends to change the friendship base. Some same-gender relationships survive separately, especially among women of all social classes and working-class men. Companionate marriage, however, makes the assumption that husbands and wives are each other's friends. In fact, men often list their wives as best friends, whereas wives continue using another woman as the main confidant. Some friends from the past are converted into couple-companionate relationships, and new couple friendships are pulled in from work, the neighborhood, and a variety of social encounters.

Couple-companionate friendships and friendly relations dependent on "coupledom" or on the husband as the main link suffer with widowhood. The symmetry of couple activity is broken, and the widowed woman and her married friends become increasingly distant, first because of the former woman's needs and later because of divergence in lifestyle and interests. Widows find that they have more in common with other unmarried women, but not necessarily with widows, once the role of widow withers. Some old friendships are revitalized and new ones are formed, or else the widow can withdraw from such relationships, becoming dependent on relatives. Of course, some women, more likely of the working class than of the middle or upper class, never develop close nonkin relationships.

Cross-gender friendships are difficult in a society with vestiges of the two-sphere world in which men and women are perceived as having little in common besides romance and sexual interaction. Most people assume that cross-gender intimacy typical of friendship must include sexual involvement or at least its potential. That possibility is tolerated among the young unmarrieds but discouraged among those people who are judged to be unavailable for sexual encounters. Lack of availability applies to married men and women, despite the fact that such people are in frequent contact in most educational, occupational, recreational, and other public settings.

Nonsexual or nonromantic cross-gender friendship among widowed women does exist, although the frequency of opportunity for contact appears to decrease with older age. Romantic relationships also abound, sometimes despite disapproval, which often comes from children. These relationships can involve only "dating" or "seeing" each other, but they also can lead to cohabitation or remarriage. A whole subculture surrounds remarriage, especially among older widowed people—with the definition of the appropriate age cutoff varying considerably, often by ethnic group. The subculture includes stories of happiness and of misery, factors contributing to both, lists of advantages and problems, and suggestions on how to avoid pitfalls. Such a wealth of stories is not surprising, because close relationships are subject to personal scrutiny by associates. American society in general does not really care who is widowed or who is remarried, and even, although to a lesser degree of tolerance, who is cohabiting. The close intimates who knew the people involved in their past lives, however, usually have strong opinions as to the movement of a man and a woman into intimacy, sexual or asexual.

All in all, there is no evidence that widowhood decreases social involvement with friends, except maybe at the very end of life when health and other constraints make continued contact difficult. The myth of the elderly moving slowly does not appear to apply to courtship involving widows. Realization of the shortage of future life speeds up courtship patterns. Older widows are, of course, much less apt to remarry, due to demographic factors as well as to complicated attitudes and emotions concerning reentrance into the role of wife.

Notes

1. The concept of "side bets" refers to the consciously decided on action or unintended consequences of prior action that support a given commitment. For example, the decision to take a certain job may contribute to a continuation of a friendship, whereas a different job may make it difficult to maintain the friendship.

2. I had to withdraw questions pertaining with sexual activity from my support system of widows interviews due to the concern of the U.S. Office of Management and Budget officials that it might be criticized for approving such questions in a research contract.

8

Community and Societal Responses to American Widows

ANNETTE PROSTERMAN

> Myth: Widows are valued and respected members of American society.
>
> Myth: The American society has always supported and assisted with the social integration of widows.

If you were one of eight shipwrecked people in a lifeboat that could carry only seven, which person would you decide to throw overboard to save the group: the single, unemployed, 22-year-old college dropout; the single, 29-year-old surgical nurse supporting her mother; the married, 41-year-old union executive who has teenage children; the 72-year-old widow who volunteers at a day care center; the 50-year-old bank president with adult children; the housewife who is married to the bank president; the 21-year-old retail management trainee; or the pregnant (with her second child), 18-year-old high school dropout? This is the question asked during *Lifeboat,* a role-playing game designed to explore the social worth and relative value that people assign to others who are faced with possible death. In contemporary America, the person who invariably is chosen by the group to be thrown overboard is the elderly widow, regardless of her social position or occupational status (Thorson, 1978).

The repeated outcome of this game suggests that, in relative terms, elderly widows are not valued members of American society. Unfortunately, we do not know if the results of the lifeboat game would be different if the widow had instead been a widower or if the widow/widower had been younger. We do know, however, that in "real" life, older people in modern America generally have a lower status than younger people, and women have a lower status than men (Matras, 1990; Matthews, 1979). Because most people experiencing widowhood in the United States are late middle-aged or older and because most are women, these are primary issues in the perception and treatment of widows in American society.

Perceptions of the
Elderly in American Society

In most societies, people with wealth and power generally are perceived as more valuable and worthy of respect than those who have relatively little wealth and power. Many people lose wealth and power as they grow older (Matras, 1990). In the United States, people also lose something else as they age—the perception that they can productively contribute to society. In a nation founded on the Protestant work ethic, this is a serious deficiency (Neuhaus & Neuhaus, 1982). More stigmatizing than to be perceived as nonproductive is to be seen as dependent on others, and many older people are also viewed as dependent (Achenbaum, 1978; Matthews, 1979).

Yet as recently as the founding of this nation, older people had not been regarded so poorly (Achenbaum, 1978; Fischer, 1977). According to Achenbaum, older Americans at the end of the 18th century were generally regarded as valuable, contributing members of society; respected for their accumulated experiences and seasoned insights; perceived as having remarkably achieved longevity through the preservation of a healthy, virtuous lifestyle; and revered as worthy examples for the young. Viewed in this way, the elderly were expected to work as long as they were physically able to do so; there was no mandatory retirement or societal pressure to deny them access to work or to force them to resign on the basis of their age. Fischer (1977) noted that this veneration of the elderly included married women and that, in the domestic realm as well as the public realm, older people were seen as important contributors and were not released from tasks on account of their age.

Many factors worked together to change this perception over the next 200 years—although perhaps more slowly over the course of the 19th century than the 20th century. Achenbaum (1978) cited the attention of science and medicine on the debilitating aspects of old age as an influence on societal perception of the elderly following the Revolutionary War. He also attributed the change in perception of the elderly to the growing reliance of the public on the scientific knowledge of "experts" over the experiential knowledge of older people. In addition, Fischer (1977) pointed out that, due to advances in science and medicine, more people were beginning to live longer, and as longevity became more common, it became less awe inspiring. The infant mortality rate also began to decrease as a result of these advances, and with a growing mass of young people, a "cult of youth" emerged (Achenbaum, 1974; Fischer, 1977).

Achenbaum (1974, 1978) also attributed the growing perception of the elderly as obsolete with the rise of bureaucratic structures during the 19th century. Higher education, precise skills, and efficiency were considered crucial to the effective functioning of business and industrial organizations. The "modern" knowledge of the youth was deemed more valuable in this changing societal context than the "outdated" knowledge of the elderly. During the last part of the 19th century, the development of pension schemes and mandatory retirement began to spread throughout the industrial and business sectors (Achenbaum, 1978; Fischer, 1977).

The greatest shift in the perception of the elderly, however, seems to have occurred during the 20th century. In 1890, 43% of all men over 65 were gainfully employed in farming, but this dwindled to about 3% by 1970 as farmers were expelled from the labor force due to the consolidation of family farms and the advances of agribusiness (Achenbaum, 1978). Younger farmers who had not already done so were often able to find work in urban areas, but older people were unable to do so, in large part due to the growing devaluation of their abilities and their lack of education.

During the Depression, a greater competition for wage labor further barred or eliminated older people from the labor force. The growing number of impoverished older Americans became alarmingly apparent, and the elderly poor began to be seen as a social problem.

It was their age, rather than their unemployed condition, that became socially defined as the problem (Matthews, 1979).

This "problem" was addressed through the creation of Social Security for elderly, former workers. Some social researchers have suggested that a hidden agenda of many of the political leaders who were helping to shape the Social Security Act was to justify the elimination of the elderly from jobs in favor of younger, unemployed workers and to deny the elderly access to the labor market (e.g., Graebner, 1980; Lopata & Brehm, 1986; Matthews, 1979). As the destitution of the elderly increased during the Depression, however, easing the plight of the elderly became the primary objective of many supporters of Social Security legislation.

Politicians favoring this legislation tended, regardless of their mo- tivations, to focus on the biological decline involved in aging as an argument for financial assistance to the elderly. Matthews (1979) effectively explained how the perception of "oldness as a disability" became socially constructed through the legislative process, showing how the Social Security Act (1935) and especially the Older Americans Act (OAA) (1965) had further lowered the social status of the people they had been designed to financially assist. In adopting the definition of old age itself as physically disabling, the passage of the OAA helped to solidify and give legal credence to a stigmatized perception of the elderly. Whereas before the OAA was passed, the elderly had come to be seen as no longer productively contributing to society, today they are also pictured as dependent on society. Now, older people are gen- erally assumed to be diminished in capacity and deficient in physical or mental competence or both. Once venerated for their accumulated knowledge and skill, they are now not taken altogether seriously (Matthews, 1979).

Many accounts of the decline in value and respect of the elderly have treated the experience of being elderly as if it was the same for men and women. Nonetheless, the attitude toward elderly women was actually more negative than the attitude toward men. Matras (1990) pointed out that people tend to be more respectful toward older individuals who are able to maintain control over wealth and power. A relatively small number of women are in positions of wealth and power; most women have gone through their lives being perceived as adjuncts to their husbands.

The social value that came to be placed on earning and income through wage labor during industrialization affected men differently than it did women, because men were the ones who got most of the paying jobs and had access to the higher incomes (Matthews, 1979; Ryan, 1979; Sapiro, 1986). Prior to this century, a significant portion of the goods now produced and services now rendered in the public sector were generated by families within the home, and women were an integral part of the family economic system (Lopata & Brehm, 1986; Ryan, 1979). But with the rise of industry, men left the homes and went out to earn a living for their families through wage labor. While the productive labor needs of the expanding economy were filled by men, women became socially responsible primarily for reproductive work within the home—including a variety of activities such as "purchasing household goods, preparing and serving food, laundering and repairing clothing, maintaining furnishings and appliances, socializing children, providing care and emotional support for adults, and maintaining kin and community ties" (Glenn, 1992, p. 1). The kind of work for which women were responsible was devalued by default (Lopata, 1993b).

In this society, work that is valued the most is paid the highest wages, and work that is valued the least is paid the lowest wages. Activity for which no wages are received is not considered very important, nor is the person who performs it. Thus, men lose respect when they become older and are no longer allowed to be engaged in "productive" work, but women often did not have that respect to begin with. The social standing of those considered the "dependents" of their husbands certainly does not increase as they, with age, become the dependents of society.

Furthermore, the increased emphasis and value placed on youth since the 1800s has not been equal in its effect on men and women. Older women are thought of as lacking not only physical vitality and mental agility (as are men) but also beauty. In addition to being perceived as physically and mentally inadequate, they are also seen as unattractive. This is particularly significant for women, as Rice (1989a) explained, because women are "viewed primarily in terms of their physical beauty and ability to entertain and amuse other people" (p. 246).

The lack of social regard for older women is reflected in many ways, one of which is the way that elderly women are portrayed on television. Vernon, Williams, Phillips, and Wilson (1990) found that older people are underrepresented in prime-time television programs, thus connoting a perceived lack of importance or significance. Elderly women are portrayed only half as often as elderly men, and when older women do appear, they are often shown as unpleasant, unintelligent, passive, or socially isolated.

Widows as a Minority Group

"American women," Lopata (1976b) noted, "often report that they are being discriminated against simply because they are widows" (p. 349). This can, no doubt, be attributed to the fact that widows are women and most of them are elderly. Apparently, however, discriminatory treatment toward widows in American society is not only a function of their gender and age. Fischer (1977) found that, even in colonial times, older women in America were generally well-respected members of society *unless* they happened to be widowed. The few widows who were able to retain some of their husbands' wealth and power continued to be venerated. But according to Fischer, many fell into poverty and were then treated with the same scorn as other "paupers." Today, widows are definitely at risk for poverty, having a higher likelihood of experiencing poverty than both never-married and still-married women (Morgan, 1989).

The lower economic status of widows is very often connected to gender and age, but it also can be brought about by widowhood through the loss of the wages, pension, or benefits that the husband was contributing to the family and that the widow cannot replace. Many widows have been out of the paid job force for several years or have been working only part-time while raising a family. Because of putting more energy into their families, they are less likely to have obtained higher education or training or to have developed well-paying careers (Lopata, 1979; Rice, 1989b). The age at which a wife becomes a widow affects her ability to obtain employment if she had not been a part of the paid labor force prior to the death of her husband. If she is elderly, she may be considered unemployable, and if she is young, she may have dependent children requiring a great amount of her attention (Lopata, 1979). Often, widows are forced to move from the homes they had shared with their husbands as a result of their changed economic circumstances, and some may not be able to maintain a car (Lopata, 1975b, 1976b). These conditions set the widows apart because they may be financially unable to live at the same level and participate in many of the activities they had before the deaths of their husbands. Furthermore, these conditions often place them in the lowly regarded social category of the poor, in which members are generally assumed to belong by their own doing (Lopata, 1976b; Lopata & Brehm, 1986).

For many women in America, race and ethnicity also lengthen the distance and compound the discrimination they feel from mainstream American society in widowhood (Lopata, 1976b). The first women who have been able to move into men's positions in the paid labor force and gain access to financial resources have been white American women. Other women have been able to fill these positions only as white American women moved on to better positions (Glenn, 1992; Ryan, 1979). The social prejudice that women of racial or ethnic minorities face affects them also in widowhood. In addition, if they are new to the United States, their "foreignness" has probably isolated them more than it has their husbands and children, who likely have had more opportunities for acculturation through activities outside the home (Lopata, 1976b). For this reason, they may have a particularly difficult time in adjusting to life without their husbands.

Widows are often set apart from the mainstream of social life in more direct ways in consequence of having lost their spouses. No longer having husbands, they can no longer attend functions where a male escort is expected or engage in couple-companionate socializing without feeling self-conscious (Lopata, 1970, 1976b). In addition, they are often avoided by their former friends who would rather not be reminded of death and would rather not face the possibility of having to deal with tears and grief (Lopata, 1976b; Silverman, 1986). Thus, widows are no longer welcome to participate in some of their previous social circles.

Married women have a higher status in American society than widows. The status of widows, however, appears to be better than that of divorced or single women with children. Divorced women are often considered at fault for not "making" their marriage work, and single women with children are often viewed as immoral (Schwartz & Kaslow, 1985). An advantage for widowed women with children over divorced or never-married women with children is that they are considered more worthy and thus deserving of societal financial assistance. More public assistance is granted to widows with dependent children than to divorced mothers or unmarried mothers whose children were born out of wedlock (Vinovskis, 1990).

Regardless of the more favorable perception and financial support of widowed over divorced or single women with children, other never-married women without children may have certain advantages over recently widowed women in terms of the personal resources they have developed. Rice (1989b), in her study of 30 never-married and 30 widowed elderly, single, childless women in Los Angeles County, found significantly higher levels of life satisfaction for never-married women than for widowed women. She suggested that this might be due, in large part, to the major role adjustments a woman faces as a result of losing her spouse. A never-married woman has a higher role consistency and has alternate lifestyles that continue over time, whereas a widow must make changes in her self-identity and social relationships. Although they are not married or necessarily living with significant other persons, single women may still be involved in strong, supportive relationships with men or with other women. Not being limited to the exclusive interaction that some marriages entail, they may be involved with friends and with the community in a more extensive manner than wives, whose prior social network may also wither on widowhood.

New challenges presented by widowhood, although formidable, may provide women with opportunities to initiate and cultivate rich relationships and experiences that they would not have had as married women (Gibbs, 1979). Of course, it must not be assumed that the development of new relationships is always necessary or beneficial for widows. Social interaction is not synonymous with social support, and social interaction can often create more problems for a widow than it solves (Rook, 1984). The establishment of new social relationships does not always have positive outcomes for widows. Widowhood can leave women, especially those who were in highly dependent relationships with their husbands, particularly vulnerable due to their relative lack of experience in handling their affairs and relationships with others. Forty percent of the widows I (Lopata, 1973d) interviewed in 1970 felt that they had been exploited as widows. Generally speaking, however, interactions that build social relationships and enhance social networks have positive effects on a widow's well-being (Osterweis, Solomon, & Green, 1984; Schuster & Butler, 1989).

Social isolation often does not increase during the months or the first few years following the death of a woman's husband because this is the time when friends and family rally to support the widow through her early stages of grieving. Often, social isolation does increase after 5 years or more (Pihlblad & Adams, 1972). Thus, there is a need not only for immediate attention but also for ongoing sources of social interaction for widows and for resources to assist in maintaining them.

Personal Limitations and
Resources for Social Involvement

In American society, formal and informal programs and resources for widows exist, and these can assist them to move beyond the bereavement stage and to shed some of the stigmatizing and isolating aspects of widowhood. These programs and resources will be discussed within the next few pages. Widows vary considerably in the extent to which they take advantage of such opportunities, depending on their personal limitations and resources for social involvement.

As discussed before, Lopata (1973a) found that, of the Chicago widows I interviewed, those likely to remain socially isolated were of working-class backgrounds with limited education, were unemployed or worked sporadically, and were not closely connected with a church or other religious group. These women had never had above-average incomes, and they became even more financially restricted in widowhood. Other studies have since supported my findings (e.g., Arling, 1976; Gibbs, 1979).

Lack of transportation is a major barrier to social interaction for many widows who do not, or are afraid to, drive. It is also a barrier for those who cannot afford to maintain a car and do not have access to (or are afraid to use) public transportation (Kinderknecht, 1989; Lopata, 1973d). Especially hindered by a lack of safe and viable transportation are elderly and minority widows (who grew up in times and places in which women were not expected to drive) and widows who live either in inner cities or rural areas.

Many urban, elderly widows are afraid to go out by themselves for necessary activities (e.g., grocery shopping or visiting the doctor), let alone for recreational or social activities (e.g., meeting new acquaintances for dinner or attending religious gatherings) due to the real or perceived threat of crime (Kahana & Kiyak, 1981; Lopata, 1973d, 1978; O'Bryant, Donnermeyer, & Stafford, 1991). This makes it difficult for them to form new relationships. In addition, age places older widows at a disadvantage in terms of social isolation because the number of available, contemporary peers dwindles due to increasing immobility and death (Roberto & Scott, 1986).

Poor health may further inhibit the mobility of widows and thus their exposure to new social situations (Arling, 1976; Gibbs, 1979; Lopata, 1973d). Language or literacy barriers often prevent women from being aware of or participating in existing opportunities for involvement (Lopata, 1973b, 1979; Salcido, Nakano, & Jue, 1980). Finally, widows with passive personalities who wait for people to come to them rather than reach out to others are more likely to be isolated than those who are more outgoing (Lopata, 1973d).

A factor related to most of the limitations mentioned earlier is the degree to which the widows depended on their husbands. Those who lived somewhat independently of their husbands and developed personal resources—for example, circles of friends in which the husbands were not a part, or education that left them able to support themselves economically—are better equipped to overcome limitations and adjust to single life than those who had been less self-sufficient (Lopata, 1979).

Programs for the
Social Involvement of Widows

American society has developed several resources to assist the social involvement of widows. These have been concentrated in three areas: economic, emotional, and social support. Before the 20th century, however, any kind of organized societal support specifically for widows was virtually nonexistent. Community authorities often took children away from widows (and other husbandless women) and placed them in workhouses on the recommendation of one "respectable" citizen or another. It was assumed that these women could not adequately care for their children if they were poor and had to work. Few paying jobs were available for women in many areas of the country, and those women who were unable to support themselves were "put out" of their homes. If relatives or family friends did not take them in, they were often either placed in the care of farmers or townspeople, who saw to their basic needs for a small fee from community funds, or they were forced to enter an almshouse (Lopata & Brehm, 1986).

By the turn of the century, some social reformers were pushing for mothers' pensions to help keep husbandless mothers and their children at home, constructing an ideology of keeping families together and defining public institutions as inadequate in "properly" socializing children. As a result of a 1909 White House Conference on the Care of Dependent Children, many states began passing legislation for mothers' pensions to be provided for "fit" mothers with "suitable" homes. These pensions were not well dispersed. Minority women, in particular, rarely received them. Well into the 1930s, however, the public assumed that the needs of widows and their children were being met by the mothers' pensions (Lopata & Brehm, 1986).

Through the early part of the 20th century, there was little societal concern regarding the needs of elderly widows who had no children or whose children had grown. It was generally assumed that they all had children who were caring for them. Rather, the focus of American public concern during the early decades of the century was primarily on unemployed men and, to some extent, on the elderly men among them. The Social Security Act of 1935 was designed to relieve older wage laborers. It had no provision for the dependent wives of those older male workers or the dependent widows and children of younger male workers. It was not until amendments to the Social Security Act were made in 1939 that those who were dependent on the workers were eligible to receive benefits (Lopata & Brehm, 1986).

Social Security benefits offer many widows economic support. Because economic problems can hinder a widow's social involvement, Social Security benefits may thus be viewed as a societal program that potentially facilitates social involvement. As such, however, these benefits have limited effect because many women have to use them for their more basic necessities in life (Lopata, 1978b; Lopata & Brehm, 1986). These funds were intended to be supplemental because the government assumed that widows would have other sources of income available to them. Most widows, however, are heavily or even totally dependent on Social Security, even though it leaves them below the adequate income levels set by the U.S. Labor Department (Lopata, 1978b; Lopata & Brehm, 1986).

In addition, many women are not eligible for regular Social Security benefits as widows. Widows who are younger than 65 are not entitled to full benefits unless they are disabled, although they may receive reduced benefits at 62 years of age (Lopata & Brehm, 1986). Those women not eligible for benefits receive only a lump sum payment intended to assist with funeral expenses.

Some widows of military veterans may qualify for a survivor's pension from the federal government (Wildhaber, Abrams, Stichman, & Addlestone, 1991). Benefits may also include limited educational assistance. For the widow to be eligible for these benefits, however, the husband must have actively served in the military during wartime. Furthermore, the widow must have limited income and net worth. Although this form of economic support is not available to a great many widows, those widows who are entitled to survivor's benefits may find that, when combined with other resources, these benefits can help to improve their social circumstances and involvement.

Other societal programs and resources exist to help widows cope with their bereavement, make necessary adjustments in their lives, and build new social relationships, thus providing both emotional and social support. For example, the government provides some assistance in the form of supplementary grants, and other support comes from community organizations and religious groups (DiGiulio, 1989). Such programs have a variety of formats and styles of functioning. The most effective in providing assistance in adjusting to widowhood have been mutual help or self-help groups, which emphasize widows helping other widows in a process of mutual support (Folken, 1990, 1991; Lieberman & Videka-Sherman, 1986; Silverman, 1986). These programs have been in existence only for the past 30 to 40 years.

A major pioneer and proponent of the mutual support program is Phyllis Silverman of Harvard University's Laboratory of Community Psychiatry. She organized and directed the Widow to Widow program as an experimental project from 1967 to 1973 (Silverman, 1986). Silverman recruited five widows of various races and religions to serve as aides. These aides would send letters to newly bereaved widows, stating that they would come and visit at a particular time on a particular day unless the widows called to ask them not to come. Once personal contact was established, the aides would offer understanding, advice, and friendship. The project also included group discussions and gatherings where problems in adjusting to widowhood could be discussed and relationships formed between a wider group of women.

The concept of a mutual help program for widows arose from Silverman's observations that many professional counselors cannot really relate to the specific feelings, experiences, and needs of the widows. Other widows, however, can truly empathize with new widows and can act as role models for dealing with the feelings and situations that they have already encountered as widows (Silverman, 1986, p. 66). Often, the widow who is helping others also benefits. For example, she can gain a different perspective on a situation that she had also been experiencing, and she can gain a new friend. Although Silverman's original Widow to Widow program is no longer in existence, many groups and organizations have designed programs for widows that are based on her model (Folken, 1990, 1991; Shuchter, 1986).

Some of these mutual help groups cater to specific groups of widows. The Widowed Person's Service (WPS), established by the American Association for Retired Persons in conjunction with the National Retired Teacher's Association, focuses on older widowed men and women (DiGiulio, 1989). Like the Widow to Widow program, the Widowed Person's Service provides an outreach program in many communities through which volunteers (who are themselves widowed) visit people who have recently lost a spouse. The bereaved are encouraged to attend group sessions designed to provide mutual support and assistance. Starting with a program in Morristown, New Jersey, in 1973, the number of WPS programs had risen to more than 200 across the United States by the late 1980s (Folken, 1990, 1991).

Another such group is THEOS (They Help Each Other Spiritually), which aims its services primarily toward young and middle-aged widows and widowers. THEOS is a grassroots network of mutual support groups with a spiritual but nondenominational orientation. The first THEOS group was started in 1962 by Bea Decker, a newly widowed mother of three (DiGiulio, 1989). There are currently about 90 THEOS chapters across the United States and Canada (Bins, 1992).

The Naim Conference is a Catholic organization specifically for widowed Catholics or widowed spouses of Catholics. It was founded in the late 1950s by Jean and William Delaney, both of whom had been widowed before their marriage to each other (Steinberg & Miles, 1979). Naim originally focused on the social needs of the younger widowed, but some chapters later were formed to address the needs of older widows as well. Naim primarily provides a forum for group discussion and has established chapters in Illinois and other central states (DiGiulio, 1989).

Another network of support groups that serves primarily younger (but not exclusively widowed) people is Parents Without Partners. In these community-based groups, single parents who may be widowed, divorced, or never married offer mutual support and share coping strategies (Levy, 1979). Some chapters also have support groups for the children of their members. By 1989, there were 1,000 local chapters of Parents Without Partners across the United States and Canada (DiGiulio, 1989).

Such support groups offer a forum for widows to express their feelings, discuss and solve common problems, share valuable information and encouragement, and build new friendships between people who understand and share in their newly obtained widowhood status (DiGiulio, 1989; Folken, 1991; Lieberman, 1993, 1994; Silverman, 1986). As one widow told DiGiulio (1989) when she met with such groups across the United States and Canada, "Nobody wants a widow. It's a married world out there. A widow is a fifth wheel. But at least here I'm not out of place. And it sure beats sitting home alone doing nothing" (p. 150). Temes (1984) uses the following incident shared by two workshop "graduates" to illustrate the new relationships that can arise as a result of participation:

> Sara Jane, the petite widow of a prominent physician from Savannah, Georgia, was in a workshop with "Big Bertha," a janitor's widow who scrubbed office floors at night and cared for her seven children during the day. Shortly after the eighth workshop meeting, Sara Jane was wheeling her cart down the supermarket aisle when she heard a familiar voice. It was "Big Bertha" shopping for her brood. They were so delighted to see one another that each abandoned her cart and ran to embrace the other. Onlookers were puzzled by the incongruous pair. Sara Jane and Bertha simultaneously turned to explain, "We're almost family." (p. 86)

These groups often help the widow to move away from the need for intensive support, distance herself from some of the more emotionally painful aspects of widowhood, and make the transition to life as a single woman intimately involved in a new social network (DiGiulio, 1989; Lieberman & Videka-Sherman, 1986; Lund & Caserta, 1992). Often, this occurs in the "splintering off" of smaller groups of people who branch out on their own and do other things together, such as taking a cruise or enrolling as a group in dance lessons (DiGiulio, 1989).

Of course, not all widows have the financial resources to be involved in such splinter activities. Indeed, the self-help movement of which these widow-to-widow programs are a part is, in many ways, a middle-class phenomenon. Thus, these groups often have not attracted or sustained the participation of those who are of lower socioeconomic backgrounds (Riessman, Moody, & Worthy, 1984).

Service supports designed specifically for widows are limited, but some do exist. The Widowed Persons Service, for example, provides a telephone service for information and assistance and publishes a referral listing of local services for widows in the United States and Canada. This service helps to fill a need for advice and information regarding matters of widowhood about which a widow's family and friends may not be familiar (DiGiulio, 1989; Temes, 1984).

Programs for the Social Involvement of the Elderly

Most widows can take advantage of other kinds of societal programs in building and maintaining social interaction by virtue of their age. Direct economic support through Social Security benefits to elderly women workers is often not greater than those they receive as a widow, unless there was a well-paying career uninterrupted by child rearing. Unfortunately, elderly widows cannot claim both forms of economic support (Lopata & Brehm, 1986). Again, the use of Social Security funds for social involvement is preempted by the greater need for material sustenance.

The federal government, largely through the OAA (1965), either fully or partially funds a wide variety of programs for individuals aged 60 and over, supplying both service and social supports for older widows. The OAA was designed to be a "comprehensive service system for the elderly," but it provides social supports as well (Huttman, 1985, p. 51). OAA projects are carried out through a system of state units on aging (SUAs) and local area agencies on aging (AAAs). One of the most important projects funded by the OAA, in terms of assisting widows to build and maintain social relationships, are senior citizens' centers.

Senior citizens' centers are designed as places where older people can come together for a variety of social activities and services. Although about a third of the nation's 5,000+ senior centers have buildings of their own, others are located (temporarily or permanently) in rooms or sections of community or recreation centers, churches, public housing facilities, or other buildings (Huttman, 1985). These centers often make arrangements with government agencies for congregate eating, which, in addition to helping to meet the nutritional needs of elderly people, provides widows with another opportunity for social interaction. As Huttman explained, "The center serves as a bridge to reconnect the elderly with the community, decreasing their isolation: It allows the participant to belong to a group again, while establishing a new identity" (p. 111). The senior center usually offers a wide range of social activities, from art classes to excursions to the zoo. It also "serves as an accessible and acceptable vehicle through which the elderly can tap the resources of the community as needed" (Huttman, 1985, p. 111). There, elderly widows can sometimes find listings of employment or housing opportunities and find free or discounted services, such as hearing tests or legal aid (Huttman, 1985; Matthews, 1979). Also, counseling services are sometimes available through senior citizens centers to assist elderly widows to deal with the confusion, loneliness, and depression they may feel as a result of the loss of their spouses.

In a subsample of women 65 and older, taken from a survey done for the National Council on the Aging in 1981, Ishii-Kuntz (1990) found that lifelong single and widowed elderly women (25% and 22%, respectively) were the most likely to participate in senior center activities, followed by married women (16%). Divorced or separated women participated least (11%). Participants at senior centers reported higher incomes than nonparticipants, but neither age, education, nor race made a significant difference in participation.

The OAA's special outreach efforts to include minorities in senior centers is apparently beginning to have an effect: Ishii-Kuntz (1990) found that race made no significant difference in participation. Earlier studies (e.g., Leanse & Wagner, 1975) showed that minorities were relatively infrequent users. The participation of the poor, whom the OAA has also been making special efforts to include, is still low (Huttman, 1985; Ishii-Kuntz, 1990). Many nonusers, according to Huttman (1985), are in rural areas where such services often are not available or where the elderly are "often not inclined to use any service that seems like government charity" (p. 110).

Other programs from which an older widow could gain the emotional and social support she might need are mutual support groups for the elderly. Foremost of these is Senior Actualization and Growth Encounter (SAGE), which was founded in California during the 1970s by Gay Luce (Riessman et al., 1984). With the working assumption that many of the problems the elderly face are due to their own acceptance of negative stereotypes and myths about aging, SAGE provides an opportunity for elderly participants to support each other in an effort to overcome these obstacles and develop new relationships in the process (Lieberman & Gourash, 1979).

Service supports designed to assist the elderly may help the older widow to achieve and maintain social involvement by making participation more accessible. Some community and religious organizations or congregate living facilities offer transportation or escort services to places such as shopping malls, senior citizens' centers, or churches (Huttman, 1985). In conjunction with the Urban Mass Transportation Act (UMTA) and the Older Americans Transportation Service (OATS), the OAA has also provided some programs that make safe transportation more accessible for the elderly in many urban and rural areas. These programs often provide special routes or schedules for elderly riders and have reduced rates or free service (Huttman, 1985). For example, funding through the OAA makes available a minibus to the older citizens in the small town (population less than 1,000) of Alma, Kansas. The bus is available through personally arranged scheduling, free of charge, to take elderly people to larger cities in Kansas where they can find the social and personal services and facilities that are not available in this rural community (Gibbs, 1979).

Some elderly widows are unable to take advantage of such transportation services due to ill health or other disabilities. For housebound, elderly individuals, the government funds service programs that may provide some measure of social interaction. One such program is a home delivery (Meals-on-Wheels) lunch service, through which volunteers or paid staff put together (in institutions, such as schools, hospitals, or churches) packaged meals and deliver them. Depending on the number of deliveries to be made, a volunteer may have time to sit for a while and interact with the recipient (Huttman, 1985).

Some service supports are available, funded by government agencies or community organizations, to assist elderly women with household and self-maintenance. These services may also provide ongoing opportunities for social contact. They may include home cleaning, lawn mowing, making household repairs, running errands, cooking, and washing clothes (Gibbs, 1979; Huttman, 1985). Like the Meals-on-Wheels programs, these services rely heavily on community volunteers.

To my knowledge, a study has not been conducted regarding the number and kinds of home assistance services that are available throughout the United States. The size of the community and its available social and economic resources, however, seem to affect the number and kind of services it provides (Gibbs, 1979). For example, Gibbs found several home assistance services among the 23 services and agencies for older citizens listed by the Council of Social Agencies in a compilation titled "Services to Older Citizens" for the small city (population 34,000) of Manhattan, Kansas. These included Meals-on-Wheels, "Wonderwoman" (home chore workers), Handyman Services, Health-Homemaker Services, Homemaker Service, and Nursing Services. In contrast, the smaller town (population less than 1,000) of Alma, Kansas, had no such organized services.

Another kind of community-level service support that can contribute to ongoing social involvement for elderly widows is assistance in finding housemates. Often, widows would prefer to keep the homes they shared with their husbands. But they may need physical or financial assistance to maintain the home, or they may prefer to live with another person rather than live alone (Jaffe, 1989; Kahana & Kiyak, 1981; O'Bryant, 1987). Responding to this need, some community organizations have developed programs to help widows arrange to share their homes with other, unrelated individuals. These programs are sometimes partially funded by Housing and Urban Development (HUD) or area agencies on aging (Robbins & Howe, 1989).

An article by Green (1993) in the *Chicago Tribune* described several home-sharing situations arranged by various organizations in Michigan. One such screening and brokering service was the Housing Bureau for Seniors in Washtenaw County. Based in the college town of Ann Arbor, it linked older women not only to each other but sometimes also to younger students. Arrangements varied depending on the needs of those involved. The person who moved to the housing unit might pay rent or, in exchange for living rent free, run errands, do chores, and provide companionship.

In addition to addressing practical housing needs, shared housing can address a widow's need to adjust to a different life by providing her with at least one new, ongoing pattern of interaction (Jaffe, 1989; Rice, 1989a). Shared housing involving elderly persons appears to be a rising trend throughout the United States (Mantell & Gildea, 1989;

Robbins & Howe, 1989). Nonetheless, a city population of at least 100,000 is usually necessary to provide an adequate pool of potential home sharers to support such a program (Robbins & Howe, 1989).

For widows who either do not wish or are unable to maintain their own homes (either alone or with the assistance of others), apartment complexes for the elderly are available in many towns and cities. These complexes cater specifically to the elderly by providing some services and facilities to meet their needs. For example, some may offer a noontime meal or have on-site medical staff available but leave daily tasks, such as cooking and cleaning, for the resident to perform (Huttman, 1985). These complexes may have recreational facilities, meeting rooms, and lounges where residents can gather and engage in social activities. Also, a minibus or van may be available to take residents to appointments, stores, or churches (Huttman, 1985).

Another form of congregate housing that can provide ample opportunity for an elderly widow's social involvement is the residential hotel or complex with hotel-like rooms. Those catering to the elderly often provide housekeeping and on-site medical staff. Meals are served in a central dining room. Other central rooms may serve as libraries or television rooms, and these facilities also often provide minibus service. Like apartment complexes for the elderly, these congregate housing facilities are usually privately owned and operated (Huttman, 1985).

Governmentally subsidized housing programs can also facilitate a woman's social involvement indirectly through the auxiliary service and social supports. Federally funded low-income congregate living sites or housing projects for the elderly are found in many localities throughout the country. They are usually available on a sliding scale based on income (Kinderknecht, 1989). These facilities often lack the range of services and social supports available in privately owned, more expensive facilities, but they sometimes provide basic service supports (e.g., congregate meals) that bring elderly residents together and the van service that allows them to get out into the community (Huttman, 1985).

A last resort in housing in the minds of many elderly widows—but still a living arrangement that provides widows opportunities for social interaction—is the nursing home. These facilities are usually inhabited by elderly who are suffering chronic, long-term health problems that interfere with their daily functioning and make them highly dependent on others (Huttman, 1985). Only about 26% of white women and

14% of black women who are over age 85 live in nursing homes (National Caucus and Center on Black Aged, 1987). Yet through group meal and recreational activities, widows are often able to make new friends who can contribute to their sense of well-being.

Although the federal government has responded to the need of older people for opportunities to engage in social interaction by making funding available for a variety of projects, it is through community organizations and institutions that these funds are put to use. OAA-sponsored senior centers are often held in community or religious organization facilities. The staff or volunteers who assist with these senior programs are often members of the organizations or affiliates of the institutions.

Societal and Community
Resources for All People

Because many widows are elderly, much of the focus of this chapter has dealt with opportunities and resources for social involvement that are available specifically to older people. Younger widows often do not have access to programs designed for the elderly. Still, there are several channels through which a younger widow can reenter the social world without her role as a wife. Furthermore, elderly widows are not limited to the programs specially designed for them. For widows of any age, many other avenues can lead away from social isolation and back into mainstream community life.

One of the best ways in which a widow can become involved in the greater community and find opportunities for social interaction is through volunteer activities. Some of these are sponsored by formal service organizations, such as the American Red Cross or the Retired Senior Volunteer Program (Kinderknecht, 1989). Other volunteer activities are less formal, such as the programs at local libraries where adults can make themselves available for tutoring or reading to children. Local hospital auxiliaries and church groups often provide ample occasions for volunteering. Various opportunities to volunteer can be found in communities of any size. Anyone willing to help with these efforts is usually welcomed.

Special interest groups and clubs, such as bird watching, quilt making, dancing, and "great books" reading, are other potential sources of social interaction for widows of various ages. Adult classes offered at community colleges can also provide interesting interactions. Although some of these activities may be prohibitive in cost for some widows, others may be accessible with no cost at all.

Religious activities are another potential source of ongoing interaction for widows of any age. Through her study of Chicago widows, Lopata (1979) received few indications that widows were receiving support or guidance from clergy after the period immediately following the deaths of the husbands. Silverman (1986) found that the clergy with whom she spoke were not *trained* to attend to the bereaved: Instead, they had received training on how to conduct funerals. Still, religiosity and the outlet for social involvement that religions provide seem to help widows deal with bereavement and adjust to the changes in their lives. As a result of their study of widows whose husbands had perished in the 1972 Sunshine Mine fire (in Kellogg, Idaho), Bahr and Harvey (1979) suggested that involvement in church activity and religious organizations may be especially effective in overcoming the deep sense of personal loneliness that is often associated with the loss of a spouse. Some churches provide transportation to the elderly or other members who would not otherwise be able to attend. Others allow the use of their facilities by senior citizens' groups and even widow self-help groups (DiGiulio, 1989; Huttman, 1985).

Although not established primarily for the purpose of doing so, places of employment can provide workers an opportunity for ongoing social interaction (Lopata, 1979). For the widow who did not hold a job at the time of her husband's death, the workplace may be an arena for social activity and for building new relationships. As indicated earlier, this form of social participation may not be accessible to all widows—especially those who are elderly, have never been employed outside of the home, have been out of the workforce for a number of years, or have very small children. For many widows, however, a workplace can be a source of social as well as financial support.

For some widows who have been employed, unions, professional associations, or retirement associations are also a potential source of ongoing social involvement. Within the Florida retirement community she studied, Neale (1987) found that one sixth of the widows held membership in these organizations. Membership in these groups may not be as available to widows as they are to other nonmarried women because of the kind of work widowed women are likely to have done. Rice (1989b) found that 90% of the never-married women she studied in Los Angeles County had careers (e.g., teaching or social work), whereas 47% of the widows had menial jobs (e.g., clerical or factory work). For many widows, however, professional associations are an option, if not immediately, then perhaps once a new career is established.

Summary

Widows have not been assigned much social value in our society, and as a result, few social resources have been allocated to them. Few societal programs exist specifically for widows beyond limited economic support from the federal government and emotional/social support provided by mutual support groups. Older widows can tap into the more abundant supports for social involvement that are provided to the elderly in general. The disadvantage of their age, however, is that they are viewed as needing attention due to being dependent on society. As a result, they are less respected. Ageism and sexism indeed have combined to make many older women unemployable and thus truly at the mercy of society. Many younger widows today have the advantage of having been employed in the wage labor force due to the need for dual paychecks in families. They can, at least to some degree, continue to support themselves and their families financially following the death of their husbands.

Although the American society's lack of a distinct and permanent role for widows may be at first unsettling for one experiencing widowhood, it offers in the long run an advantage in being vague and temporary. Unlike the immutable stigma attached to many minorities in America, the pervasive influence of widowhood can be left behind. A widow can adjust and develop new relationships that—although never taking the place of the relationship she lost with her husband—can still provide meaningful interaction. Society may not go out of its way to provide her with opportunities, but it does not stand in her way.

9

Widowhood in Variation

Past, Present, and Future

This book traces changes in the relationships of a woman as she moves from the role of wife, mother married to the father of their children, married kin member, married friend, and so forth into the role of widow and then into the life of a widowed woman with a reorganized role cluster, social life space, and identity. The processes by which a woman becomes a wife require change in all her prior relationships. The processes by which she becomes established as a widowed woman involve the development or recognition, more or less consciously, of new changes. Of course, the degree and direction of all the modifications of a widow's world vary by the many factors that we have examined throughout this volume. This includes her location in the society and community and her personal resources. Also important is her dependence on the husband, on the life they lived while he was alive, and on the financial, health, and other personal resources she has to restructure her life space and self-concept. Age, length of marriage, the presence of children, and the other roles in her role cluster influence what she can do after the role of widow and the period of heavy grief are over. Of course, these factors often are clustered. The woman's position in the social system and her resources are strongly influenced by the status of her family of orientation, education, occupation, and these characteristics of her husband. Young widows are more likely to have dependent children than are older widows. The need to modify her prior support systems and the ease with which she can do that are also influenced by the availability of societal resources.

Dramatic changes in the life and the self of a woman after she becomes widowed may be visible to everyone, including herself. Less drastic changes may differentially involve associates at varying social distances from the widow. Her primary associates (relatives and friends, neighbors, and maybe group comembers) may know of, and take into consideration, her identities as a former wife of a particular husband and a widowed person. Other aspects of her total self may be more or less important to their relationships once heavy grief is over. Many other people and groups may not even be aware of a widow's marital status as she goes about performing roles in her social circles. Thus, especially in modern, urban America, there is no institutionalized role of widow—only a pervasive identity of widow that enters, more or less intrusively, into the relationships of her various social roles, much as do the identities of woman, person of color, Polish American, and so forth.

On the other hand, widowhood may not be strongly disorganizing to life and the self, as in the case of a separated couple or as in traditional matrilineal and matrilocal societies. The latter situation is exemplified in parts of Africa and in several tribes of the American Southwest, as we saw earlier.

Social History and Widowhood

The lives of widows any place in the world, in the past, present, and future, illustrate C. Wright Mills's (1959) thesis of the interweave of societal history and personal biography. The culture and social structure of a society at any period of time influence the whole pattern of a member's existence. The culture contains beliefs about human nature and about people of different societal categories, such as gender, race, social class, and age. These beliefs are built into the socialization system and form the foundation of people's behavior toward members of the category, identified by symbolic "characteristics." The most effective socialization system ensures that the person being socialized believes what the society considers appropriate to that kind of person. Thus, whole myths develop around social categories, building behavioral and attitudinal expectations and therefore directing interactional attitudes and behavior. These beliefs are hierarchically arranged: In American society, it is better to be a man than a woman, to be defined as white rather than as a "person of color," to be upper class rather than lower class, and to be young rather than old. For a woman, being single is still good when she is young, and being married is good for the rest of life. Being divorced or being widowed is not so good. At this time in history, however, in this society, being widowed is not as bad as it has been at other times and other places. Being a widow in traditional, patriarchally encrusted India was not an enviable situation, especially with the prevailing myth that widows caused the death of their husbands. Whatever people wanted to force on a widow in terms of work or degradation was justified by this myth.

The location of the widow in the social structure of a society—in a specific caste or class, urban or rural, dominant or minority community—at any time makes an enormous amount of difference on her social life space and self-images. This was particularly true of more stable, less mobile societies of the past and more isolated present. Modern, complex, urban society makes less obvious many characteristics of a person that can be used to categorize her or him, unless they are physically visible. It is virtually impossible to hide gender, race, or age, so these pervasive identities are carried into all social situations.

The status of widows in most communities depended to a great extent on their age, possessions, and the numerical proportion of women to men. Age has been an important factor in myths concerning people's abilities and resources. In past times, widows were usually of childbearing and hardworking years. In modern times in American society, most women do not become widowed until at least late middle age. Thus, many current myths concerning widows are old age myths. In addition, widows are women, about whom there are still important belief vestiges of patriarchy, the British common law lack of rights, and the two-sphere mentality.

To better understand the connection between societal history and personal biography in widowhood in its broadest form, I have used the concept of social development, modernization, or increasing scale of complexity, whichever one best covers all the recent changes in societies.

Traditional societies were, for the most part, patriarchal, patrilineal, and often also patrilocal. The position of the wife in the male line system depended on the position of her husband, which was usually determined by his relative age and birth order. The position of the widow depended on the power of the male line and their determination of how she can best fit into it now that the husband was dead. This power was strongest if she could not return to her family of origin, had no adult sons responsible for her welfare, and had no means of developing alternative support systems and lifestyles. Many of the attitudes of those people who had power over a widow in different places and times depended on their definition of her usefulness in terms of wisdom and knowledge, as an owner or inheritor of property, as the producer of valuable children in the past or in the future, as a member of a work team, or as a special contributor to the group's status or welfare. Cultural and even religious expectations of existing behaviors toward widowed women could make their lives very restricted or, on the contrary, could open up previously closed opportunities.

Transitional times, in which societies move from mainly traditional toward modern social structures and cultures, frequently remove prior support networks or diminish their contributions to widows. During such times, the male line loses most of its power over its adult members, who can maintain themselves externally to it. Throughout recent centuries, the male line has become more distanced and the wife less dependent on its members. Although the wife's family of orientation gradually increased in importance, it rarely formed as strong a support system as is true of the traditional patriarchal extended family.

Early modernization in American society, seen here as part of the transitional time, divided the constructed world into two spheres—the private, managed by women, and the public, dominated by men. The introduction of a money economy and the organization of much work into paying jobs outside of agriculture, open for the most part to men or single women, made wives and children personal dependents on the husband and father. In fact, the need for money as a major means of self-maintenance disadvantaged all those people who had no direct means of obtaining it.

In transitional times and places, the death of the husband deprived the wife of a major supplier of income unless he made special provisions or she received sufficient inheritance. Some of the new widow's supports that had been supplied by the later husband are taken over by community or societally developed resources, but there has remained a need for informal support supplied by a varying number and type of associates. These supports are often provided by a daughter.

These transitional times have been difficult for many widowed women, especially for those who were socialized into more traditional cultures and who lived within the domestic sphere. Many such women have had minimal formal education and knowledge of modern urban resources. Many lack self-confidence as full members of society, acceptable to new personal relationships or roles in the public sphere. Some are also restricted by other characteristics, surrounded by stereotypes and discriminatory practices. In an environment oriented toward youth and progress, being old, being a woman, lacking power and wealth, and, in many cases, being a member of a racial, ethnic, or religious minority have proved extremely disadvantageous. Any of these characteristics can restrict opportunities, making such widows unable to enjoy the benefits of modernizing life.

The more "modern," large, urbanized, mobile societies and the communities within them depend increasingly on the ability of adult members to voluntaristically and flexibly use the ever-expanding societal resources and build their own support networks. America's social structure and culture have changed some of the traditional stereotypes, albeit slowly and only with great pressure from new organizing groups demanding their rights and greater independence. The society is developing new resources for such a voluntaristically flexible life, in the form of education, job training, private and public organizations, and a culture encouraging change. Of course, this varies by community, as we noted in Kansas. As the society changes, so do personal relationships. Women are decreasingly economically dependent on their husbands, although it will take more time before they can earn an equal share of family income or earn enough to provide for themselves and children in the absence of a cosupporting partner. It will take even more time before the sharing of the breadwinner contributions are converted into sharing of other contributions to family life.

All these changes, combined with vestiges of the past and the anticipated future, are developing a complex world, one organized differently than in the past (McCrea & Costa, 1993). Many traditional forms of stigmatization and discrimination of women, older people, and widows remain, although some are being modified by various factors. One factor is, of course, demographic—America's population, especially the large number of baby boomers, is aging. In addition, an increasing number of these people have built, and continue to occupy, full social life spaces as they age. Thus, the size and activity of this segment of the population have resulted in a rather substantial increase in its influence upon the society. This means that, although the elderly as individuals and widowed women as individuals may lack high status and power, aggregated senior power is real, as evidenced, for example, by the defense of Social Security and the political action by such groups as the American Association of Retired Persons. This has produced benefits, especially in economic and public policy areas. This increase in power, however, may have negative repercussions in a society with dwindling resources. Younger generations and their representatives repeatedly express concern, even anger, over the uneven distribution of benefits by age group. Stigmatizing stereotypes of older people may again increase, this time defined as selfish in demanding so many benefits at the cost of, especially, children. Even on the personal level, the middle generation, which is decreasing in numbers, may revolt against having too many elderly relatives and "nonproductive" widowed mothers to support emotionally, socially, economically, and with the services they need.

The demographic trends in America's population have been mixed, however, and will undoubtedly have mixed results, camouflaged by the stereotype of an explosion of dependent elderly. Starting in the early 19th century, several changes have transformed widowhood (and widowerhood). Life expectancy lengthened, and younger widows became rarer. To an increasing extent, widowhood has become synonymous with old age (see Blom, 1991, p. 193). In 1920, 10.8% of the women aged 14 and over were widowed. This percentage kept increasing until 1970, when it reached a peak of 13.9%. Since then, however, it has been dropping so that it was only 11.2% in 1992 (U.S. Department of Commerce, 1975, 1992b). This is not due to an increase in the proportion of divorced women, although this did increase from 0.8% in 1920 to 8.4% in 1992. These women formed only 6.7% of women aged 65 to 74 and only 3.9% of those aged 75 and over. Although the percentage of single women decreased from 29.4% in 1920 to 12.4% in 1965, it began to rise again to 23.0% in

1992. Obviously, the proportion of women in any marital status depends on the proportions of those in the other marital situations. This becomes apparent when we look at the marital status by age. Among women aged 18 and over in 1991, the proportion of single women decreased from a high at early years to a low of 3.7% at ages 55 to 64. Married women peaked between ages 35 to 39, at 74.2%. The highest proportion of widowed women (65.7%) is present among those 75 years and older, whereas the highest proportion of divorced women (15.8%) is found at ages 45 to 54 (see Eshleman, 1994, p. 32). These proportions are likely to change as an increasing number of divorced baby boomers reach older ages, displacing some widows and possibly changing the stereotype of older women.

Another very recent change has been in the increasing age of women who are still married as the male age at death has increased. White male life expectancy rose from 54 years in 1920 to 70.7 years in 1980 (see Barrow, 1986, p. 17). It must be remembered that although the age at widowhood has been increasing, 30% of widows were under the age of 65 as late as 1983 (Strong & DeVault, 1986).

Despite the rising life expectancy of American men, women still outnumber them by far, increasingly so in each age category. In 1991, for example, there were 29 unmarried men aged 65 and over for every 100 unmarried older women (see Eshleman, 1994, p. 494). Nearly 60% of previously widowed brides and grooms in 1988 were aged 55 or older. The median interval between the death of a spouse and remarriage was 2.3 years for men and 4.6 years for women (see Ahlburg & De Vita, 1992, p. 17).

Those elderly people who are not married, for the first time or in remarriage, and who are not living with relatives or other individuals, live alone. In 1991, 34% of women and only 13% of men aged 65 to 74 were living alone; at age 75 and older, 53% of the women and 21% of the men were living alone (see Ahlburg & De Vita, 1992, p. 10).

According to a hypothetical life cycle created by Mary Jo Bane (1976, p. 25), women born between 1846 and 1855 were likely to lose a spouse at the age of 56.4 and to die themselves by age 60.7. This means that they were widowed for a little more than 4 years. Women born between 1946 and 1955, on the other hand, did not lose their husband until they were 67.7 and did not die themselves until age 77.1 (see Gill, Glazer, & Thernstrom, 1992, p. 410). Women were thus married until an older age than the earlier cohort by more than 11 years, and their period of widowhood thus lasted 9.4 years.

Although more people live longer and die of more old-age complications than in prior centuries and decades, the changes indicate more years of independence by more competent people. That is, there appears to be a definite decrease of dependency on the part of widowed women. Many women, in rapidly increasing numbers, have been able to lead flexible, multidimensional lives at any stage of their life course and to learn new means of social engagement as old ones become unavailable or unacceptable. Flexibility of the life course is made easier by the decreasing distance between the private and public spheres as people move back and forth between them. The boundaries of the spheres are more open and overlapping as people carry forth paid employment at home and previously private activities in public. The educational system is finally acknowledging that it must prepare both men and women for full participation in primary and secondary social relations and social roles. This flexibility is helping to break down some of the old myths that box people into gender, racial, and other stereotypical identity packages. Ideas that personality is fixed by the time one reaches adulthood are giving way to ideas of personal development throughout the life span. Research into all forms of identities using in-depth, rather than survey, analysis is invalidating many stereotypes.

Personal Processes of Current Widowhood

The modern wife is becoming less economically dependent on her husband and more likely to be involved in a multidimensional life, much of which is also socially and emotionally independent of that partner, than was true of her ancestresses. Nevertheless, marriage is still very important to Americans. Continued life together prior to the death of the husband inevitably builds strong emotional bonds, even if some are ambivalent. Although in many societies the worst thing that can happen to a wife in widowhood is a drop in status and being controlled by often indifferent or hostile others, in America, the strongest effect appears to be a personal one. It is personal not only in the loss and modification of personally built resources in marriage but also in the emotional loss of what was probably the most significant other in her life. Marriage in traditional times was more embedded in a complex of social relationships and so was not as salient as in modern American times. Marriage is now supposed to be the most important relationship for the partners, although the mother-child relationship is still considered important for the woman, the father-child relationship increasingly important for the man, and the occupational role important to both of them. The alleged salience of marriage to the wife means that the aftereffect of the death of her husband is likely to be highly emotional. So many sentiments concerning the self, others, and life in general are likely to have been influenced by the responses and behaviors of the husband. We really do not know enough about the differences in emotional consequence of widowhood on women with flat and with multidimensional social life spaces. One can hypothesize that the more multidimensional the life space, and the more important the other roles, the less disorganizing and traumatizing is the death of the husband. On the other hand, a multidimensional life may require deep personal commitments with one person, which is likely to be a husband. Again, both possibilities need examination. Much of friendly social interaction is still couple companionate, at least for the middle class, although each partner may have independent same-gender and cross-gender friendships. Of course, couple-companionate situations do not need to involve marital units. On the other hand, single men are hard to find at increasing widowhood age.

That the death of her husband can leave a woman alone in the household need not lead to social isolation. Independent living arrangements can provide her with comfortable alternatives of social interaction and privacy. This is particularly true if the woman living independently is easily able to continue interacting due to her history of movement between the private and the public spheres. Of course, living without a husband may not necessitate living alone in that various residential arrangements are possible.

One aspect of current widowhood that still needs study is remarriage. Different widows report different attitudes toward entering another marriage, as do the same widows at different times. Many factors affect the probability and the attractiveness of remarriage, including the recognized advantages and disadvantages. The ever-present statistical asymmetry of available partners looms in the minds of many widowed women, but they also often hold conflicting attitudes toward reentrance into the role of wife. They weigh the pleasure of companionship versus the loss of personal independence (as perceived by many), mutual caring versus the probability of having to care for another ill person, possible family disapproval versus children's happiness that the mother may be happy in a new relationship, economic security versus concern regarding the financial consequences of a new legal relationship, and so forth. The increasing openness and permissiveness of temporary or permanent cohabitation has attracted unnumbered widows. So have, although less openly, lesbian relationships.

Myths and Stereotypes: Popular and "Scientific"

I will end this final chapter with a review of the main myths discussed in this book and reiterate how they misrepresent the processes and characteristics of widowhood.

Scientific theories about the effects of social development or "modernization" of societies, filtered and spread through the mass media, have led to many semiscientific, often mistaken, assumptions about its effects on societal members. Few people would reject all theories about the changes in societies as they move into more complex social structures and cultures with the help of industrialization, postindustrial developments, urbanization, mass education, social and geographical mobility, the market economy, and so forth (Inkeles, 1983; Inkeles & Smith, 1974). These changes have undoubtedly influenced the members of the "developing" and "developed" nations. Pop sociology or pop psychology versions of these theories have led to overgeneralizations concerning people. The modernization trends have not changed all members to the same degree and in the same direction. Few, if any, cultures form a tightly woven fabric, and few, if any, societies form an integrated social structure. As Gusfield (1967, 1976) points out, allegedly modern cultural elements do not necessarily replace traditional ones; they can coexist side by side or even be interwoven, as evident in many cultural-religious adaptations. Papanek (1978) also points out that the initial studies of the effects of modernization on societal members were focused only on men. Although this has been somewhat modified, the enormity of the task of determining the effects of these tremendous changes results in large gaps in our knowledge. Yet the mass media and people at various levels of familiarity with the theories tend to treat cultures as whole fabrics and to generalize way beyond actual knowledge of specific situations.

These comments apply with relevance to ideas that people hold about widowhood and widows the world over. Frequently, contradictory myths and stereotypes are fused into broad misconceptions. For example, societies defined as "developing" are assumed to contain widows living in large, extended, mainly patriarchal, family households. Yet as we saw in the case of Turkey, most people live in nuclear households. The myth that families in traditional societies take care of their members with problems is certainly questioned by what happened in the past, and is still happening, to many widows in India. The lives of widows in rural areas are very different from the lives of those in urban areas, as exemplified in Korea. Even within the latter areas, there is a great deal of variation in social life space and multidimensionality of involvement based on the personal resources of a particular widow or group of widows, as evidenced in Chicago. The location of a widow in the social structure in terms of social class and minority community is a major influence on these resources. These resources include her knowledge of what is available and how to reach her goals, plus—and this is an important plus—her self-concept.

We found great variations in widowhood in different parts of the world and then learned of variations in historical and current America. The piecemeal and irregular change summarized as modernization—or the increasing complexity of structure, culture, and individual life—has not affected this society or its members evenly and in the same way. Heterogeneity of this world leads to heterogeneity of its members, carrying forth into a heterogeneity of widowed women. Yet people need to explain the world and each other despite all this complexity. This is where myths, overgeneralizations, and stereotypes come into the picture—as explanations and predictions of behavior. Myths can often be traced back to the original cultures of America's immigrant groups. They are added to by ideas drawn from modernization and similar theories or hypotheses. The mixture of sources leads to a great deal of contradiction. Do women lose or gain status in widowhood? Has modernization benefited widows? Are widows valued in American society? Are there extensive family support networks available to widowed women? Do interactional networks provide positive or negative "help" to widows? Was life for widows in colonial America better than it is now? Do African Americans have more complex households that provide more positive supports than do other Americans?

There are no single answers to these questions, because so many factors influence all the situations. This certainly applies to the various myths about widowhood. Yet people, even a widow's close associates, tend to draw on this "commonsense" or semiscientific knowledge to make assumptions about her, often to provide her with supports that are inappropriate. There are enough autobiographies by articulate women (Buck, 1962; Caine, 1974; Lerner, 1978; see also van den Hoonaard, 1993, for personal reminiscences of authors) to make us realize how inadequate are many attempts of other people to understand what a widowed woman is experiencing. Thus, the myths provide overgeneralized ideas as to what is a needed support and result in many efforts that actually contribute to a new widow's depression (Morgan, Neal, & Carder, n.d.).

The assumptions concerning widowhood in general are carried over to various aspects of becoming and being a widow. Many people believe that sudden death is harder on the survivors than prolonged dying or that families generally do not need to care for the dying patient because hospitals have taken over that task. The absence of the husband allegedly leaves the widow starved for sexual interaction or else relieved by not having to go on with it. Remarriage is seen as highly desired or completely unwanted unless there are children in need of a father. Friendships are expected to be increasingly important or a cause of problems. Cross-gender friendships are seen as impossible or as only a precursor to a romantic involvement. The reality of the situation, in most cases, falls somewhere between these conflicting assumptions and varies by person.

A basic theme of the book is that there is no permanent role of widow in American society. The temporary role of widow follows the death of the husband and goes through the processes by which the widow and her social circle accomplish the funeral rituals, including the anchoring of the social person of the deceased in the memory of the participants, disposing of the body, mourning, and initial grieving. These processes take a varied amount of time. One of the problems of the role of widow in modern times, with the deinstitutionalization of so many death rituals, is its indefinite ending. The circle supporting the woman as a widow may dissolve before she is ready. On the other hand, the circle may insist on treating her as a widow long after she wishes to give up that role.

All in all, however, the image of widowhood that is emerging from current research is of a resilient widowed woman, able to work through her grief, cutting ties with the deceased, accepting life without him, modifying existing social relationships and roles and building new ones, and reconstructing the self into an independent, whole human being. Younger widows often remarry, the frequency decreasing with age for various demographic and personal reasons. Generally, widows maintain a social lifestyle that is basically similar to the one they led in marriage, modifying it in response to self-defined needs within a variety of social roles. The main discovery in pulling together and reanalyzing the theory and research on current widowhood is that the increasing heterogeneity of American widowed women is due to unique combinations of factors rather than to group differences. There are still many widowed women in American society who are embedded in group identities and support systems, some with more advantages than others. Such group differences will continue as new groups enter the society or as older ones face discriminating barriers. For an increasing number of women—and undoubtedly for men, too—the various group and individually idiosyncratic identities are combined uniquely throughout the life course.

References

Abbott, E. (1913). *Women in industry: A study in American economic history.* New York: Appleton.

Achenbaum, W. A. (1974). The obsolescence of old age in America, 1865-1914. *Journal of Social History, 8,* 45-64.

Achenbaum, W. A. (1978). *Old age in the new land.* Baltimore: Johns Hopkins University Press.

Adams, B. (1968). *Kinship in an urban setting.* Chicago: Markham.

Adams, B. N. (1995). *The family: A sociological interpretation* (5th ed.). New York: Harcourt Brace Jovanovich.

Adams, R. G. (1985). People would talk: Normative barriers to cross-sex friendships for elderly women. *The Gerontologist, 25,* 605-611.

Adams, R. G. (1989). Conceptual and methodological issues in studying friendships of older adults. In R. G. Adams & R. Blieszner (Eds.), *Older adult friendship: Structure and process* (pp. 17-41). Newbury Park, CA: Sage.

Adams, R. G., & Blieszner, R. (Eds.). (1989). *Older adult friendship: Structure and process.* Newbury Park, CA: Sage.

Ahlburg, D. A., & De Vita, C. J. (1992). New realities of the American family. *Population Bulletin, 47,* 2-17.

Allan, G. A. (1979). *Sociology of friendship and kinship.* Boston: Allen & Unwin.

Allan, G. A., & Adams, R. G. (1989). Aging and the structure of friendship. In R. G. Adams & R. Blieszner (Eds.), *Older adult friendship: Structure and process* (pp. 45-64). Newbury Park, CA: Sage.

Altergott, K. (1985). Marriage, gender and social relations in late life. In J. Quadagno & W. Peterson (Eds.), *Social bonds: Aging and interdependence* (pp. 28-48). Beverly Hills, CA: Sage.

Anderson, T. B., & McCulloch, B. J. (1993). Conjugal support: Factor structure for older husbands and wives. *Journal of Gerontology, 48,* S133-S142.

Aries, P. (1965). *Centuries of childhood.* New York: Random House.

Aries, P. (1981). *The hour of our death.* New York: Knopf.

Arling, G. (1976). The elderly widow and her family, neighbors, and friends. *Journal of Marriage and the Family, 38,* 757-768.

Atchley, R. (1975). Dimensions of widowhood in later life. *The Gerontologist, 15,* 176-178.

Aulette, J. R. (1994). *Changing families.* Belmont, CA: Wadsworth.

Backer, B. A., Hannon, N., & Russell, N. A. (1994). *Death and dying: Understanding and care.* Albany, NY: Delmar.

Bahr, H. M., & Harvey, C. D. (1979). Correlates of loneliness among widows bereaved in a mining disaster. *Psychological Reports, 44,* 367-385.

Bane, M. J. (1976). *Here to stay: American families in the twentieth century.* New York: Basic Books.

Bankoff, E. A. (1990). Effects of friendship support on the psychological well-being of widows. In H. Z. Lopata & D. R. Maines (Eds.), *Friendship in context* (pp. 109-139). Greenwich, CT: JAI.

Barrow, G. M. (1992). *Aging, the individual, and society.* (5th ed.) St. Paul, MN: West.

Baruch, G., & Barnett, R. (1983). Adult daughters' relationships with their daughters: The era of good feelings. *Journal of Marriage and the Family, 45,* 601-606.

Baruch, G., & Brooks-Gunn, J. (Eds.). (1984). *Women in midlife.* New York: Plenum.

Barusch, A. S., & Spaid, W. M. (1989). Gender differences in caregiving: Why do wives report greater burden? *The Gerontologist, 29,* 557-576.

Becerra, R. M. (1988). The Mexican American family. In C. H. Mindel, R. Habenstein, & R. Wright, Jr. (Eds.), *Ethnic families in America: Patterns and variations* (3rd ed., pp. 141-159). New York: Elsevier.

Bell, R. R. (1981). *Worlds of friendship.* Beverly Hills, CA: Sage.

Bengtson, V. L., & Robertson, J. F. (Eds.). (1985). *Grandparenthood.* Beverly Hills, CA: Sage.

Berardo, F. (1970). Survivorship and social isolation: The case of the aged widower. *The Family Coordinator, 1,* 11-25.

Berger, B. (1960). *Working class suburb.* Berkeley: University of California Press.

Berger, P., & Kellner, H. (1970). Marriage and construction of reality. In H. Dreitzel (Ed.), *Patterns of communicative behavior* (pp. 50-73). London: Collier-Macmillan.

Bernard, J. (1956). *Remarriage.* New York: Holt, Rinehart & Winston.

Bernard, J. (1973). *The future of marriage.* New York: Bantam.

Bernard, J. (1983). The good provider role: Its rise and fall. In A. S. Skolnick & J. H. Skolnick (Eds.), *Family in transition* (pp. 155-175). Boston: Little, Brown.

Bins, S. (1992). THEOS foundation chapters—United States and Canada. *The Communicator,* p. 5.

Blau, Z. S. (1961). Structural constraints on friendships in old age. *American Sociological Review, 26,* 429-439.

Blauner, R. (1966). Death and social structure. *Psychiatry, 29,* 378-394.

Blieszner, R. (1989). Developmental processes of friendship. In R. G. Adams & R. Blieszner (Eds.), *Older adult friendship: Structure and process* (pp. 108-126). Newbury Park, CA: Sage.

Blom, I. (1991). The history of widowhood: A bibliographic overview. *Journal of Family History, 16,* 191-210.

Blumer, H. (1969). *Symbolic interactionism: Perspective and method.* Englewood Cliffs, NJ: Prentice Hall.

Bohannan, P. (1963). *Social anthropology.* New York: Holt, Rinehart & Winston.

Booth, A., & Hess, E. (1974). Cross-sex friendship. *Journal of Marriage and the Family, 36,* 38-47.

Bott, R. (1957). *Family and social network.* London: Tavistock.

Breton, R. (1964). Institutional completeness of ethnic communities and the personal relations of immigrants. *American Journal of Sociology, 70,* 193-205.

Brody, E. M. (1986). Filial care of the elderly and changing roles of women (and men). *Journal of Geriatric Psychiatry, 19,* 175-201.

Brody, E. M. (1990). *Women in the middle: Their parent care years.* New York: Springer.

Brody, E. M., Kleban, M. H., Johnson, P. T., Hoffman, C., & Schoonover, C. B. (1987). Work status and parent care: A comparison of four groups of women. *The Gerontologist, 27,* 201-208.

Brody, E. M., Litvin, S. J., Hoffman, C., & Kleban, M. H. (1995). Marital status of caregiving daughters and co-residence with dependent parents. *The Gerontologist, 35,* 75-85.

Buck, P. (1962). *A bridge in passing.* New York: John Day.

Bulcroft, K., & Bulcroft, R. (1985). Dating and courtship in late life: An exploratory study. In W. A. Peterson & J. Quadagno (Eds.), *Social bonds in later life* (pp. 115-126). Beverly Hills, CA: Sage.

Burton, L. M., & Bengtson, V. L. (1985). Black grandmothers: Issues of timing and continuity of roles. In V. L. Bengtson & J. F. Robertson (Eds.), *Grandparenthood* (pp. 61-77). Beverly Hills, CA: Sage.

Butler, R. (1963). The life review: An interpretation of the reminiscence in the aged. *Psychiatry, 26,* 65-70.

Cain, A. C. (1977). Survivors of suicide. In S. G. Wilcox & M. Sutton (Eds.), *Understanding death and dying: An interdisciplinary approach* (pp. 229-233). Dominguez Hills: California State University Press.

Caine, L. (1974). *Widow.* New York: William Morrow.

Carnegie, D. (1936). *How to win friends and influence people.* New York: Simon & Schuster.

Chandler, J. (1991). *Women without husbands: An exploration of the margins of marriage.* New York: St. Martin's.

Charmaz, K. (1980). *The social reality of death: Death in contemporary America.* Reading, MA: Addison-Wesley.

Cherlin, A. J. (1978). Remarriage as an incomplete institution. *American Journal of Sociology, 84,* 550-634.

Cherlin, A. J. (1981). *Marriage, divorce, remarriage.* Cambridge, MA: Harvard University Press.

Cherlin, A. J. (1992). *Marriage, divorce, remarriage* (2nd ed.). Cambridge, MA: Harvard University Press.

Cherlin, A. J., & Furstenberg, F. J. (1986). *The new American grandparent.* New York: Basic Books.

Chevan, A., & Korson, H. (1972). The widowed who live alone: An examination of social and demographic factors. *Social Forces, 51,* 45-53.

Chevan, A., & Korson, H. (1975). Living arrangements of widows in the United States and Israel, 1960 and 1961. *Demography, 12,* 505-518.

Chodorow, N. (1978). *The reproduction of mothering: Psychoanalysis and the sociology of gender.* Berkeley: University of California Press.

Cicirelli, V. G. (1982). Sibling influence throughout the lifespan. In M. E. Lamb & B. Sutton-Smith (Eds.), *Sibling relationships: Their nature and significance across the lifespan* (pp. 267-284). Hillsdale, NJ: Lawrence Erlbaum.

Clignet, R. (1992). *Death, deeds, and descendants: Inheritance in modern America.* New York: Aldine de Gruyter.

Clipp, E. C., & George, L. K. (1990). Caregiver needs and patterns of social support. *Journal of Gerontology: Social Sciences, 45,* S102-S111.

Connidis, I. A. (1989). Siblings as friends in later life. *American Behavioral Scientist, 33,* 81-93.

Cool, L., & McCabe, J. (1983). The "scheming hag" and the "dear old thing": An anthropology of aging women. In J. Sokolovsky (Ed.), *Growing old in different societies* (pp. 56-68). Belmont, CA: Wadsworth.

Coontz, S. (1992). *The way we never were: American families and the nostalgia trap.* New York: Basic Books.

Coser, L. (Ed.). (1974). *Greedy institutions.* New York: Free Press.

Coser, L., & Coser, R. L. (1974). The housewife and her "greedy family." In L. Coser (Ed.), *Greedy institutions* (pp. 89-100). New York: Free Press.

Coser, R. (1991). *In defence of modernity: Role complexity and individual autonomy.* Stanford, CA: Stanford University Press.

Cumming, E., & Henry, W. I. (1961). *Growing old: The process of disengagement.* New York: Basic Books.

Daniels, A. K. (1988). *Invisible careers: Women community leaders in the volunteer world.* Chicago: University of Chicago Press.

Davidson, J. K., & Moore, N. B. (1992). *Marriage and family.* Dubuque, IA: William C. Brown.

De Hoyos, A., & De Hoyos, G. (1966). The amigo system and alienation of the wife in the conjugal Mexican family. In B. Farber (Ed.), *Kinship and family organization* (pp. 102-115). New York: John Wiley.

Denzin, N. K. (1970). Rules of conduct and the study of deviant behavior: Some notes on the social relationship. In G. J. McCall, M. A. McCall, N. K. Denzin, G. D. Suttles, & S. B. Kurth (Eds.), *Social relationships* (pp. 62-94). Chicago: Aldine.

DeSpelder, L. A., & Strickland, A. L. (1992). *The last dance: Encountering death and dying* (3rd ed.). Mountain View, CA: Mayfield.

Diamont, S. (Ed.). (1957). *Kibbutz and shtetl: Politics and public policy.* New York: Longman.

DiGiulio, R. (1989). *Beyond widowhood: From bereavement to emergence and hope.* New York: Free Press.

di Leonardo, M. (1984). *The varieties of ethnic experience: Kinship, class and gender among California Italian-Americans.* Ithaca, NY: Cornell University Press.

Dulles, F. R. (1965). *A history of recreation: America learns to play.* New York: Appleton-Century-Crofts.

Durkheim, E. (1946). *The elementary forms of religious life* (J. W. Swan, Trans.). London: Allen & Unwin. (Original work published 1915)

Durkheim, E. (1951). *Suicide* (J. A. Spaulding & G. Simpson, Trans.). Glencoe, IL: Free Press.

Dwyer, J. W., & Coward, R. T. (1991). Multivariate comparison of the involvement of adult sons versus daughters in the care of impaired parents. *Journal of Gerontology: Social Sciences, 46,* S259-S269.

Ebaugh, H. R. F. (1988). *Becoming an ex: The process of role exit.* Chicago: University of Chicago Press.

Ehrenreich, B., & English, D. (1979). *For her own good.* Garden City, NY: Basic Books.

Eichler, M. (1973). Women as personal dependents. In M. Stephenson (Ed.), *Women in Canada* (pp. 36-55). Toronto: New Press.

Eren, N. (1963). *Turkey today—and tomorrow: An experiment in westernization.* New York: Praeger.

Eshleman, J. R. (1994). *The family* (7th ed.). Boston: Allyn & Bacon.

Felton, M. (1966). *A child widow's story.* New York: Harcourt, Brace & World.

Finch, J. (1983). *Married to the job: Wives' incorporation in men's work.* Boston: Allen & Unwin.

Fischer, D. H. (1977). *Growing old in America.* New York: Oxford University Press.

Fischer, L. R. (1981). Transitions in the mother-daughter relationship. *Journal of Marriage and the Family, 43*, 613-622.

Fischer, L. R. (1983). Mothers and mothers-in-law. *Journal of Marriage and the Family, 45*, 187-192.

Fischer, L. R. (1986). *Linked lives: Adult daughters and their mothers.* New York: Harper & Row.

Folken, M. H. (1990). Moderating grief of widowed people in talk groups. *Death Studies, 14*, 171-176.

Folken, M. H. (1991). The importance of group support for widowed persons. *Journal for Specialists in Group Work, 16*(3), 172-177.

Franks, D. D. (Ed.). (1985). The sociology of emotions [Special issue]. *Symbolic Interaction, 8*(2), 161-341.

Fry, C. L., & Gavrin, L. (1987). American after lives: Widowhood in community context. In H. Z. Lopata (Ed.), *Widows: North America* (pp. 32-47). Durham, NC: Duke University Press.

Gans, H. (1962). *The urban villagers.* New York: Free Press.

Gentry, M., Rosenman, L., & Shulman, A. D. (1987). Comparison of the needs and support systems of remarried and nonremarried widows. In H. Z. Lopata (Ed.), *Widows: North America* (pp. 158-180). Durham, NC: Duke University Press.

Ghosh, S. K. (1984). *Women in a changing society.* New Delhi: Ashish Publishing House.

Gibbs, J. M. (1979). *The social world of the older widow in the non-metropolitan community.* Unpublished doctoral dissertation, Kansas State University, Manhattan.

Gill, R. T., Glazer, N., & Thernstrom, S. A. (1992). *Our changing population.* Englewood Cliffs, NJ: Prentice Hall.

Gladstone, J. (1993, July). *Exploring the impact of institutional relocation on older married couples.* Paper presented at the 15th International Congress of Gerontology, Budapest, Hungary.

Glaser, B., & Strauss, A. L. (1965). *Awareness of dying.* Chicago: Aldine.

Glaser, B., & Strauss, A. L. (1968). *Time for dying.* Chicago: Aldine.

Glenn, E. (1992). From servitude to service work: Historical continuities in the racial division of paid reproductive labor. *Signs, 18*(1), 1-43.

Glick, I. O., Weiss, R. S., & Parkes, C. M. (1974). *The first year of bereavement.* New York: John Wiley.

Gorer, G. (1967). *Death, grief and mourning.* Garden City, NY: Anchor/Doubleday.

Gouldner, H., & Strong, M. S. (1987). *Speaking of friendship—Middle-class women and their friends.* New York: Greenwood.

Graebner, W. (1980). *A history of retirement: The management and function of an American institution 1885-1978.* New Haven, CT: Yale University Press.

Greeley, A. M., & Rossi, P. H. (1968). *The education of Catholic Americans.* Garden City, NY: Doubleday.

Green, S. A. (1993, October 24). A room of their own. *Chicago Tribune*, Sec. 16, p. 5D.

Grubb, N. W., & Lazerson, M. (1983). *Broken promises: How Americans fail their children.* New York: Basic Books.

Gujral, J. S. (1987). Widowhood in India. In H. Z. Lopata (Ed.), *Widows: The Middle East, Asia and the Pacific* (pp. 43-55). Durham, NC: Duke University Press.

Gusfield, J. R. (1967). Tradition and modernity: Misplaced polarities in the study of social change. *American Journal of Sociology, 72*, 351-362.

Gusfield, J. R. (1976). [Review of the book *Becoming modern: Individual changes in six developing countries.*] *American Journal of Sociology, 82*, 443-448.

Hacker, A. (Ed.). (1983). *U/S: A statistical portrait of the American people.* New York: Viking.

Hagestad, G. O. (1985). Continuity and connectedness. In V. L. Bengtson & J. F. Robertson (Eds.), *Grandparenthood* (pp. 31-48). Beverly Hills, CA: Sage.

Hart, N. (1976). *When marriage ends: A study in status passage.* London: Tavistock.

Heaton, T. B., & Hoppe, C. (1987). Widowed and married: Comparative change in living arrangements, 1900 and 1980. *Social Science History, 11,* 261-278.

Heisel, M. (1987). Women and widows in Turkey: Support systems. In H. Z. Lopata (Ed.), *Widows: The Middle East, Asia and the Pacific* (pp. 79-105). Durham, NC: Duke University Press.

Hess, B. B. (1972). Friendship. In M. Riley, M. Johnson, & A. Foner (Eds.), *Aging and society: A sociology of age stratification* (pp. 357-393). New York: Russell Sage.

Hess, B. B., & Markson, E. W. (1980). *Aging and old age.* New York: Macmillan.

Hill, C. D., Thompson, L. W., & Gallagher, D. (1988). The role of anticipatory bereavement in older women's adjustment to widowhood. *The Gerontologist, 28,* 792-796.

Hite, S. (1987). *Women and love: A cultural revolution in progress.* Harmondsworth, UK: Penguin.

Hochschild, A. (1973). *The unexpected community.* Englewood Cliffs, NJ: Prentice Hall.

Hochschild, A. (1989). *The second shift: Working parents and the revolution at home.* New York: Viking Penguin.

Horowitz, A. (1985). Sons and daughters as caregivers to older parents: Differences in role performance and consequences. *The Gerontologist, 25,* 612-617.

Hunt, M. (1966). *The world of the formerly married.* New York: McGraw-Hill.

Hunter, A. (1974). *Symbolic communities: The persistence and change of Chicago's local communities.* Chicago: University of Chicago Press.

Hunter, S., & Sundel, M. (1989). Introduction: An examination of key issues concerning midlife. In S. Hunter & M. Sundel (Eds.), *Midlife myths: Issues, findings, and practice implications* (pp. 8-28). Newbury Park, CA: Sage.

Huttman, E. D. (1985). *Social services for the elderly.* New York: Free Press.

Hyman, H. H. (1983). *Of time and widowhood.* Durham, NC: Duke University Press.

Inkeles, A. (1983). *Exploring individual modernity.* New York: Columbia University Press.

Inkeles, A., & Smith, D. H. (1974). *Becoming modern: Individual change in six developing countries.* Cambridge, MA: Harvard University Press.

Irish, D. P., Lundquist, K. F., & Nelson, V. J. (Eds.). (1993). *Ethnic variations in dying, death and grief: Diversity in universality.* Washington, DC: Taylor & Francis.

Ishii-Kuntz, M. (1990). Formal activities for elderly women: Determinants of participation in voluntary and senior center activities. *Journal of Women and Aging, 2,* 79-97.

Jackson, M. R., & Crane, M. (1986). "Some of my best friends are black . . .": Interracial friendships and whites' racial attitudes. *Public Opinion Quarterly, 50,* 459-486.

Jacobs, R. H., & Vinick, B. H. (1979). *Re-engagement in later life: Re-employment and remarriage.* Stamford, CT: Gaylock.

Jaffe, D. J. (1989). *Caring strangers: The sociology of intergenerational homesharing.* Greenwich, CT: JAI.

Jerrome, D. (1981). The significance of friendship for women in later life. *Ageing and Society, 1,* 175-197.

Johnson, C. L., & Troll, L. E. (1994). Constraints and facilitators to friendships in late life. *The Gerontologist, 34,* 79-87.

Johnston, J. A. (1992, October 25). You may want to get expert advice before you remarry. *Chicago Sun Times,* p. 62.

Kahana, E. F., & Kiyak, H. A. (1981). The older woman: Impact of widowhood and living arrangements on service needs. *Journal of Gerontological Social Work, 3,* 17-29.

Kalish, R. A. (1981). *Death, grief, and caring relationship.* Monterey, CA: Brooks/Cole.

Kastenbaum, R. J. (1991). *Death, society and human experience* (4th ed.). New York: Macmillan.

Katz, R., & Ben-Dor, N. (1987). Widowhood in Israel. In H. Z. Lopata (Ed.), *Widows: The Middle East, Asia and the Pacific* (pp. 133-147). Durham, NC: Duke University Press.

Keyssar, A. (1974). Widowhood in 18th century Massachusetts: A problem in the history of the family. *Perspectives in American History, 8,* 83-119.

Kimmel, M. S., & Messner, M. A. (1995). *Men's lives* (3rd ed.). New York: Macmillan.

Kinderknecht, C. H. (1989). What's out there and how to get it: A practical resource guide for the helpers of older women. In J. D. Garner & S. O. Mercer (Eds.), *Women as they age: Challenge, opportunity, and triumph* (pp. 363-395). New York: Haworth.

Kitson, G., Lopata, H. Z., Holmes, W. M., & Meyering, S. M. (1980). Divorcees and widows: Similarities and differences. *American Journal of Orthopsychiatry, 50,* 291-301.

Kleinberg, S. (1973). *Technology's stepdaughters: The impact of industrialization upon working class women, Pittsburgh, 1865-1890.* Unpublished doctoral dissertation, University of Pittsburgh.

Komarovsky, M. (1967). *Blue-collar marriage.* New York: Random House.

Koo, J. (1982). *Korean women in widowhood.* Unpublished doctoral dissertation, University of Missouri—Columbia.

Koo, J. (1987). Widows in Seoul, Korea. In H. Z. Lopata (Ed.), *Widows: The Middle East, Asia and the Pacific* (pp. 56-78). Durham, NC: Duke University Press.

Kübler-Ross, E. (1969). *On death and dying.* New York: Macmillan.

Kurth, S. B. (1970). Friendship and friendly relations. In G. J. McCall, M. M. McCall, N. K. Denzin, G. D. Suttles, & S. B. Kurth (Eds.), *Social relationships* (pp. 136-170). Chicago: Aldine.

Lamm, M. (1969). *The Jewish way in death and mourning.* New York: Jonathan David.

Laslett, P. (1976). Characteristics of the Western family considered over time. *Family History, 2,* 89-115.

Lawson, H. (1990). *Service values=profit goals: The divided selves of car sales women.* Unpublished doctoral dissertation, Loyola University of Chicago.

Leanse, J., & Wagner, S. (1975). *Senior centers: Report of senior group programs in America.* Washington, DC: National Council on Aging.

Lerner, G. (1978). *A death of one's own.* New York: Simon & Schuster.

Levy, L. H. (1979). Processes and activities in groups. In M. A. Lieberman & L. D. Borman (Eds.), *Self-help groups for coping with crisis* (pp. 234-271). San Francisco: Jossey-Bass.

Lieberman, M. A. (1993). Bereavement self-help groups: A review of conceptual and methodological issues. In M. S. Stroebe, W. Stroebe, & R. O. Hansson (Eds.), *Handbook of bereavement: Theory, research and intervention* (pp. 411-426). New York: Cambridge University Press.

Lieberman, M. A. (1994). *Must widows wear black: Growth beyond grief.* Unpublished manuscript.

Lieberman, M. A., & Gourash, N. (1979). Effects of change groups on the elderly. In M. A. Lieberman & L. D. Borman (Eds.), *Self-help groups for coping with crisis* (pp. 67-79). San Francisco: Jossey-Bass.

Lieberman, M. A., & Videka-Sherman, L. (1986). The impact of self-help groups on the mental health of widows and widowers. *American Journal of Orthopsychiatry, 56,* 435-449.

Lieberson, S. (1963). *Ethnic patterns in American cities.* New York: Free Press.

Lindemann, E. (1944). Symptomology and management of acute grief. *American Journal of Psychiatry, 101,* 141-148.

Litwak, E. (1989). Forms of friendship among older people in an industrial society. In R. G. Adams & R. Blieszner (Eds.), *Older adult friendship: Structure and process* (pp. 65-88). Newbury Park, CA: Sage.

Lofland, L. H. (1985). The social shaping of emotion: The case of grief. *Symbolic Interaction, 8,* 171-190.

Lopata, H. Z. (1969). Loneliness: Forms and components. *Social Problems, 17,* 248-260.

Lopata, H. Z. (1970). The social involvement of American widows. *American Behavioral Scientist, 14,* 41-57.

Lopata, H. Z. (1971a). Living arrangements of urban widows and their married children. *Sociological Focus, 5*(1), 41-61.

Lopata, H. Z. (1971b). *Occupation: Housewife.* New York: Oxford University Press.

Lopata, H. Z. (1973a). The effect of schooling on social contacts of urban women. *American Journal of Sociology, 79,* 604-619.

Lopata, H. Z. (1973b). Self-identity in marriage and widowhood. *Sociological Quarterly, 14,* 407-418.

Lopata, H. Z. (1973c). Social relations of black and white widowed women in a northern metropolis. *American Journal of Sociology, 78,* 241-248.

Lopata, H. Z. (1973d). *Widowhood in an American city.* Cambridge, MA: Schenkman.

Lopata, H. Z. (1975a). Couple-companionate relationships in marriage and widowhood. In N. Glazer-Malbin (Ed.), *Old family/New family* (pp. 119-149). New York: D. Van Nostrand.

Lopata, H. Z. (1975b). On widowhood: Grief work and identity reconstruction. *Journal of Geriatric Psychiatry, 8*(2), 41-55.

Lopata, H. Z. (1976a). *Polish Americans: Status competition in an ethnic community.* Englewood Cliffs, NJ: Prentice Hall.

Lopata, H. Z. (1976b). Widows as a minority group. In B. D. Bell (Ed.), *Contemporary social gerontology* (pp. 348-355). Springfield, IL: Charles C Thomas.

Lopata, H. Z. (1977). Widowhood in Polonia. *Polish American Studies, 34,* 7-25.

Lopata, H. Z. (1978a). Contributions of extended families to the support systems of metropolitan area widows: Limitations of the modified kin network. *Journal of Marriage and the Family, 40,* 355-364.

Lopata, II. Z. (1978b). The absence of community resources in support systems of urban widows. *The Family Coordinator, 27,* 383-388.

Lopata, H. Z. (1979). *Women as widows: Support systems.* New York: Elsevier.

Lopata, H. Z. (1981). Widowhood and husband sanctification. *Journal of Marriage and the Family, 43,* 439-450.

Lopata, H. Z. (1986a). Becoming and being a widow: Reconstruction of self and support systems. *Geriatric Psychiatry, 14,* 203-214.

Lopata, H. Z. (1986b). Time in anticipated future and events in memory. *American Behavioral Scientist, 29,* 695-709.

Lopata, H. Z. (1987a). Widowhood and social change. In H. Z. Lopata (Ed.), *Widows: The Middle East, Asia and the Pacific* (pp. 217-229). Durham, NC: Duke University Press.

Lopata, H. Z. (1987b). Widowhood: World perspectives on support systems. In H. Z. Lopata (Ed.), *Widows: The Middle East, Asia and the Pacific* (pp. 1-23). Durham, NC: Duke University Press.

Lopata, H. Z. (Ed.). (1987c). *Widows: North America.* Durham, NC: Duke University Press.

Lopata, H. Z. (1987d). Widows: North American perspective. In H. Z. Lopata (Ed.), *Widows: North America* (pp. 3-31). Durham, NC: Duke University Press.

Lopata, H. Z. (Ed.). (1987e). *Widows: The Middle East, Asia and the Pacific.* Durham, NC: Duke University Press.

Lopata, H. Z. (1990). Friendship: Historical and theoretical introduction. In H. Z. Lopata & D. R. Maines (Eds.), *Friendship in context* (pp. 1-19). Greenwich, CT: JAI.

Lopata, H. Z. (1991a, July). *In-laws and the concept of family.* Paper presented at the Family Research Symposium of the International Sociological Association on "What Is Family?" Oslo, Norway.

Lopata, H. Z. (1991b). Which child? The consequences of social development on the support systems of widows. In B. B. Hess & E. W. Markson (Eds.), *Growing old in America* (pp. 39-49). New Brunswick, NJ: Transaction.

Lopata, H. Z. (1993a). Career commitments of American women: The issue of side bets. *Sociological Quarterly, 34,* 257-277.

Lopata, H. Z. (1993b). The interweave of public and private: Women's challenge to American society. *Journal of Marriage and the Family, 55,* 220-235.

Lopata, H. Z. (1994a). *Circles and settings: Role changes of American women.* Albany: State University of New York.

Lopata, H. Z. (1994b). *Polish Americans* (2nd ed.). New Brunswick, NJ: Transaction.

Lopata, H. Z., Barnewolt, D., & Harrison, K. (1987). Homemakers and household composition. In H. Z. Lopata (Ed.), *Current research on occupations and professions* (pp. 219-245). Greenwich, CT: JAI.

Lopata, H. Z., Barnewolt, D., & Miller, C. A. (1985). *City women: Work, jobs, occupations, careers. Vol. 1: Chicago.* New York: Praeger.

Lopata, H. Z., & Brehm, H. (1986). *Widows and dependent wives: From social problem to federal policy.* New York: Praeger.

Lopata, H. Z., & Maines, D. R. (Eds.). (1990). *Friendship in context.* Greenwich, CT: JAI.

Lopata, H. Z., Miller C. A., & Barnewolt, D. (1986). *City women in America: Work, jobs, occupations, careers.* New York: Praeger.

Ludwig, C. (1977). *The social role of the grandmother among Puerto Ricans on the mainland.* Unpublished master's thesis, Loyola University of Chicago.

Lund, D. A., & Caserta, M. S. (1992). Older bereaved spouses' participation in self-help groups. *Omega, 25*(1), 47-61.

Lund, D. A., Caserta, M. S., & Diamond, M. F. (1993). The course of spousal bereavement in later life. In M. S. Stroebe, W. Stroebe, & R. O. Hansson (Eds.), *Handbook of bereavement: Theory, research and intervention* (pp. 240-254). New York: Cambridge University Press.

Lund, D. A., Caserta, M. S., Diamond, M. F., & Gray, R. M. (1986). Impact of bereavement on the self-conceptions of older surviving spouses. *Symbolic Interaction, 9,* 235-244.

Malatesta, V. J., Chambless, D. L., Pollack, M., & Cantor, A. (1988). Widowhood, sexuality and aging: A life span analysis. *Journal of Sex and Marital Therapy, 14,* 49-62.

Mantell, J., & Gildea, M. (1989). Elderly shared housing in the United States. In D. J. Jaffe (Ed.), *Shared housing for the elderly* (pp. 13-23). New York: Greenwood.

Marris, P. (1958). *Widows and their families.* London: Routledge and Kegan Paul.

Martin, J. L., & Dean, L. (1993). Bereavement following death from AIDS: Unique problems, reactions and special needs. In M. S. Stroebe, W. Stroebe, & R. O.

Hansson (Eds.), *Handbook of bereavement: Theory, research and intervention* (pp. 317-330). New York: Cambridge University Press.

Martin Matthews, A. (1987). Support systems of widows in Canada. In H. Z. Lopata (Ed.), *Widows: North America* (pp. 225-250). Durham, NC: Duke University Press.

Martin Matthews, A. (1991). *Widowhood in later life.* Toronto: Butterworths.

Matras, J. (1990). *Dependency, obligations, and entitlements: A new sociology of aging, the life course, and the elderly.* Englewood Cliffs, NJ: Prentice Hall.

Matthews, S. H. (1979). *The social world of old women: Management of self-identity.* Beverly Hills, CA: Sage.

McCrea, R. R., & Costa, P. T. (1993). Psychological resilience among widowed men and women: A 10-year follow-up of a national sample. In M. S. Stroebe, W. Stroebe, & R. O. Hansson (Eds.), *Handbook of bereavement: Theory, research and intervention* (pp. 196-207). New York: Cambridge University Press.

McDonald, J. M. (1987). Support systems of American black wives and widows. In H. Z. Lopata (Ed.), *Widows: North America* (pp. 139-157). Durham, NC: Duke University Press.

McKaine, W. C. (1969). *Retirement marriage.* Chicago: University of Chicago Press.

Middleton, W., Raphael, B., Martinek, N., & Misso, V. (1993). In M. S. Stroebe, W. Stroebe, & R. O. Hansson (Eds.), *Handbook on bereavement: Theory, research and intervention* (pp. 44-61). New York: Cambridge University Press.

Miller, B. (1987). Gender and control among spouses of the cognitively impaired: A research note. *The Gerontologist, 29,* 447-453.

Miller, B., & Kaufman, J. E. (1993, June). *Gender stereotypes of care among spouse caregivers of persons with dementia.* Paper presented at the National Institute on Aging Conference on Men's Caregiving Roles in an Aging Society, Washington, DC.

Mills, C. W. (1959). *The sociological imagination.* New York: Oxford University Press.

Min, P. G. (1988). The Korean American family. In C. Mindel, R. W. Habenstein, & R. Wright, Jr. (Eds.), *Ethnic families in America: Patterns and variations* (3rd ed., pp. 199-229). New York: Elsevier.

Mitford, J. (1963). *The American way of death.* New York: Simon & Schuster.

Morgan, D. L., Neal, M. B., & Carder, P. C. (n.d.). *How differences in the timing of social support affect depression among recent widows.* Unpublished manuscript.

Morgan, L. A. (1986). The financial experience of widowed women: Evidence from the LRHS. *The Gerontologist, 26,* 663-668.

Morgan, L. A. (1989). Economic well-being following marital termination: A comparison of widowed and divorced women. *Journal of Family Issues, 10,* 86-101.

Morgan, L. A. (1991a). *After marriage ends: Economic consequences for midlife women.* Newbury Park, CA: Sage.

Morgan, L. A. (1991b). Economic security of older women: Issues and trends for the future. In B. B. Hess & E. W. Markson (Eds.), *Growing old in America* (2nd ed., pp. 275-292). New Brunswick, NJ: Transaction.

Moss, M. S., Lawton, M. P., Kleban, M. H., & Duhamel, L. (1993). Time use of caregivers of impaired elders before and after institutionalization. *Journal of Gerontology, 48,* 102-111.

Moynihan, P. (1963). *The Negro family: The case for national action.* Washington, DC: U.S. Department of Labor, Office of Policy Planning and Research.

Murstein, W. I. (1974). *Love, sex and marriage through the ages.* New York: Springer.

Nardi, P. M. (Ed.). (1992). *Men's friendships.* Newbury Park, CA: Sage.

National Caucus and Center on Black Aged. (1987). *The status of the black elderly in the United States.* Washington, DC: Government Printing Office.

Neale, A. V. (1987). Widows in a Florida retirement community. In H. Z. Lopata (Ed.), *Widows: North America* (pp. 71-94). Durham, NC: Duke University Press.

Nelson, S. M. (1988). Widowhood and autonomy in the Native-American Southwest. In A. Scandron (Ed.), *On their own: Widows and widowhood in the American Southwest, 1848-1939* (pp. 22-41). Urbana: University of Illinois Press.

Neugarten, B. L., & Hagestad, G. O. (1976). Age and the life course. In E. Shanas & R. Binstock (Eds.), *Handbook of aging and the social sciences* (pp. 35-55). New York: Van Nostrand Reinhold.

Neuhaus, R., & Neuhaus, R. H. (1982). *Successful aging.* New York: John Wiley.

Nye, I. F., & Berardo, F. M. (1973). *The family.* New York: Macmillan.

Oakley, A. (1974a). *The sociology of housework.* Bath, UK: Pitman.

Oakley, A. (1974b). *Women's work: A history of the housewife.* New York: Pantheon.

O'Bryant, S. L. (1987). Attachment to home and support systems of older widows in Columbus, Ohio. In H. Z. Lopata (Ed.), *Widows: North America* (pp. 48-70). Durham, NC: Duke University Press.

O'Bryant, S. L. (1988a). Sex differentiated assistance in older widows' support networks. *Sex Roles, 19,* 91-106.

O'Bryant, S. L. (1988b). Sibling support and older widows' well-being. *Journal of Marriage and the Family, 50,* 173-183.

O'Bryant, S. L. (1991a). Forewarning of a husband's death: Does it make a difference for older widows? *Omega, 23,* 227-239.

O'Bryant, S. L. (1991b). Older widows and independent lifestyles. *International Journal of Aging and Human Development, 32,* 41-51.

O'Bryant, S. L., Donnermeyer, J. F., & Stafford, K. (1991). Fear of crime and per-ceived risk among older widowed women. *Journal of Community Psychology, 19,* 166-177.

O'Bryant, S. L., & McGloshen, T. H. (1987). Older widows' intention to stay or move from their homes. *Home Economics Research Journal, 15,* 177-183.

O'Bryant, S. L., & Murray, C. I. (1986). Attachment to home and other factors related to widows' relocation decision. *Journal of Housing for the Elderly, 4*(1), 53-72.

O'Bryant, S. L., Straw, L. B., & Meddaugh, D. I. (1990). Contributions of the care-giving role to women's development. *Sex Roles, 23,* 645-658.

O'Connor, P. O. (1993). Same-gender and cross-gender friendships among the frail elderly. *The Gerontologist, 33,* 24-30.

Osterweis, M., Solomon, F., & Green, N. (1984). *Bereavement: Reactions, consequences, and care.* Washington, DC: National Academy Press.

Oxford Universal Dictionary. (1955). Oxford, UK: Clarendon.

Papanek, H. (1973). Men, women and work: Reflections on the two-person career. *American Journal of Sociology, 78,* 852-872.

Papanek, H. (1978). Comment on Gusfield's review essay on "Becoming modern." *American Journal of Sociology, 83,* 1507-1511.

Papanek, H. (1979). Family status production: The "work" and "nonwork" of women. *Signs, 4,* 775-781.

Parkes, C. M. (1972). *Bereavement.* London: International Universities Press.

Parkes, C. M. (1993). Bereavement as a psychosocial transition: Processes of adaptation to change. In M. S. Stroebe, W. Stroebe, & R. O. Hansson (Eds.), *Handbook on bereavement: Theory, research and intervention* (pp. 91-101). New York: Cam-bridge University Press.

Patil, G. D. (1990). *Hindu widows: A study of deprivation.* Unpublished doctoral dissertation, Karnatak University, India.

Peterson, J. A., & Payne, B. (1975). *Love in the later years: The emotional, physical, sexual and social potential of the elderly.* New York: Association Press.

Pihlblad, C. T., & Adams, D. L. (1972). Widowhood, social participation, and life satisfaction. *Aging and Human Development, 3,* 323-330.

Pine, V. R., & Phillips, D. L. (1977). The cost of dying: A sociological analysis of funeral expenditures. In R. Fulton (Ed.), *Death and identity* (pp. 420-434). Bowie, MD: Charles Press.

Polish Welfare Association. (1991). *Annual report.* Chicago: Author.

Raphael, B. (1978). *The anatomy of bereavement.* New York: Basic Books.

Rice, S. (1989a). Sexuality and intimacy for aging women: A changing perspective. *Journal of Women and Aging, 1,* 245-264.

Rice, S. (1989b). Single older childless women: Differences between never-married and widowed women in life satisfaction and social support. *Journal of Gerontological Social Work, 13,* 35-47.

Riessman, F., Moody, H. R., & Worthy, E. H., Jr. (1984). Self-help and the elderly. *Social Policy, 14,* 19-26.

Roach, M. J., & Kitson, G. C. (1989). Impact of forewarning on adjustment to widowhood and divorce. In D. A. Lund (Ed.), *Older bereaved spouses* (pp. 185-200). New York: Hemisphere.

Robbins, B., & Howe, E. (1989). Patterns of homesharing in the United States. In D. J. Jaffe (Ed.), *Shared housing for the elderly* (pp. 25-36). New York: Greenwood.

Roberto, K. A., & Scott, J. P. (1986). Confronting widowhood: The influence of informal supports. *American Behavioral Scientist, 29,* 497-511.

Rook, K. S. (1984). The negative side of social interaction: Impact on psychological well-being. *Journal of Personality and Social Psychology, 46,* 1097-1108.

Rook, K. S. (1989). Strains in older adults' friendships. In R. G. Adams & R. Blieszner (Eds.), *Older adult friendship: Structure and process* (pp. 166-194). Newbury Park, CA: Sage.

Rosenberg, M. (1979). *Conceiving the self.* New York: Basic Books.

Rosenblatt, P. C. (1993). Grief: The social context of private feelings. In M. S. Stroebe, W. Stroebe, & R. O. Hansson (Eds.), *Handbook of bereavement: Theory, research and intervention* (pp. 102-111). New York: Cambridge University Press.

Rosenblatt, P. C., Walsh, R. P., & Jackson, D. A. (1976). *Grief and mourning in cross-cultural perspective.* New Haven, CT: HRAF.

Ross, A. (1962). *The Hindu family in its urban setting.* Toronto: University of Toronto Press.

Rossi, A. S., & Rossi, P. H. (1990). *Of human bonding: Parent-child relations across the life course.* New York: Aldine de Gruyter.

Rubin, L. (1985). *Just friends: The role of friendship in our lives.* New York: Harper & Row.

Rubin, S. S. (1993). The death of a child is forever: The life course impact of child loss. In M. S. Stroebe, W. Stroebe, & R. O. Hansson (Eds.), *Handbook of bereavement: Theory, research and intervention* (pp. 285-299). New York: Cambridge University Press.

Ryan, M. (1979). *Womanhood in America.* New York: New Viewpoints.

Salcido, R. M., Nakano, C., & Jue, S. (1980). The use of formal and informal health and welfare services of the Asian-American elderly: An exploratory study. *California Sociologist, 3,* 213-229.

Sanchez, C. D. (1989). Informal support systems of widows over 60 in Puerto Rico. In American Association of Retired Persons (Ed.), *Midlife and older women* (pp. 265-278). Washington, DC: Pan American Health Organization.

Sanchez-Ayendez, M. (1988). The Puerto Rican American family. In C. H. Mindel, R. W. Habenstein, & R. Wright, Jr. (Eds.), *Ethnic families in America: Patterns and variations* (3rd ed., pp. 173-195). New York: Elsevier.

Sanders, C. M. (1993). Risk factors in bereavement outcome. In M. S. Stroebe, W. Stroebe, & R. O. Hansson (Eds.), *Handbook of bereavement: Theory, research and intervention* (pp. 255-267). New York: Cambridge University Press.

Sapiro, V. (1986). *Women in American society.* Palo Alto, CA: Mayfield.

Savage, T. (1992, October 25). Marrying again? Read this book. *Chicago Sun Times,* p. 62.

Scandron, A. (Ed.). (1988). *On their own: Widows and widowhood in the American Southwest, 1848-1939.* Urbana: University of Illinois Press.

Schlegel, A. (1988). Hopi family structure and the experience of widowhood. In A. Scandron (Ed.), *On their own: Widows and widowhood in the American Southwest, 1848-1939* (pp. 42-64). Urbana: University of Illinois Press.

Schulz, R., & Ewen, R. B. (1993). *Adult development and aging: Myths and emerging realities* (2nd ed.). New York: Macmillan.

Schuster, T. L., & Butler, E. W. (1989). Bereavement, social networks, social support, and mental health. In D. A. Lund (Ed.), *Older bereaved spouses: Research with practical applications* (pp. 55-68). New York: Hemisphere.

Schwartz, L. L., & Kaslow, F. W. (1985). Widows and divorcees: The same or different? *American Journal of Family Therapy, 13*(4), 72-76.

Shaie, K. W., & Willis, S. L. (1986). *Adult development and aging* (2nd ed.). Boston: Little, Brown.

Shamgar-Handelman, L. (1986). *Israeli war widows: Beyond the glory of heroism.* South Hadley, MA: Bergin & Garvey.

Shanas, E. (1973). Family-kin networks and aging in cross-cultural perspective. *Journal of Marriage and the Family, 35,* 505-511.

Shanas, E. (1979). Social myth as hypothesis: The case of the family relations of old people. *The Gerontologist, 19,* 3-9.

Shanis, H. S. (1985). Impact of Medicare certification on the hospice movement. *Death Studies, 9,* 365-382.

Shuchter, S. R. (1986). *Dimensions of grief: Adjusting to the death of a spouse.* San Francisco: Jossey-Bass.

Shuchter, S. R., & Zisook, S. (1993). The course of normal grief. In M. S. Stroebe, W. Stroebe, & R. O. Hansson (Eds.), *Handbook of bereavement: Theory, research and intervention* (pp. 23-43). New York: Cambridge University Press.

Silverman, P. R. (1986). *Widow to widow.* New York: Springer.

Silverman, P. R. (1987). Widowhood as the next stage in the life course. In H. Z. Lopata (Ed.), *Widows: North America* (pp. 171-190). Durham, NC: Duke University Press.

Silverman, P., & Worden, J. W. (1993). Children's reactions to the death of a parent. In M. S. Stroebe, W. Stroebe, & R. O. Hansson (Eds.), *Handbook of bereavement: Theory, research and intervention* (pp. 300-316). New York: Cambridge University Press.

Simon, B. L. (1987). *Never married women.* Philadelphia: Temple University Press.

Smith, K. R., Zick, C. C., & Duncan, G. J. (1991). Remarriage patterns among recent widows and widowers. *Demography, 28,* 361-375.

Sommers, T., & Shields, L. (1987). *Women take care: The consequences of caregiving in today's society.* Gainesville, FL: Triad.

Squier, D. A., & Quadagno, J. S. (1988). The Italian American family. In C. Mindel, R. W. Habenstein, & R. Wright, Jr. (Eds.), *Ethnic families in America: Patterns and variations* (pp. 109-137). New York: Elsevier.

Stack, C. S. (1974). *All our kin: Strategies for survival in a black community.* New York: Harper & Row.

Stack, C. S. (1981). Sex roles and survival strategies in the urban black community. In F. C. Steady (Ed.), *The black woman cross-culturally* (pp. 349-367). Cambridge, MA: Schenkman.

Stein, D. (1978). Women to burn: Suttee as a normative institution. *Signs, 4,* 253-268.

Stein, D. (1989). Burning widows, burning brides: The perils of daughterhood in India. *Pacific Affairs, 4,* 253-268.

Steinberg, M., & Miles, C. (1979). Transformation of a group for the widowed. In M. A. Lieberman & L. D. Borman (Eds.), *Self-help groups for coping with crisis* (pp. 67-79). San Francisco: Jossey-Bass.

Steinhart, F. (1977). Labor force participation as a resource. In H. Z. Lopata (Ed.), *Support systems involving widows in a metropolitan area of the United States* (Report to the Social Science Administration, Chapter 5). Chicago: Loyola University of Chicago Press.

Straw, L. B., O'Bryant, S. L., & Meddaugh, D. L. (1991). Support system participation in spousal caregiving: Alzheimer's disease versus other illness. *Journal of Applied Gerontology, 10,* 359-371.

Stroebe, M. S., & Stroebe, W. (1993a). The mortality of bereavement: A review. In M. S. Stroebe, W. Stroebe, & R. O. Hansson (Eds.), *Handbook of bereavement: Theory, research and intervention* (pp. 175-195). New York: Cambridge University Press.

Stroebe, M. S., Stroebe, W., & Hansson, R. O. (Eds.). (1993). *Handbook of bereavement: Theory, research and intervention.* New York: Cambridge University Press.

Stroebe, W., & Stroebe, M. S. (1987). *Bereavement and health: The psychological and physical consequences of partner loss.* New York: Cambridge University Press.

Stroebe, W., & Stroebe M. S. (1993b). Determinants of adjustment to bereavement in younger widows and widowers. In M. S. Stroebe, W. Stroebe, & R. O. Hansson (Eds.), *Handbook of bereavement: Theory, research and intervention* (pp. 208-226). New York: Cambridge University Press.

Strong, B., & DeVault, C. (1986). *The marriage and family experience* (3rd ed.). New York: West.

Sussman, M. (1965). Relationships of adult children with their parents in the United States. In E. Shanas & G. Streib (Eds.), *Social structure and the family: Generational relations* (pp. 62-72). Englewood Cliffs, NJ: Prentice Hall.

Sussman, M., Cates, J. N., & Smith, D. T. (1970). *The family and inheritance.* New York: Russell Sage.

Suttles, G. D. (1970). Friendship as a social institution. In G. J. McCall, M. M. McCall, N. K. Denzin, G. D. Suttles, & S. B. Kurth (Eds.), *Social relationships* (pp. 95-135). Chicago: Aldine.

Temes, R. (1984). *Living with an empty chair: A guide through grief.* New York: Irvington, New Horizon.

Thomas, W. I., & Znaniecki, F. W. (1958). *The Polish peasant in Europe and America.* New York: Dover. (Original work published 1918-1920)

Thompson, E. H., Jr., Futterman, A. M., Gallagher-Thompson, D., Rose, J. M., & Lovett, S. B. (1993). Social support and caregiving burden in family caregivers of frail elders. *Journal of Gerontology, 48,* 245-254.

Thorson, J. A. (1978). Lifeboat: Social values and decision making. *Death Education, 1,* 459-464.

Touliatos, J., Perlmutter, B. F., & Holden, G. W. (1990). *Handbook of family measurement techniques.* Newbury Park, CA: Sage.

Tucker, M. B., Taylor, R. J., & Mitchell-Kerman, C. (1993). Marriage and romantic involvement among aged African Americans. *Journal of Gerontology: Social Sciences, 48,* 123-132.

Turner, R. (1962). Role-taking: Process versus conformity. In A. Rose (Ed.), *Human behavior and social processes* (pp. 20-40). Boston: Houghton Mifflin.

Turner, R. (1970). The real self: From institution to impulse. *American Journal of Sociology, 81,* 989-1016.

Ullrich, H. E. (1988). Widows in a South India society: Depression as an appropriate response to cultural factors. *Sex Roles, 19,* 169-187.

U.S. Department of Commerce. (1975). *Statistical abstracts.* Washington, DC: Government Printing Office.

U.S. Department of Commerce. (1992a). *Global aging 1991: Comparative indicators and future trends.* Washington, DC: Bureau of the Census.

U.S. Department of Commerce. (1992b). *Statistical abstracts.* Washington, DC: Government Printing Office.

U.S. Department of Commerce. (1993). *Statistical abstracts.* Washington, DC: Government Printing Office.

van den Hoonaard, D. K. (1992). *Aging in a retirement community.* Unpublished doctoral dissertation, Loyola University of Chicago.

van den Hoonaard, D. K. (1993, May). *Widows tales: Experiences in widowhood.* Paper presented at the Qualitative Research Conference: Studying Human Lived Experience: Symbolic Interaction and Ethnographic Research '93. University of Waterloo, Canada.

van den Hoonaard, D. K. (1994). Paradise lost: Widowhood in a Florida retirement community. *Journal of Aging Studies, 8,* 121-132.

Vernon, J. A., Williams, J. A., Jr., Phillips, T., & Wilson, J. (1990). Media stereotyping: A comparison of the way elderly women and men are portrayed on prime-time television. *Journal of Women and Aging, 2*(4), 55-68.

Vinovskis, M. A. (1990). Death and family life in the past. *Human Nature, 1,* 109-122.

Vlassoff, C. (1990). The value of sons in an Indian village: How widows see it. *Population Studies, 44,* 5-20.

Weber, M. (1958). *The Protestant ethic and the spirit of capitalism* (T. Parsons, Trans.). New York: Scribner. (Original work published 1904)

Weiss, S. S. (1973). *Loneliness: The experience of emotional and social isolation.* Cambridge: MIT Press.

Wildhaber, M. E., Abrams, R. B., Stichman, B. F., & Addlestone, D. F. (1991). *Veterans benefits manual: An advocate's guide to representing veterans and their dependents* (Vol. 1). Washington, DC: National Veterans Legal Services Project.

Willie, C. V. (1976). *A new look at black families.* Bayside, NY: General Hall.

Wilson, W. J. (1978). *The declining significance of race.* Chicago: University of Chicago Press.

Wilson, W. J. (1987). *The truly disadvantaged.* Chicago: University of Chicago Press.

Wiseman, J. P. (1986). Friendship: Bonds and binds in a voluntary relationship. *Journal of Social and Personal Relationships, 3,* 191-211.

Wood, V., Traupmann, J., & Hay, J. (1984). Motherhood in the middle years: Women and their adult children. In G. Baruch & J. Brooks-Gunn (Eds.), *Women in midlife* (pp. 227-244). New York: Plenum.

Wortman, C. B., Silver, R. C., & Kessler, R. C. (1993). The meaning of loss and adjustment to bereavement. In M. S. Stroebe, W. Stroebe, & R. O. Hansson (Eds.), *Handbook of bereavement: Theory, research and intervention* (pp. 349-366). New York: Cambridge University Press.

Wright, L. K., Clipp, E. C., & George, L. K. (1993). Health consequences of caregiver stress. *Medicine, Exercise, Nutrition, and Health, 2,* 181-195.

Wright, P. H. (1989). Gender differences in adults' same- and cross-gender friendship. In R. G. Adams & R. Blieszner (Eds.), *Older adult friendship: Structure and process* (pp. 197-221). Newbury Park, CA: Sage.

Young, R. F., & Kahana, E. (1989). Specifying caregiver outcomes: Gender and relationship aspects of caregiving strain. *The Gerontologist, 29,* 658-666.

Znaniecki, F. W. (1952). *Modern nationalities.* Urbana: University of Illinois Press.

Znaniecki, F. W. (1965). *Social relations and social roles.* San Francisco: Chandler.

Index

About the Authors

Helena Znaniecka Lopata is Professor of Sociology and Director of the Center for the Comparative Study of Social Roles at Loyola University of Chicago. She came to the United States during World War II and obtained her PhD from the University of Chicago in 1954. Her books include *Occupation: Housewife* (1971); *Widowhood in an American City* (1973); *Polish Americans: Status Competition in an Ethnic Community* (1976); *Women as Widows: Support Systems* (1979); *City Women: Work, Jobs, Occupations, Careers* (with Debra Barnewolt and Cheryl Allyn Miller, 1985); *Widows and Dependent Wives: From Social Problem to Federal Policy* (with Henry Brehm, 1987); *Widows: The Middle East, Asia and the Pacific* and *Widows: North America* (edited, 1987); *Polish Americans* (1994); and *Circles and Settings* (1994).

Annette Prosterman, who authored a chapter in this book, is working toward a PhD in sociology at Loyola University of Chicago where she has served as Dr. Lopata's research assistant. She received a bachelor's degree from Northwestern University in 1989 and a master's degree from Loyola University in 1994. Her primary areas of sociological interest are in social change, social movements, and community, and her research has included ethnographic studies of sociospatial relationships within a neighborhood public library and the organizational culture of an economic development project in Chicago.

0836